Prioritizing Mental Health: A Guide to Overcoming Despair and Rediscovering Hope

Amanda Ventura

Published by Amanda Ventura, 2024.

While every precaution has been taken in the preparation of this book, the publisher assumes no responsibility for errors or omissions, or for damages resulting from the use of the information contained herein.

PRIORITIZING MENTAL HEALTH: A GUIDE TO OVERCOMING DESPAIR AND REDISCOVERING HOPE

First edition. October 23, 2024.

Written by Amanda Ventura.

Also by Amanda Ventura

Echoes Of Divinity
Determined Heart
Rising From The Ashes
Unyielding Faith
Vanessa's Miracle, A Journey Through Kidney Cancer
Prioritizing Mental Health: A Guide to Overcoming Despair and
Rediscovering Hope

Table of Contents

Prioritizing Mental Health: A Guide to Overcoming Despair and Rediscovering Hope

Introduction

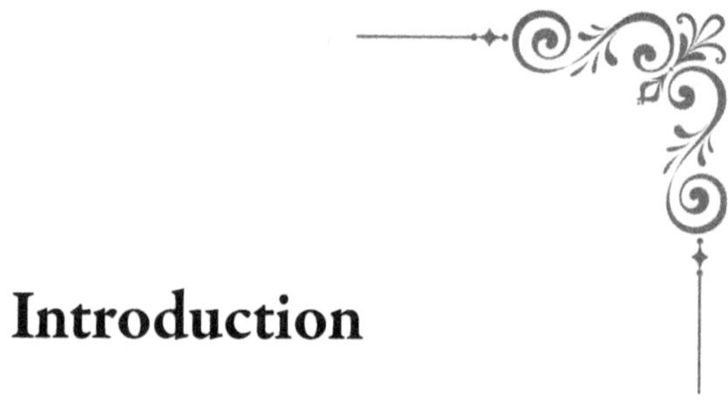

Life can often feel overwhelming, and for many, there comes a time when the weight of despair seems insurmountable. In the depths of such darkness, thoughts of suicide may emerge as a misguided solution to the pain that feels unending. This book is written for anyone who has felt that their situation is hopeless or that they have exhausted all means of finding relief. It is a compassionate guide designed to illuminate the path toward healing, resilience, and ultimately, hope.

The experience of struggling with suicidal thoughts is often shrouded in stigma and silence. Many people feel isolated, believing that they are alone in their suffering. However, it is crucial to recognize that these feelings, while intensely personal, are shared by countless others. Understanding that you are not alone is the first step toward healing. This book aims to create a safe space where you can explore your emotions and experiences without judgment.

In the chapters that follow, we will delve into the nature of despair, the importance of acknowledging and expressing your feelings, and the value of seeking help. You will learn about coping strategies that can provide immediate relief and long-term solutions. We will explore the significance of building a robust support system and the power of communication, both with others and within yourself.

We will also discuss the role of mental health professionals and the various treatment options available, including therapy, medication, and self-care practices. You will find stories of resilience and recovery from individuals who have walked this difficult path and emerged stronger on the other side. Their journeys serve as a reminder that hope is always possible, even in the darkest times.

This book is not just about survival, it's about thriving. It is about rediscovering your purpose and passion for life, even when everything seems bleak. By taking small, actionable steps, you can begin to navigate through your pain and emerge with a renewed sense of self and a deeper understanding of what it means to live.

Remember, reaching out for help is not a sign of weakness, it is a courageous act of self-preservation. If you are in crisis, please speak to someone who can help you right now. Your life matters. As we embark on this journey together, I encourage you to keep an open heart and mind. Healing is possible, and you are worthy of a life filled with hope, joy, and meaning. Let us begin this journey toward finding light in the darkness together.

4

Table of Contents

Chapter One:

Understanding the Depth of Despair

Chapter Two:

R ecognizing the Signs of Crisis

Chapter Three:

The Stigma Surrounding Mental Health

Chapter Four:

The Importance of Acknowledging Your Feelings

Chapter Five:

What It Means to Feel Overwhelmed

Chapter Six:

The Cycle of Hopelessness

Chapter Seven:

Life: A Series of Challenges

Chapter Eight:

The Strength in Vulnerability

Chapter Nine:

Finding the Right Support System

Chapter Ten:

Professional Help: Therapists and Counselors

Chapter Eleven:

E xpressing Your Feelings

Chapter Twelve:

Talking to Friends and Family

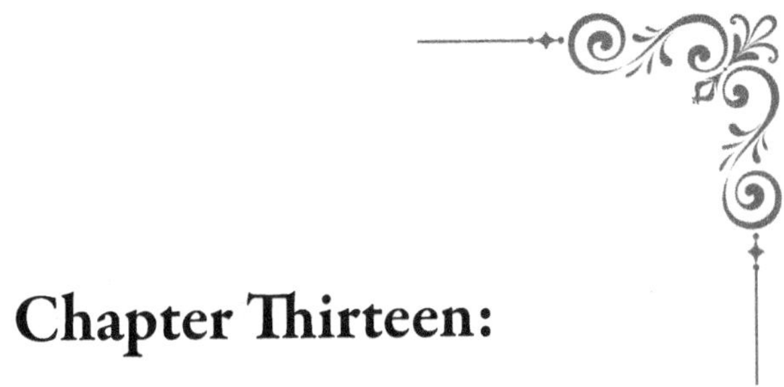

Chapter Thirteen:

Writing as a Therapeutic Tool

Chapter Fourteen:

Creating a Supportive Environment

Chapter Fifteen:

Identifying Trustworthy Individuals

Chapter Sixteen:

Establishing Boundaries for Your Well-being

Chapter Seventeen:

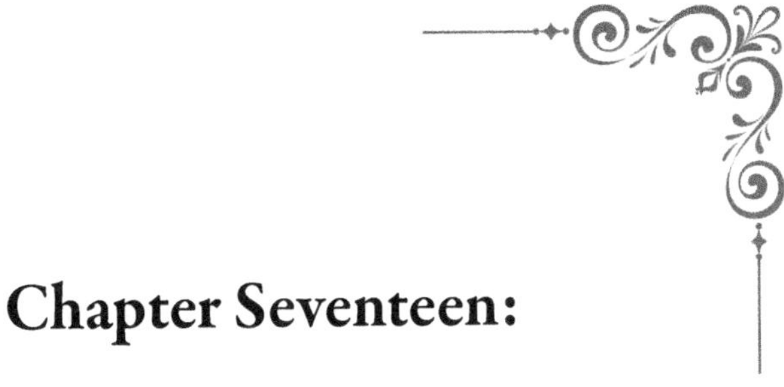

M indfulness and Meditation

Chapter Eighteen:

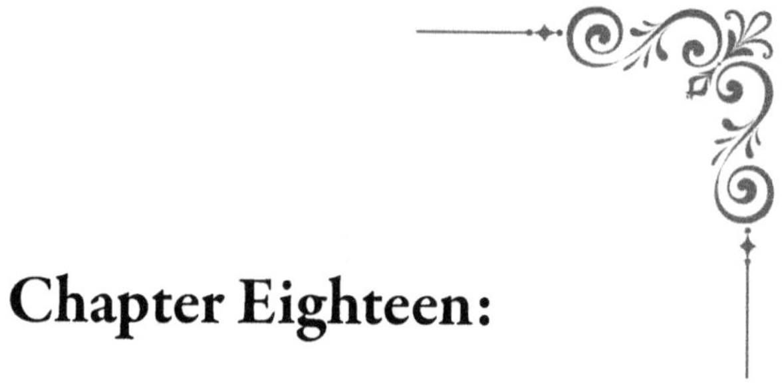

Journaling Your Thoughts

Chapter Nineteen:

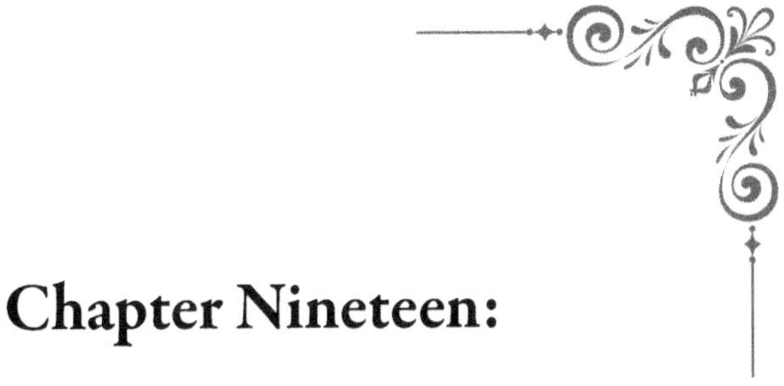

P hysical Activity and Its Benefits

Chapter Twenty:

The Power of Hobbies and Interests

Chapter Twenty One:

Volunteering and Helping Others

Chapter Twenty Two:

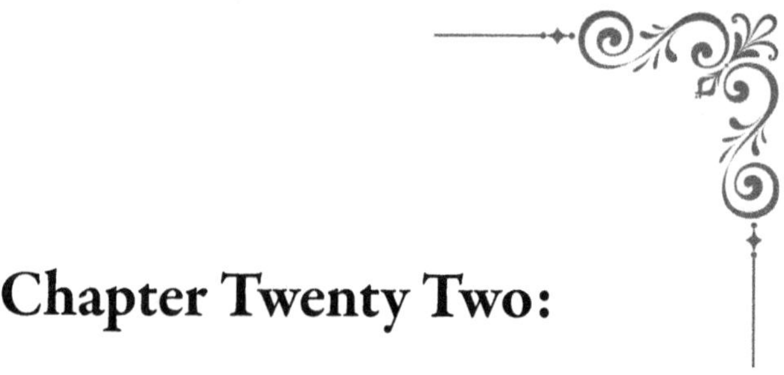

E ngaging in Community Activities

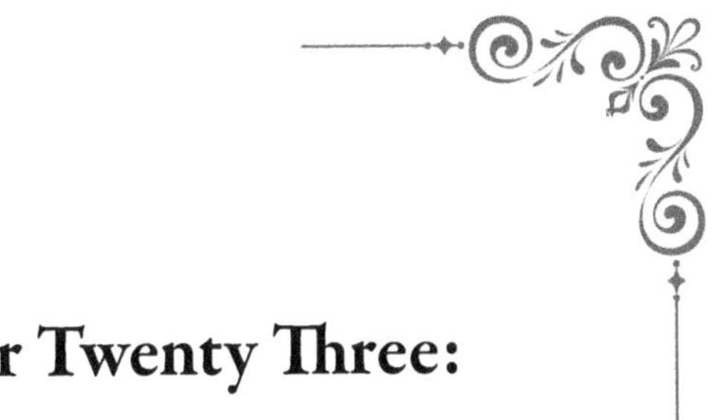

Chapter Twenty Three:

U nderstanding Your Values and Beliefs

Chapter Twenty Four:

Setting Small, Achievable Goals

Chapter Twenty Five:

The Importance of Daily Routines

Chapter Twenty Six:

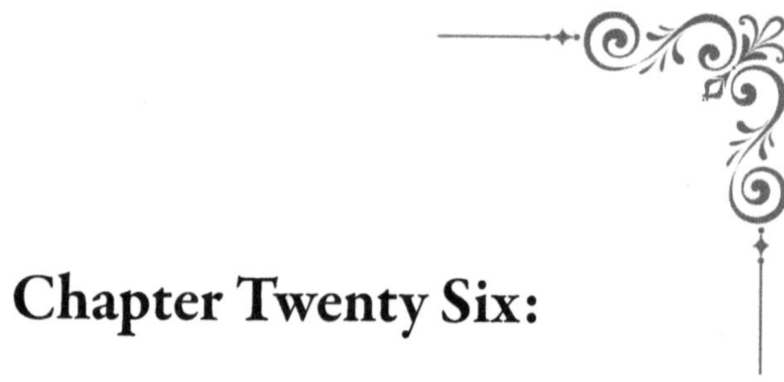

Recognizing Cognitive Distortions

Chapter Twenty Seven:

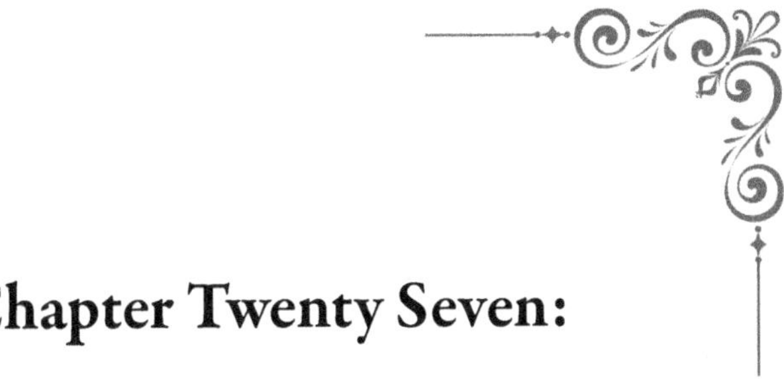

Practicing Positive Affirmations

Chapter Twenty Eight:

Reframing Your Perspective

Chapter Twenty Nine:

Understanding Mental Health Medications

Chapter Thirty:

Working with Healthcare Providers

Chapter Thirty One:

When to Reassess Your Treatment Plan

Chapter Thirty Two:

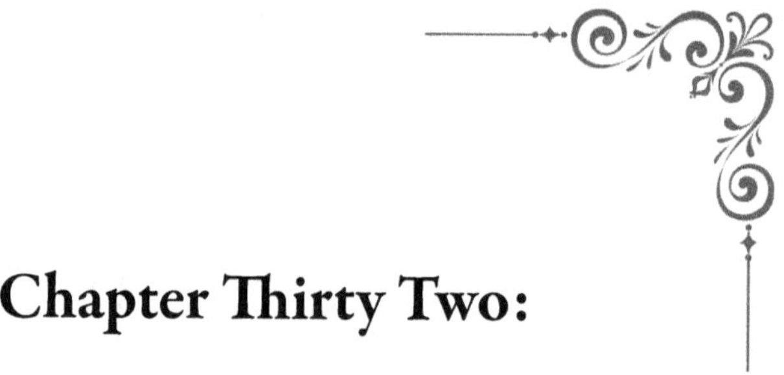

Crisis Hotlines and Text Lines

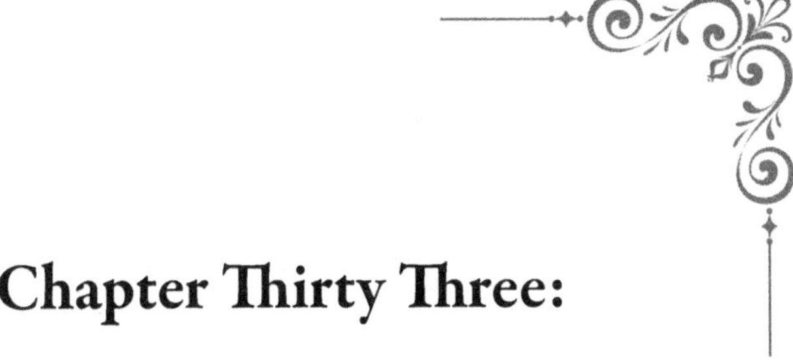

Chapter Thirty Three:

Local Mental Health Services

Chapter Thirty Four:

C reating an Emergency Plan

Chapter Thirty Five:

Real-Life Stories of Overcoming Despair

Chapter Thirty Six:

The Role of Resilience in Recovery

Chapter Thirty Seven:

L earning from Others' Experiences

Chapter Thirty Eight:

Nutrition and Mental Health

Chapter Thirty Nine:

The Importance of Sleep

Chapter Forty:

E ngaging in Relaxation Techniques

Chapter Forty One:

Understanding Your Emotions

Chapter Forty Two:

D eveloping Empathy and Compassion

Chapter Forty Three:

Managing Stress Effectively

Chapter Forty Four:

Nurturing Healthy Relationships

Chapter Forty Five:

Letting Go of Toxic Connections

Chapter Forty Six:

The Importance of Forgiveness

Chapter Forty Seven:

Accepting That Recovery Takes Time

Chapter Eight:

Celebrating Small Victories

Chapter Forty Nine:

M oving Forward: Life After Crisis

Chapter Fifty:

E mbracing Life: Finding Joy and Purpose Again

Chapter One

Understanding the Depth of Despair

Despair is a profound emotional state that often transcends simple sadness or disappointment. It can be described as a state of utter hopelessness, where individuals feel trapped in a cycle of negativity and find it difficult to see any possibility for change or improvement in their circumstances. This emotional condition can stem from various sources, including traumatic experiences, chronic stress, or overwhelming life challenges, and it can manifest in different ways, affecting mental, emotional, and physical well-being.

At the core of despair lies a sense of loss. Loss of hope, loss of purpose, or even loss of identity. When individuals find themselves in this state, they may feel as if they have been stripped of their ability to envision a brighter future. This loss can be particularly acute in situations involving grief, where the death of a loved one or a significant life transition can lead to feelings of emptiness and disconnection from the world. The weight of such despair can be crushing, leaving individuals feeling isolated and misunderstood.

The psychological implications of despair are profound. It often leads to a cycle of negative thinking, where individuals become trapped in their own minds, replaying their failures and disappointments. Cognitive distortions, such as catastrophizing or black-and-white thinking, can exacerbate this state, making it difficult for individuals to see the nuances of their experiences. This mental fog can prevent them from recognizing potential solutions or support systems that could help them navigate their challenges.

Moreover, despair can have physical manifestations that further complicate the emotional struggle. Many individuals experiencing deep despair report symptoms such as fatigue, changes in appetite, and sleep disturbances. These physical symptoms can create a feedback loop, where the lack of physical well-being exacerbates feelings of hopelessness, making it even harder to engage in self-care or seek help. This interplay between mind and body emphasizes the importance of a holistic approach to understanding and addressing despair.

Social isolation is another critical aspect of despair. Individuals may withdraw from friends, family, and social activities as they wrestle with their feelings. This withdrawal can further entrench their despair, as the lack of social support can lead to feelings of loneliness and alienation. The stigma surrounding mental health issues often exacerbates this isolation, as individuals may be reluctant to share their struggles for fear of judgment or misunderstanding. Consequently, the very connections that could offer support become severed, deepening the despair.

Understanding the depth of despair also requires recognizing its complexity. It is not simply an emotional response, it can be influenced by various factors, including genetic predispositions, environmental influences, and personal history. For some, a history of trauma or mental health disorders can create a vulnerability to despair, while for others, situational factors may trigger this emotional state. This complexity underscores the importance of a personalized approach to treatment and support.

Addressing despair often requires professional intervention. Therapy can provide individuals with tools to process their feelings, challenge negative thought patterns, and develop coping strategies. Cognitive-behavioral therapy (CBT), for example, has been shown to be effective in helping individuals reframe their thoughts and beliefs, fostering a more hopeful outlook. In some cases, medication may also be prescribed to help alleviate symptoms of depression and anxiety that accompany despair.

Support groups can also play a vital role in combating despair. Connecting with others who have faced similar struggles can validate feelings and foster a sense of community. Sharing experiences can help individuals feel less alone in their journey, and hearing stories of recovery can ignite hope. These groups can offer practical advice, emotional support, and a safe space for individuals to express their feelings without fear of judgment.

Mindfulness and self-care practices can also be beneficial for individuals grappling with despair. Techniques such as meditation, journaling, and physical exercise can help ground individuals in the present moment, reducing the tendency to ruminate on past failures or future worries. Engaging in creative outlets or hobbies can provide a sense of accomplishment and joy, countering the feelings of hopelessness that often accompany despair.

Ultimately, understanding the depth of despair requires empathy and compassion, both for oneself and for others who may be struggling. It is essential to recognize that despair is a complex emotional state that can affect anyone, regardless of their circumstances. Encouraging open conversations about mental health, reducing stigma, and fostering supportive environments can help individuals feel more empowered to seek help and navigate their journey through despair.

In conclusion, despair is a multifaceted emotional experience that requires a nuanced understanding. By acknowledging its origins, manifestations, and effects, we can better support those who are struggling. Whether through professional help, social support, or personal practices, there are pathways to healing and hope, reminding us that even in the depths of despair, light can emerge.

Building on the understanding of despair, it's crucial to explore the role of resilience in overcoming this emotional state. Resilience is not merely a trait but a dynamic process that enables individuals to adapt and thrive in the face of adversity. While despair may feel all-consuming, cultivating resilience can provide a counterbalance, helping individuals navigate their emotional landscapes more effectively. This process often involves acknowledging one's feelings of despair while also recognizing one's strengths and capacities for growth and recovery.

Resilience can be fostered through various practices and mindsets. For instance, developing a growth mindset, which emphasizes the belief that abilities and intelligence can be developed through effort and learning, can shift one's perspective on challenges. When individuals view setbacks as opportunities for growth rather than insurmountable obstacles, they can begin to distance themselves from feelings of despair. Engaging in positive self-talk and affirmations can also reinforce resilience, allowing individuals to challenge negative thought patterns that contribute to their hopelessness.

Support from loved ones plays an integral role in fostering resilience as well. Strong social connections provide emotional support and practical assistance during difficult times. Friends and family can offer a listening ear, encouragement, and a sense of belonging, which can be particularly protective against the isolating effects of despair. Building and maintaining these relationships may require intentional effort, especially when individuals are in a state of despair and may not feel inclined to reach out. However, even small gestures of connection can make a significant difference in one's emotional well-being.

Moreover, engaging in meaningful activities can act as a powerful antidote to despair. Pursuing hobbies, volunteering, or participating in community activities can instill a sense of purpose and fulfillment. These activities can redirect focus away from negative feelings and foster a sense of achievement and connection to others. When individuals engage in experiences that resonate with their values and passions, they can rekindle a sense of hope and motivation, even amidst challenging circumstances.

It is also essential to address the societal factors that contribute to despair. Social inequalities, economic hardship, and systemic barriers can exacerbate feelings of hopelessness, particularly for marginalized communities. Understanding the broader context of despair requires acknowledging these external factors and advocating for systemic change. Creating supportive environments that promote mental health awareness, access to resources, and community support can help mitigate the impacts of despair on individuals and communities alike.

Education about mental health is a crucial step in combating despair at both individual and societal levels. By fostering open discussions about emotions, mental health struggles, and resilience, we can reduce stigma and promote understanding. Schools, workplaces, and community organizations can play a pivotal role in equipping individuals with the knowledge and tools to recognize and address despair. Workshops, training sessions, and resources can empower individuals to seek help and support others in their journeys, creating a culture of empathy and understanding.

Finally, it is vital to remember that recovery from despair is a journey, not a destination. Each individual's path will be unique, shaped by personal experiences and circumstances. Embracing this journey with patience and compassion can allow individuals to navigate their feelings without judgment. By recognizing that despair is a part of the human experience, we can cultivate a more profound understanding of ourselves and others, fostering a sense of solidarity and hope in the face of life's challenges. In this way, understanding the depth of despair becomes not only a means of acknowledging suffering but also a pathway toward healing and connection.

Chapter Two

Recognizing the Signs of Crisis

Crisis situations can arise unexpectedly, affecting individuals, families, and communities. Recognizing the signs of a crisis is crucial for timely intervention and support. A crisis may be triggered by various factors, including personal trauma, significant life changes, or societal events. Understanding the indicators that someone may be experiencing a crisis can help friends, family, and professionals provide the necessary support and resources to navigate these challenging moments.

One of the most prominent signs of a crisis is a noticeable change in behavior. Individuals experiencing a crisis may exhibit sudden shifts in mood, energy levels, or social engagement. For instance, someone who has been outgoing and energetic may become withdrawn and irritable. Conversely, a person who has been reserved may become overly emotional or aggressive. These behavioral changes can serve as critical signals that something is amiss, prompting those around them to take notice and reach out.

Another common indicator of a crisis is a decline in performance, whether at work, school, or in personal responsibilities. Individuals may struggle to meet deadlines, find it challenging to concentrate, or experience a drop in the quality of their work. This decline can stem from overwhelming stress, emotional turmoil, or an inability to cope with their circumstances. Recognizing these changes in performance can be vital for identifying someone in crisis, as it often reflects their internal struggles.

Physical symptoms can also manifest during a crisis, serving as both a warning sign and a consequence of emotional distress. Individuals may experience changes in appetite or sleep patterns, leading to weight loss or gain, fatigue, or insomnia. Headaches, gastrointestinal issues, and other stress-related ailments may arise as well. These physical symptoms can indicate that a person is experiencing significant emotional pain, and addressing both the physical and emotional aspects of their crisis is crucial for effective support.

Isolation is another significant sign that someone may be in crisis. Individuals may withdraw from social interactions, avoid activities they once enjoyed, or cease communicating with friends and family. This withdrawal can be a coping mechanism, as individuals may feel overwhelmed or ashamed of their struggles. Recognizing this isolation is vital, as it can lead to further emotional distress and reinforce feelings of loneliness. Encouraging connection and providing support can help break this cycle.

Changes in communication patterns are also key indicators of a crisis. Individuals may express feelings of hopelessness, worthlessness, or despair more openly than before. They might make comments about wanting to escape their situation or express a desire to give up entirely. Verbal expressions of distress, whether through direct statements or more subtle hints, should be taken seriously, as they can signal a need for immediate intervention and support.

In some cases, individuals in crisis may engage in self-destructive behaviors, such as substance abuse, self-harm, or reckless decisions. These behaviors can serve as a means of coping with overwhelming emotions or as a cry for help. Recognizing these signs is crucial for intervening before the situation escalates further. It is essential to approach individuals exhibiting these behaviors with empathy and understanding, as they may feel trapped in their circumstances and unsure of how to seek help.

Additionally, crises can manifest in relationships, leading to conflicts or breakdowns in communication. Individuals may find themselves in heightened states of anger, frustration, or despair, resulting in arguments or distancing from loved ones. This relational strain can exacerbate feelings of isolation and despair. Observing changes in relationship dynamics and encouraging open communication can help individuals navigate their crises and maintain supportive connections.

Recognizing the signs of crisis is not solely the responsibility of those close to the individual; it also extends to community members, colleagues, and mental health professionals. Training programs that educate individuals on the signs of crisis can empower more people to identify when someone may be in distress. These programs can promote awareness, reduce stigma around seeking help, and create a culture of support within communities and organizations.

When signs of crisis are recognized, timely intervention is essential. Approaching someone in crisis with compassion, understanding, and a willingness to listen can make a significant difference in their experience. Encouraging them to seek professional help, whether through counseling, support groups, or crisis hotlines, can provide them with the tools and resources they need to navigate their challenges.

Finally, it's important to remember that recognizing the signs of a crisis does not always lead to immediate solutions. It requires ongoing support and understanding to help individuals through their struggles. Building a supportive environment that fosters open communication, empathy, and access to mental health resources can empower those in crisis to seek help and find their path to recovery. By being vigilant and proactive in recognizing the signs of crisis, we can create a more compassionate society where individuals feel valued and supported during their most challenging times.

In addition to individual behaviors, it is vital to pay attention to environmental factors that can signal a crisis. Changes in one's surroundings, such as the loss of a job, a family member's illness, or a community event that causes widespread distress, can contribute to emotional upheaval. These external stressors can exacerbate existing mental health issues or create new challenges. Being aware of the context in which someone is functioning can provide insight into their emotional state and signal a potential crisis.

Cultural factors also play a significant role in recognizing the signs of crisis. Different cultures may have varying expressions of distress, which can impact how individuals communicate their struggles. For instance, some cultures may emphasize stoicism and discourage open displays of emotion, making it challenging to identify when someone is in crisis. Understanding cultural nuances and being sensitive to different expressions of pain can enhance our ability to recognize when someone needs support.

Moreover, the digital age has introduced new dimensions to recognizing signs of crisis. Social media platforms can provide insights into a person's emotional state through their posts, comments, and interactions. Sudden changes in online behavior, such as posting distressing content, withdrawing from social media, or engaging in negative online interactions, can serve as red flags. While online communication may not capture the full complexity of an individual's situation, it can offer valuable clues that warrant further investigation and support.

It is also important to recognize that crises can occur at any age, from childhood through adulthood. Each developmental stage presents unique challenges that can lead to a crisis. For instance, adolescents may face pressures related to identity, peer relationships, and academic performance, while older adults may grapple with issues related to health, loss of independence, or the death of loved ones. Tailoring our approach to recognize and support individuals across the lifespan is crucial for effective intervention.

In educational settings, teachers and school staff can play a vital role in recognizing the signs of crisis among students. By fostering supportive classroom environments and developing strong relationships with students, educators can create spaces where young people feel safe to express their emotions. Training staff to identify behavioral changes, academic struggles, and social withdrawal can empower them to intervene early and connect students with appropriate resources.

In the workplace, managers and colleagues can also be instrumental in recognizing signs of crisis. A supportive work environment that encourages open communication can help identify employees who may be struggling. Regular check-ins, mental health initiatives, and employee assistance programs can create a culture where individuals feel comfortable sharing their challenges and seeking help. Recognizing the signs of crisis in the workplace can lead to early intervention and prevent further deterioration of an employee's mental health.

Community organizations and local resources can enhance the ability to recognize and respond to crises. Establishing partnerships with mental health professionals, crisis centers, and advocacy groups can create a network of support for individuals in distress. Training community members to identify the signs of crisis and connect individuals with local resources can foster a culture of care and resilience. This community-based approach can extend the reach of support beyond immediate relationships, ensuring that help is accessible.

As we seek to recognize signs of crisis, it is essential to prioritize self-care for those providing support. Supporting someone in distress can be emotionally taxing, leading to compassion fatigue or burnout.

Caregivers, friends, and family members must also attend to their own mental health and well-being. Engaging in self-care practices, seeking support, and setting boundaries can help maintain the strength needed to assist others effectively.

Recognizing the signs of crisis is an ongoing process that requires vigilance, compassion, and a willingness to engage. It is essential to approach those in distress without judgment, creating a safe space for them to express their feelings. Empowering individuals to seek help and providing them with the tools to navigate their challenges can lead to more positive outcomes. Building a culture of understanding and support is crucial for fostering resilience in individuals facing crises.

Lastly, it is important to remember that while recognizing the signs of crisis is a significant step, it is only the beginning of a larger conversation about mental health. Advocating for mental health awareness, reducing stigma, and promoting access to resources can help create an environment where individuals feel safe to express their struggles. By prioritizing mental health at the community, organizational, and societal levels, we can work towards a future where recognizing and addressing the signs of crisis is viewed as an essential part of caring for one another.

In conclusion, recognizing the signs of crisis is a critical skill that can save lives and facilitate healing. By fostering awareness, understanding, and compassion, we can create supportive environments that empower individuals to seek help and navigate their challenges. Whether through personal connections, community initiatives, or organizational support, the ability to recognize and respond to crises is a shared responsibility that ultimately strengthens our collective resilience.

Chapter Three

The Stigma Surrounding Mental Health

Mental health stigma refers to the negative attitudes, beliefs, and behaviors that society holds towards individuals experiencing mental health issues. This stigma can manifest in various forms, ranging from overt discrimination to subtle social exclusion, and can profoundly impact those affected. Understanding the origins and consequences of this stigma is crucial for fostering a more supportive environment for individuals struggling with mental health challenges.

Historically, mental health issues have been misunderstood and misrepresented in society. In many cultures, mental illness was viewed as a personal failing, a sign of weakness, or even a moral failing. These misconceptions often stem from a lack of knowledge and awareness about mental health conditions. Consequently, individuals who experience mental health challenges may feel ashamed, isolated, and reluctant to seek help due to the fear of being judged or discriminated against.

One of the most damaging aspects of mental health stigma is its impact on individuals' willingness to seek help. Many people suffering from mental health conditions delay or avoid seeking treatment due to fears of being labeled or stigmatized. This can lead to a cycle of worsening symptoms and increased isolation, as individuals may feel they have to suffer in silence rather than risk facing societal judgment. By not seeking help, they miss out on effective treatments and support that could significantly improve their quality of life.

In addition to affecting individuals' willingness to seek help, stigma can also lead to social exclusion and discrimination in various settings. People with mental health conditions may experience negative attitudes from family members, friends, colleagues, and even healthcare providers. This can manifest in unfair treatment in the workplace, difficulty maintaining relationships, or a lack of understanding from others. Such exclusion not only exacerbates feelings of isolation but can also hinder recovery and overall well-being.

The media plays a significant role in shaping public perceptions of mental health. Unfortunately, portrayals of mental illness in movies, television shows, and news articles often perpetuate stereotypes and exaggerate the dangers associated with mental health conditions. These negative representations can reinforce stigma and create fear among the general public, further alienating those living with mental health challenges. Promoting accurate and compassionate representations of mental health in media can help counteract these harmful narratives.

Education is a powerful tool in combating mental health stigma. By increasing awareness and understanding of mental health issues, communities can foster a more supportive atmosphere for those affected. Schools, workplaces, and community organizations can implement mental health education programs that provide accurate information about mental health conditions, their prevalence, and the importance of seeking help. These initiatives can help dispel myths and promote empathy, reducing stigma and encouraging individuals to seek support when needed.

Peer support and shared experiences can also play a vital role in challenging mental health stigma. When individuals share their stories and struggles with mental health, it humanizes their experiences and fosters empathy among listeners. Support groups, mental health advocacy organizations, and public forums can provide platforms for individuals to share their journeys openly, helping to normalize conversations about mental health. By breaking the silence, we can create a culture where discussing mental health is seen as a sign of strength rather than weakness.

Additionally, legislation and policy changes can address systemic stigma. Advocating for mental health parity in healthcare, workplace protections for individuals with mental health conditions, and anti-discrimination laws can help dismantle barriers to access and support. Governments and organizations must commit to prioritizing mental health alongside physical health, ensuring that individuals receive the care and support they need without fear of stigma or discrimination.

It is also essential to recognize the intersectionality of mental health stigma. Certain populations, including individuals from marginalized communities, may face compounded stigma based on race, gender, sexual orientation, or socioeconomic status. This intersectional stigma can create additional barriers to seeking help and accessing resources. Addressing mental health stigma requires a nuanced understanding of these intersecting identities and a commitment to promoting equity in mental health care.

As we work to combat the stigma surrounding mental health, it is crucial to foster an environment of compassion and understanding. Encouraging open dialogues about mental health and creating safe spaces for individuals to share their experiences can help dismantle stigma and promote healing. By supporting one another and advocating for change, we can create a society where mental health is treated with the same importance and respect as physical health.

In conclusion, the stigma surrounding mental health remains a significant barrier preventing individuals from seeking help and receiving adequate support. By understanding the roots and consequences of this stigma, we can take meaningful steps toward fostering a more compassionate and understanding society. Through education, advocacy, and open conversations, we can challenge stereotypes and create an environment where individuals feel safe to discuss their mental health and seek the help they need, ultimately promoting a healthier and more inclusive community for all.

To further understand the stigma surrounding mental health, it is essential to explore the role of language in perpetuating negative perceptions. The words we choose to describe mental health conditions can significantly influence public attitudes. Phrases that evoke fear or portray individuals as dangerous can reinforce harmful stereotypes. Conversely, using person-first language, such as "a person with depression" instead of "a depressed person" can promote a more compassionate view and remind society that mental health conditions do not define an individual's identity. Changing the conversation to focus on the person rather than the illness can help reduce stigma and foster greater understanding.

The workplace environment is another critical arena where mental health stigma manifests. Many employees hesitate to disclose their mental health struggles due to fears of retaliation, job loss, or being perceived as less competent. Consequently, organizations may benefit from implementing mental health policies that prioritize employee well-being. Creating an open and supportive workplace culture can encourage employees to seek help without fear of judgment. Training managers and colleagues to recognize signs of mental distress and to respond with empathy can cultivate a more inclusive atmosphere that values mental health as part of overall employee wellness.

The impact of mental health stigma extends beyond individual experiences; it influences public policy and funding for mental health services. Stigmatized perceptions can lead to underinvestment in mental health resources, resulting in inadequate support for those in need. Advocating for mental health initiatives at the community and governmental levels can help ensure that mental health services are prioritized alongside physical health. By raising awareness about the importance of mental health and its impact on overall societal well-being, we can work towards securing the necessary funding and resources to support those affected.

The importance of mental health education in schools cannot be overstated. Early intervention and education can play a vital role in reducing stigma among younger generations. By integrating mental health education into school curricula, students can learn about mental health issues, develop coping strategies, and understand the importance of seeking help. This proactive approach can empower young people to recognize their own mental health needs and support their peers, ultimately fostering a culture of understanding and empathy from a young age.

Furthermore, mental health advocacy organizations play a crucial role in addressing stigma. These organizations work to raise awareness, promote education, and provide resources for individuals experiencing mental health challenges. By mobilizing communities and advocating for policy changes, they can amplify the voices of those affected by mental health issues. Collaborative efforts between advocacy groups, healthcare providers, and policymakers can create a more comprehensive approach to addressing mental health stigma and improving access to care.

The role of social media in shaping perceptions of mental health cannot be ignored. While social media can sometimes perpetuate stigma through the sharing of negative stereotypes, it also offers a platform for individuals to share their experiences, connect with others, and foster community support. Online campaigns and hashtags dedicated to mental health awareness can help normalize conversations about mental health and provide a sense of solidarity for those struggling. By harnessing the positive potential of social media, we can challenge stigma and create a more informed and compassionate dialogue around mental health.

As we strive to combat mental health stigma, it is crucial to emphasize the importance of self-care and personal well-being. Encouraging individuals to prioritize their mental health and seek help when needed can help dismantle the stigma that surrounds mental health challenges. Normalizing self-care practices, such as therapy, mindfulness, and stress management, can empower individuals to take charge of their mental well-being and lead by example. When people openly discuss their mental health journeys and promote self-care, it contributes to a cultural shift that values mental health as an integral part of overall health.

In conclusion, addressing the stigma surrounding mental health requires a multifaceted approach that involves education, advocacy, and open dialogue. By challenging negative perceptions, promoting empathy, and creating supportive environments, we can help individuals feel safe to seek help and share their experiences. It is essential to work collectively across communities, organizations, and platforms, to foster a culture that values mental health and recognizes its importance in our lives. Through these concerted efforts, we can dismantle stigma and create a society where mental health is embraced, understood, and prioritized.

Chapter Four

The Importance of Acknowledging Your Feelings

Acknowledging one's feelings is a fundamental aspect of emotional health and well-being. Many people tend to suppress or ignore their emotions due to societal pressures, fear of vulnerability, or a belief that expressing feelings is a sign of weakness. However, recognizing and validating one's emotions is crucial for personal growth, self-awareness, and ultimately, mental health. When individuals allow themselves to feel and acknowledge their emotions, they can better understand their reactions and needs, paving the way for healthier relationships and life choices.

Understanding emotions is the first step toward acknowledging them. Emotions serve as important signals that provide insight into our experiences and reactions to the world around us. For instance, feelings of sadness might indicate a need for connection or support, while anger could point to unmet needs or boundaries being crossed. By tuning into these emotional signals, individuals can gain valuable insights into their needs and motivations, which can lead to healthier responses and decisions.

Moreover, acknowledging feelings can prevent emotional bottling, which often leads to negative consequences. When emotions are suppressed, they can build up, resulting in emotional outbursts, anxiety, or depression. This accumulation of unacknowledged feelings can create a cycle of avoidance, where individuals feel overwhelmed by their emotions but continue to deny their existence. By recognizing and processing these feelings as they arise, individuals can prevent emotional overload and maintain a healthier emotional balance.

Expressing emotions can also enhance interpersonal relationships. When individuals acknowledge their feelings, they can communicate more effectively with others, fostering deeper connections and understanding. For example, expressing feelings of hurt or frustration can lead to constructive conversations that strengthen relationships. On the other hand, suppressing emotions can lead to misunderstandings and resentment, making it difficult for relationships to thrive. By being honest about one's feelings, individuals create a foundation of trust and openness in their relationships.

In addition to improving relationships, acknowledging feelings plays a critical role in self-acceptance and personal growth. When individuals are honest about their emotions, they begin to accept themselves as they are, fostering a sense of authenticity. This self-acceptance can lead to greater self-esteem and confidence, allowing individuals to pursue their goals and aspirations without the burden of self-doubt. Embracing one's emotions can facilitate a journey of self-discovery, where individuals learn more about themselves and their desires.

Practicing mindfulness is an effective way to cultivate the habit of acknowledging feelings. Mindfulness encourages individuals to stay present and observe their thoughts and emotions without judgment. This practice can help individuals recognize feelings as they arise, creating a space for reflection and understanding. By developing mindfulness techniques, such as meditation or deep-breathing exercises, individuals can train themselves to notice their emotions more readily and respond to them with compassion rather than avoidance.

In the context of mental health, acknowledging feelings is particularly crucial. Many mental health conditions, such as anxiety and depression, can be exacerbated by unacknowledged emotions. Individuals struggling with these conditions may find it difficult to articulate their feelings, leading to further isolation and distress. By fostering an environment where feelings are acknowledged and validated, individuals can take significant steps toward healing. Therapists and mental health professionals often encourage clients to explore and express their emotions as part of the therapeutic process, highlighting the importance of emotional acknowledgment in recovery.

Cultural factors can also influence the way individuals acknowledge their feelings. In some cultures, expressing emotions may be discouraged, leading to the internalization of feelings. This can create a significant barrier to emotional acknowledgment and can perpetuate cycles of unprocessed feelings. It is essential to recognize these cultural influences and work towards creating safe spaces where individuals feel empowered to express their emotions without fear of judgment or retribution. Educating communities about the importance of emotional expression can help dismantle these barriers and promote a more emotionally aware society.

Additionally, acknowledging feelings can have physical health benefits. Research has shown that repressed emotions can manifest physically, leading to ailments such as headaches, gastrointestinal issues, and chronic pain. By allowing oneself to feel and express emotions, individuals can potentially alleviate these physical symptoms. The mind-body connection underscores the importance of emotional health; when individuals prioritize their emotional well-being, they are also investing in their physical health.

The process of acknowledging feelings may not always be easy, especially in a society that often prioritizes resilience and stoicism. However, it is essential to approach this process with kindness and patience. Individuals may need to unlearn habits of emotional suppression and develop healthier coping mechanisms. Seeking support from friends, family, or mental health professionals can provide the encouragement needed to navigate this journey. Creating a supportive network can help individuals feel more comfortable sharing their emotions and foster a culture of openness.

In conclusion, acknowledging one's feelings is a vital aspect of emotional well-being that has far-reaching implications for mental health, relationships, and personal growth. By allowing oneself to feel and express emotions, individuals can gain deeper insights into their needs, prevent emotional bottling, and foster healthier connections.

Furthermore, acknowledging feelings can serve as a powerful tool for emotional regulation. When individuals recognize their emotions, they gain the ability to respond to them appropriately rather than react impulsively. For instance, acknowledging feelings of frustration can allow a person to take a step back, assess the situation, and choose a constructive response rather than lashing out. This capacity for emotional regulation can lead to better decision-making and more harmonious interactions with others, ultimately enhancing one's quality of life.

Another important aspect of acknowledging feelings is the role it plays in resilience. Resilience is the ability to adapt and bounce back from adversity, and it is often cultivated through the process of facing and processing emotions. When individuals confront their feelings, they develop coping mechanisms and strategies that enable them to navigate challenges more effectively. This proactive approach to emotional health can foster a sense of empowerment, as individuals learn to view their emotions not as obstacles but as valuable sources of information that guide their actions and decisions.

Additionally, the act of acknowledging feelings can foster empathy and understanding toward others. When individuals learn to recognize and validate their own emotions, they become more attuned to the feelings of those around them. This heightened emotional awareness can lead to more compassionate interactions and a greater willingness to support others in their emotional struggles. As people become more comfortable with their own feelings, they can create a ripple effect, encouraging those in their lives to also embrace emotional openness and vulnerability.

It is also essential to recognize that acknowledging feelings does not mean dwelling on them or allowing them to dictate behavior. Instead, it is about creating a healthy space to process emotions. This might involve journaling, talking to a trusted friend, or practicing mindfulness techniques to reflect on feelings without judgment. By developing healthy outlets for emotional expression, individuals can learn to process their feelings in a constructive manner, leading to deeper self-understanding and growth.

In the workplace, fostering an environment that encourages emotional acknowledgment can enhance employee well-being and productivity. When employees feel safe to express their emotions, they are more likely to seek support when needed, leading to a healthier workplace culture. Employers can play a crucial role by promoting mental health awareness, offering resources like counseling services, and encouraging open communication. By prioritizing emotional health, organizations can cultivate a more engaged and resilient workforce.

Moreover, acknowledging feelings is particularly important in parenting and caregiving roles. Children and adolescents learn about emotional expression largely through their caregivers. When parents model healthy emotional acknowledgment, it teaches children the importance of recognizing their own feelings and expressing them in appropriate ways. This foundational skill can lead to better emotional intelligence in children, equipping them with the tools they need to navigate life's challenges and build healthy relationships.

In times of crisis or significant life changes, acknowledging one's feelings becomes even more critical. Events such as loss, trauma, or major transitions can evoke a wide range of emotions, including grief, fear, and anxiety. Avoiding these feelings can lead to prolonged distress and hinder the healing process. By facing these emotions head-on and allowing themselves to grieve or process, individuals can move toward acceptance and healing. This acknowledgment can pave the way for personal growth and a renewed sense of purpose.

Creating supportive communities is essential for fostering a culture of emotional acknowledgment. Initiatives that promote mental health awareness, such as workshops, support groups, and public campaigns, can help individuals feel less isolated in their emotional experiences. These community efforts can provide safe spaces for individuals to share their feelings, learn from one another, and develop coping strategies. By collectively promoting emotional health, communities can build resilience and support networks that benefit everyone.

In conclusion, acknowledging one's feelings is a vital component of emotional health and well-being. It allows individuals to understand and process their emotions, leading to healthier relationships, personal growth, and improved resilience. As society continues to evolve, it is essential to foster an environment that encourages emotional expression and validation. By prioritizing emotional health, individuals can lead more fulfilling lives, support one another in their journeys, and contribute to a more empathetic and understanding world. Acknowledging feelings is not just a personal endeavor; it is a collective responsibility that can have profound effects on individuals and communities alike.

Chapter Five

What It Means to Feel Overwhelmed

Feeling overwhelmed is a common emotional experience that many people encounter at various points in their lives. It often manifests as a sense of being inundated by stressors, responsibilities, or emotions, leading to feelings of helplessness or confusion. The sensation of overwhelm can arise from a multitude of sources, including work demands, personal relationships, financial pressures, or significant life changes. Understanding what it means to feel overwhelmed is crucial for recognizing the signs and developing effective coping strategies.

At its core, feeling overwhelmed is a response to perceived excessive pressure. When individuals encounter tasks or emotions that exceed their ability to cope, they may experience a flood of anxiety, frustration, or despair. This can lead to a reduction in productivity and an inability to focus or make decisions. The brain's response to overwhelming situations often triggers a fight-or-flight reaction, which can further exacerbate feelings of stress and anxiety. This reaction may inhibit one's ability to think clearly and rationally, causing a sense of paralysis in the face of challenges.

The consequences of feeling overwhelmed can be both psychological and physical. Psychologically, individuals may experience heightened levels of anxiety, irritability, or mood swings. This emotional turmoil can lead to withdrawal from social activities, decreased motivation, and a general decline in mental health.

Physically, chronic overwhelm can manifest as fatigue, headaches, or other stress-related ailments. It is essential to recognize these symptoms, as they serve as indicators that one's emotional well-being is at risk and needs attention.

A significant factor that contributes to feelings of overwhelm is the modern lifestyle, characterized by constant connectivity and high expectations. With the rise of technology, individuals are often bombarded with information, notifications, and the pressure to be constantly productive. This "always-on" culture can create an environment where it feels impossible to escape from responsibilities or take time for self-care. As a result, the line between work and personal life can blur, leading to increased stress levels and feelings of being overwhelmed.

Recognizing the specific sources of overwhelm is a crucial step in managing it. Individuals may find it helpful to identify the key stressors contributing to their feelings. This could involve reflecting on daily tasks, responsibilities, or relationships that may be causing distress. Once these sources are identified, individuals can begin to develop strategies to address them, whether through delegation, time management, or setting boundaries. This process of self-reflection can empower individuals to regain a sense of control over their lives.

Another important aspect of feeling overwhelmed is the societal stigma surrounding vulnerability and emotional struggles. Many people believe that they should be able to handle everything independently, leading them to avoid seeking help when needed. This stigma can perpetuate feelings of isolation, making individuals feel as though they are the only ones experiencing overwhelm. By fostering open conversations about mental health and emotional well-being, society can create an environment where individuals feel comfortable expressing their struggles and seeking support.

Coping with feelings of overwhelm often requires a multifaceted approach. Mindfulness practices, such as meditation and deep-breathing exercises, can help individuals ground themselves and manage stress effectively. These techniques promote self-awareness and can create a sense of calm amidst chaos. Additionally, physical activity, creative outlets, and spending time in nature can serve as powerful tools for alleviating feelings of overwhelm. Engaging in activities that bring joy and relaxation can help restore balance and perspective.

Support systems play a critical role in managing feelings of overwhelm. Friends, family, and mental health professionals can provide invaluable support, offering a listening ear and practical advice. Sharing feelings of overwhelm can lead to validation and understanding, which can alleviate some of the burdens individuals carry. Building a network of supportive individuals encourages open dialogue about emotional struggles and fosters a sense of community, helping to combat feelings of isolation.

Establishing healthy boundaries is another essential strategy for managing overwhelm. Learning to say no to additional responsibilities or recognizing when to step back from commitments can help individuals maintain their emotional balance. Setting boundaries allows individuals to prioritize self-care and ensure that they are not spreading themselves too thin. This self-advocacy is crucial for maintaining emotional health and preventing the cycle of overwhelm from becoming a chronic issue.

Ultimately, feeling overwhelmed is a natural response to life's demands, but it does not have to be a permanent state. By recognizing the signs, understanding the sources, and employing effective coping strategies, individuals can regain control over their emotional well-being. It is essential to approach feelings of overwhelm with compassion and understanding, both for oneself and for others who may be experiencing similar struggles. Acknowledging that feeling overwhelmed is a shared human experience can foster connection and support, ultimately leading to greater resilience and emotional health.

In conclusion, feeling overwhelmed is a complex emotional state that can significantly impact an individual's mental and physical well-being. By recognizing the signs and sources of overwhelm, individuals can take proactive steps to manage their emotional health. Through open dialogue, support systems, and effective coping strategies, it is possible to navigate feelings of overwhelm and cultivate a sense of balance in life. This journey toward emotional resilience involves not only understanding the individual experience of overwhelm but also recognizing the broader societal context that influences it.

One of the key components of cultivating resilience is the practice of self-compassion. It is essential for individuals to treat themselves with kindness and understanding when they feel overwhelmed. Instead of criticizing oneself for struggling to cope, practicing self-compassion allows for a more nurturing approach, where individuals can acknowledge their feelings without judgment. This can create a sense of safety and acceptance, reducing the pressure to "have it all together" and enabling individuals to take the necessary steps to address their feelings of overwhelm.

Furthermore, developing a routine that incorporates regular self-care practices can significantly alleviate feelings of being overwhelmed. Self-care is not a one-size-fits-all concept; it encompasses a wide range of activities that promote physical, emotional, and mental well-being. Whether it's setting aside time for hobbies, engaging in physical exercise, or ensuring adequate sleep, these practices can provide individuals with the energy and clarity needed to face challenges more effectively. By prioritizing self-care, individuals can create a buffer against the stressors that contribute to feelings of overwhelm.

Another vital consideration is the importance of setting realistic expectations. In a world that often glorifies busyness and productivity, it's easy to fall into the trap of believing that one must constantly achieve and excel. However, recognizing that everyone has limitations and that it's okay to ask for help can be liberating. By setting achievable goals and celebrating small victories, individuals can foster a sense of accomplishment without succumbing to the pressure of unrealistic standards. This shift in mindset can prevent overwhelm from escalating and promote a more sustainable approach to life.

Additionally, engaging in regular reflection can help individuals understand their emotional responses and identify patterns that contribute to feelings of overwhelm. Journaling, for instance, can serve as a powerful tool for self-discovery. By writing down thoughts and feelings, individuals can gain insights into their triggers and the circumstances that lead to overwhelm. This practice not only facilitates emotional processing but also allows individuals to track their progress over time, fostering a greater sense of agency in managing their emotional health.

Social connections also play a crucial role in mitigating feelings of overwhelm. Building and maintaining relationships with supportive individuals can provide a sense of belonging and community. Sharing experiences with others who understand similar challenges can be incredibly validating. Whether through informal gatherings, support groups, or online communities, fostering social connections can reduce feelings of isolation and provide a platform for sharing coping strategies. It is often through these connections that individuals find encouragement and resources to navigate overwhelming situations.

In the workplace, organizations can implement practices that support employees in managing overwhelm. This might include promoting a healthy work-life balance, offering mental health resources, and creating a culture where employees feel comfortable discussing their challenges. Employers can also encourage regular breaks and downtime, allowing employees to recharge and return to their tasks with renewed focus. By prioritizing employee well-being, organizations can not only enhance productivity but also create a more positive and supportive work environment.

Moreover, it is essential to recognize that feelings of overwhelm can sometimes signal the need for professional help. Mental health professionals, such as therapists or counselors, can provide valuable support and tools for managing overwhelming emotions. Therapy can offer a safe space to explore feelings, develop coping strategies, and work through underlying issues that contribute to overwhelm. Seeking help is a sign of strength, and it can be a transformative step toward reclaiming one's emotional health.

As individuals navigate their feelings of overwhelm, it's important to remember that this experience is often temporary. Life is dynamic, and the challenges that contribute to feelings of overwhelm can shift and change over time. By developing resilience and implementing effective coping strategies, individuals can learn to adapt to new circumstances and manage stressors more effectively. This adaptability can lead to personal growth and a deeper understanding of oneself.

In conclusion, feeling overwhelmed is a common yet complex emotional experience that can significantly impact one's life. By recognizing the signs and sources of overwhelm, practicing self-compassion, prioritizing self-care, and fostering supportive relationships, individuals can cultivate resilience and navigate life's challenges with greater ease. It is crucial to approach feelings of overwhelm with empathy and understanding, both for oneself and others. Acknowledging that these feelings are a shared human experience can pave the way for connection, support, and ultimately, a more balanced and fulfilling life.

Chapter Six

The Cycle of Hopelessness

The cycle of hopelessness is a psychological phenomenon that ensnares individuals in a repetitive spiral of despair, characterized by a pervasive sense of helplessness and a belief that change is unattainable. This cycle often begins with adverse life events or ongoing stressors that overwhelm a person's coping mechanisms. As these stressors accumulate, the individual may start to internalize negative thoughts and feelings, leading to a diminished sense of self-worth and an increasing belief that their circumstances are insurmountable. This foundational stage sets the tone for a cascade of negative emotions and behaviors that can perpetuate the cycle.

Central to the cycle of hopelessness is the development of detrimental thought patterns. Cognitive distortions, such as all-or-nothing thinking, catastrophizing, and discounting the positive, can exacerbate feelings of hopelessness. When individuals begin to view their situations through a lens of negativity, they may overlook potential solutions or support systems that could facilitate change. This cognitive trap reinforces their sense of despair, creating a feedback loop that deepens their emotional turmoil.

As negative thoughts take root, the emotional fallout can be profound. Feelings of sadness, anxiety, and irritability may become chronic, leading individuals to withdraw from social interactions and activities that once brought joy. This withdrawal further isolates them, depriving them of essential support networks that could help them navigate their struggles. The resulting loneliness can amplify feelings of hopelessness, making it even more challenging to envision a path forward.

The cycle of hopelessness is not just psychological; it manifests behaviorally as well. Individuals may engage in self-destructive behaviors, such as substance abuse, unhealthy eating, or neglecting responsibilities, as a means of coping with their emotional pain. These behaviors can lead to further negative consequences, including deteriorating relationships, job loss, and health issues, which only serve to reinforce their feelings of helplessness.

The impact of hopelessness is not confined to the mind; it also has physiological ramifications. Chronic stress and emotional distress can lead to a host of health problems, including depression, anxiety disorders, cardiovascular issues, and weakened immune function. The body's response to prolonged hopelessness can create a cycle of physical health deterioration that further entrenches the feeling of hopelessness, making it increasingly difficult for individuals to break free from this cycle.

Environmental factors play a crucial role in perpetuating the cycle of hopelessness. Socioeconomic status, community support, and access to mental health resources can significantly influence an individual's ability to cope with adversity. Those living in environments marked by poverty, violence, or social isolation may find it particularly challenging to seek help or envision a better future. The external circumstances can compound internal struggles, making it appear as though hope is an unattainable luxury.

Recognizing the cycle of hopelessness is the first step toward breaking free from it. Awareness allows individuals to identify their negative thought patterns and emotional responses, creating an opportunity for intervention. Acknowledgment of their feelings, rather than suppressing or denying them, can be empowering. This process often involves a willingness to confront uncomfortable truths about their situation and to seek help, whether through therapy, support groups, or trusted friends and family.

Various therapeutic approaches can be effective in addressing the cycle of hopelessness. Cognitive-behavioral therapy (CBT), for instance, helps individuals challenge and reframe negative thought patterns, fostering a more balanced perspective. Additionally, mindfulness and acceptance-based therapies encourage individuals to engage with their thoughts and feelings without judgment, promoting emotional resilience. These interventions can provide practical tools for navigating the challenges of life, ultimately fostering a renewed sense of agency and hope.

Community support plays a pivotal role in combating hopelessness. Building connections with others who understand or have experienced similar struggles can create a sense of belonging and validation. Peer support groups, mentorship programs, and community resources can offer both practical assistance and emotional encouragement. This social support network can serve as a lifeline, reminding individuals that they are not alone in their struggles and that change is possible.

Finally, cultivating hope is essential in breaking the cycle of hopelessness. This involves setting small, achievable goals and celebrating incremental progress, which can help restore a sense of agency and purpose. Engaging in activities that foster passion, creativity, or connection can reignite a sense of joy and fulfillment. Ultimately, the journey out of hopelessness requires patience, self-compassion, and a commitment to seeking support, but with time and effort, it is entirely possible to emerge from the shadows and embrace a brighter future.

To effectively combat the cycle of hopelessness, it is essential to understand its roots. Often, hopelessness stems from traumatic experiences, chronic stress, or prolonged exposure to negative environments. These factors can lead to a learned helplessness, where individuals come to believe that their actions have no impact on their circumstances. Understanding this background can empower individuals to recognize that their feelings of hopelessness are responses to specific experiences, rather than inherent traits. This awareness is crucial for fostering a sense of agency and the possibility of change.

Cultural narratives surrounding success, failure, and mental health can significantly influence how individuals perceive their situations. Societal expectations often emphasize resilience and self-sufficiency, leaving little room for vulnerability or acknowledgment of struggle. When individuals feel pressured to conform to these ideals, they may suppress their feelings of hopelessness, leading to increased internal conflict. Challenging these cultural narratives and promoting a more compassionate understanding of mental health can create an environment where individuals feel safe to express their struggles and seek help.

Self-compassion is a powerful antidote to hopelessness. Practicing self-compassion involves treating oneself with kindness and understanding during times of difficulty, rather than engaging in self-criticism. This shift in mindset can help individuals break free from the negative thought patterns that contribute to hopelessness. By acknowledging their suffering without judgment, individuals can create space for healing and growth. Self-compassion can also encourage individuals to reach out for support, reinforcing the idea that vulnerability is not a weakness but a vital aspect of the human experience.

Effective coping strategies are essential for breaking the cycle of hopelessness. Individuals can benefit from learning healthy coping mechanisms that allow them to manage stress and emotional pain more effectively. Techniques such as deep breathing, journaling, physical exercise, and engaging in creative activities can provide constructive outlets for emotions. By developing a toolkit of coping strategies, individuals can better navigate challenging situations and reduce the feelings of helplessness that fuel the cycle of hopelessness.

Professional help can be a critical component in breaking the cycle of hopelessness. Mental health professionals, such as therapists and counselors, can provide tailored support and guidance. They can help individuals explore the underlying causes of their feelings, develop coping strategies, and work through cognitive distortions. Therapy can also offer a safe space for individuals to express their emotions and fears, which is often a crucial step in the healing process. Recognizing the value of professional help can empower individuals to take the necessary steps toward recovery.

Building resilience is another key factor in overcoming hopelessness. Resilience is the ability to bounce back from adversity and adapt to challenging circumstances. It can be cultivated through various means, including fostering a growth mindset, developing strong problem-solving skills, and maintaining social connections. Resilient individuals often view setbacks as temporary and manageable, which can counteract feelings of hopelessness. By focusing on resilience, individuals can shift their perspective and find strength even in the face of difficulty, allowing them to break free from the cycle of despair.

Hope is a transformative force that can counteract feelings of hopelessness. It involves the belief that positive change is possible and that one has the resources to achieve their goals. Cultivating hope can be achieved through goal-setting, visualization techniques, and affirmations that reinforce positive self-belief. By envisioning a brighter future and taking actionable steps toward it, individuals can gradually shift their mindset from one of despair to one of possibility. Hope acts as a catalyst for change, providing the motivation needed to break the cycle of hopelessness.

Mindfulness practices can play a significant role in breaking the cycle of hopelessness. Mindfulness encourages individuals to be present in the moment and to observe their thoughts and feelings without judgment. This practice can help individuals detach from negative thought patterns and reduce the intensity of their emotional responses. By fostering a non-reactive awareness, mindfulness can create a space for healing and self-acceptance, allowing individuals to confront their feelings of hopelessness with compassion and understanding.

Encouraging open dialogue about mental health and hopelessness is crucial for reducing stigma and promoting healing. By fostering an environment where individuals feel safe discussing their struggles, communities can help break the isolation that often accompanies hopelessness. Support groups, educational programs, and community initiatives can facilitate these conversations, creating a culture of understanding and support. When individuals feel that their experiences are validated and understood, they are more likely to seek help and take steps toward recovery.

Breaking the cycle of hopelessness is often a complex and non-linear journey. It requires patience, self-compassion, and a commitment to seeking change. While setbacks may occur, it is essential to recognize that progress is possible.

Chapter Seven

L ife: A Series of Challenges

Life can often feel like a tumultuous journey filled with a series of challenges that test our resilience and strength. For many, these challenges are compounded by struggles with mental health, creating a seemingly endless cycle of darkness that can be difficult to navigate. Yet, within this darkness, there lies a glimmer of hope, a chance to find light, healing, and ultimately, growth. Understanding this duality is essential in recognizing that while life may present us with obstacles, it also offers opportunities for profound transformation.

The first step in confronting life's challenges is acknowledging their existence. Mental health struggles can manifest in various forms, including anxiety, depression, and overwhelming stress. These conditions can distort our perception of reality, making it hard to see beyond the shadows that cloud our minds. Recognizing and accepting these feelings is not a sign of weakness but rather a courageous act of self-awareness. It is through this acknowledgment that we can begin to address our mental health and seek the support we need.

Once we accept our challenges, the journey toward finding light can begin. This often involves reaching out for help, whether through therapy, support groups, or trusted friends and family. The act of sharing our burdens can be incredibly cathartic, allowing us to release some of the weight we carry. In these conversations, we may discover that we are not alone in our struggles; many others face similar battles, creating a sense of community and shared understanding that can be profoundly healing.

As we navigate our mental health journey, it's essential to cultivate self-compassion. Life's challenges often lead to feelings of guilt, shame, or inadequacy, causing us to be our harshest critics. Learning to treat ourselves with kindness and understanding can be a radical shift in perspective. Instead of berating ourselves for our struggles, we can practice self-acceptance, recognizing that it is okay to feel overwhelmed and that healing is a process that takes time. This shift can illuminate paths toward self-improvement and emotional well-being.

Finding light in the darkness also involves discovering healthy coping mechanisms. Engaging in mindfulness practices, such as meditation, yoga, or journaling, can provide moments of clarity and peace amidst the chaos. These practices help ground us, allowing us to reconnect with our inner selves and gain perspective on our situations. They can serve as tools to manage anxiety, reduce stress, and promote emotional regulation, enabling us to face challenges with a clearer mind and a more balanced heart.

Engaging with nature can also be a powerful source of light during difficult times. The natural world has a unique ability to soothe our minds and elevate our spirits. Whether it's taking a stroll through a park, hiking in the mountains, or simply sitting by a body of water, immersing ourselves in nature can provide a sense of calm and connection. This connection to the earth often reminds us of the beauty that exists outside of our struggles and helps us realize that there is life beyond our pain.

Creativity can serve as another beacon of light in the darkness. Expressing ourselves through art, music, writing, or any form of creative outlet can be incredibly therapeutic. It allows us to channel our emotions into something tangible, giving voice to feelings that might otherwise remain trapped inside. This creative expression can lead to moments of clarity and insight, helping us process our experiences and fears, and ultimately transforming our pain into something beautiful and meaningful.

As we work through our challenges, it's crucial to celebrate small victories along the way. Every step forward, no matter how minor it may seem, is a testament to our resilience. Acknowledging these victories helps to build confidence and reinforce the idea that we are capable of overcoming adversity. This practice of gratitude can illuminate the path ahead, reminding us that even in difficult times, there are moments of joy and achievement worth recognizing.

The journey toward mental health recovery is rarely linear; it often includes setbacks and relapses. However, these challenges do not diminish our progress or worth. Instead, they serve as reminders that healing is a complex and ongoing process. Embracing this reality and adopting a growth mindset can empower us to learn from our experiences and continue seeking the light, even when it feels elusive. Each setback can become a stepping stone toward greater understanding and strength.

Ultimately, finding light in the darkness is about cultivating hope and resilience. It's about recognizing that while life presents us with immense challenges, it also offers us the capacity to rise above them. The journey may be fraught with obstacles, but it is also filled with opportunities for growth, connection, and self-discovery. By embracing our mental health challenges, seeking support, and nurturing our inner light, we can transform our struggles into a source of strength that propels us forward.

In conclusion, life, with all its complexities, invites us to engage with our challenges head-on. By acknowledging our struggles, practicing self-compassion, and seeking out light in moments of darkness, we can navigate our mental health journeys with grace and resilience. There is profound beauty in the acknowledgment of life's challenges and the pursuit of light amidst them. Our experiences, whether joyous or painful, shape who we are and inform our understanding of the world around us. When we learn to embrace our struggles, we open the door to a more profound sense of purpose and connection. This journey toward healing is not just about overcoming obstacles but also about integrating those experiences into our identity and using them to inspire others.

Embracing vulnerability is a crucial aspect of this journey. Society often promotes the idea of strength as invulnerability, but true strength lies in our ability to be open and honest about our feelings and experiences. By allowing ourselves to be vulnerable, we create space for authentic connections with others. Sharing our stories can foster understanding and compassion, both for ourselves and those around us. As we become more comfortable in our vulnerability, we give others permission to do the same, creating a ripple effect of healing in our communities.

As we move forward, it can be beneficial to engage in acts of service or kindness. Helping others in their struggles can provide a sense of purpose and fulfillment, reminding us that we are not alone in our battles. Volunteering, offering a listening ear, or simply being present for someone in need can shift our focus from our pain to the positive impact we can have on others' lives. This shift in perspective can illuminate our path, revealing the interconnectedness of our experiences and the importance of community in the journey toward healing.

In the search for light, it is also essential to establish boundaries. Life's challenges can often lead us to overextend ourselves, whether in relationships, work, or personal commitments. Learning to set boundaries allows us to prioritize our mental health and well-being. By recognizing what drains us and what nourishes us, we can cultivate a more balanced life. This self-awareness is crucial in maintaining our energy and focus on healing, ensuring that we do not become overwhelmed by external pressures.

Reflecting on our values and passions can also guide us in finding light. Engaging in activities that resonate with our core beliefs can reignite our sense of purpose and joy. Whether it's pursuing a hobby, participating in a cause we care about, or simply spending time with loved ones, reconnecting with what brings us joy can serve as a powerful antidote to the darkness. This alignment with our values helps us create a life that feels authentic and fulfilling, even amidst challenges.

Moreover, cultivating a practice of gratitude can be transformative. Taking the time each day to reflect on what we are thankful for, no matter how small, can shift our focus from what we lack to what we have. This practice helps to foster a more positive mindset, allowing us to see the beauty in our lives, even in difficult times. Gratitude encourages us to recognize the light that exists alongside our challenges, reminding us of the moments of joy and connection that enrich our experiences.

As we navigate the complexities of life, it's important to seek out resources that support our mental health. This could include therapy, support groups, or self-help literature that resonates with us. The knowledge that we are not alone in our struggles can be incredibly comforting and empowering. These resources provide us with tools and strategies to cope with our challenges, helping us build resilience and develop a deeper understanding of ourselves.

Ultimately, the journey of finding light in the darkness is a deeply personal and transformative process. Each individual's path will be unique, shaped by their experiences, beliefs, and support systems. By embracing our challenges, cultivating self-compassion, and seeking connection with others, we can illuminate our paths and navigate the complexities of life with grace. This journey is not merely about surviving; it's about thriving, discovering our inner strength, and emerging from the darkness with a renewed sense of purpose.

In this ever-evolving journey of life, it's essential to remember that the light we seek is often within us. By nurturing our inner selves, practicing self-love, and embracing our vulnerabilities, we can find the strength to face our challenges head-on. Life may present us with obstacles, but it also offers us the gift of resilience, hope, and the capacity to shine even in the darkest of times.

Chapter Eight:

The Strength in Vulnerability

Strength in vulnerability is a profound concept that has gained increasing recognition in discussions surrounding mental health. Traditionally, society often equates strength with invincibility, encouraging individuals to hide their struggles and project an image of unwavering confidence. However, true strength emerges when one embraces vulnerability, the willingness to acknowledge and share one's fears, insecurities, and emotional pain. This willingness can foster deeper connections, promote healing, and empower others to confront their own challenges.

At its core, vulnerability is about authenticity. When individuals allow themselves to be seen in their raw, unfiltered form, they create a space for genuine connection. This authenticity breaks down the barriers of isolation often felt by those struggling with mental health issues. By sharing their experiences, individuals can find solace in knowing they are not alone. This sense of community can be incredibly healing, as it encourages mutual understanding and support, fostering a culture where seeking help is normalized rather than stigmatized.

Embracing vulnerability also plays a crucial role in self-acceptance. For many, mental health struggles can lead to feelings of shame or inadequacy. However, recognizing that vulnerability is a shared human experience can help dissolve these feelings. When individuals accept their struggles as part of their journey, they can begin to cultivate self-compassion. This self-compassion is key to healing, as it allows individuals to treat themselves with the same kindness they would offer a friend facing similar challenges.

Moreover, vulnerability invites authenticity into our relationships. When individuals open up about their mental health struggles, it encourages others to do the same. This mutual sharing creates a safe environment where individuals can express their thoughts and feelings without fear of judgment. Such openness can lead to deeper, more meaningful relationships, as it fosters trust and intimacy. In these connections, individuals can find strength and encouragement, reinforcing the idea that vulnerability is not a weakness but rather a powerful tool for building resilience.

The act of sharing one's mental health journey can also serve as a source of inspiration for others. When individuals bravely speak about their struggles, they provide a voice for those who may feel silenced by their own experiences. This visibility can help to dismantle the stigma surrounding mental health, encouraging more individuals to seek help and support. By sharing stories of resilience and recovery, individuals can empower others to embrace their vulnerabilities, illustrating that it is possible to seek help and heal.

In the context of mental health, vulnerability can also lead to personal growth. Facing one's fears and insecurities can be daunting, but it often paves the way for transformative experiences. By confronting difficult emotions and situations, individuals can develop greater emotional intelligence and resilience. This growth fosters a deeper understanding of oneself, ultimately leading to an enhanced ability to navigate future challenges. In this way, vulnerability acts as a catalyst for personal development and empowerment.

Furthermore, vulnerability can enhance creativity and self-expression. Many individuals find that their mental health struggles inspire their creative pursuits. Whether through writing, art, music, or other forms of expression, sharing one's vulnerabilities can lead to powerful and transformative creations. This creative outlet not only serves as a form of self-therapy but also resonates with others who may feel similarly. It creates a shared experience that can foster connection and understanding, reminding us that our vulnerabilities can be a source of beauty and strength.

In the professional realm, embracing vulnerability can lead to more effective leadership and collaboration. Leaders who demonstrate vulnerability create a culture of openness and trust within their teams. By acknowledging their own challenges, they set an example that encourages team members to voice their concerns and seek support. This vulnerability fosters a sense of belonging and psychological safety, which can enhance teamwork and creativity. Ultimately, leaders who embrace their vulnerabilities can inspire others to bring their authentic selves to work, leading to a more engaged and productive environment.

As society continues to evolve, it is essential to create spaces where vulnerability is celebrated rather than shamed. Mental health awareness campaigns, support groups, and community initiatives can all play a role in fostering this culture. By promoting open conversations about mental health and vulnerability, we can help dismantle the stigma that often surrounds these topics. It is crucial to remind individuals that seeking help is a sign of strength, and that embracing vulnerability can lead to healing and growth.

In conclusion, strength in vulnerability is a powerful and transformative concept, particularly in the realm of mental health. By embracing our vulnerabilities, we can build deeper connections, foster self-acceptance, and inspire others to confront their own struggles. The journey toward mental well-being is often paved with challenges, but it is through vulnerability that we can find resilience, creativity, and personal growth. As we continue to navigate our mental health journeys, let us remember that it is our willingness to be vulnerable that ultimately lights the path toward healing and connection.

The journey toward embracing vulnerability in mental health is not always easy, but it is often paramount for healing and growth. Many individuals grapple with the fear of being judged or misunderstood, which can deter them from sharing their struggles. This fear can create a cycle of silence and isolation, where individuals feel trapped in their pain. However, when one takes the courageous step to open up about their experiences, it can lead to profound relief and connection. By vocalizing their fears and emotions, individuals not only lighten their own burdens but also encourage others to share their stories, thus breaking the cycle of isolation.

Mental health education plays a vital role in fostering an environment where vulnerability is accepted and encouraged. Schools, workplaces, and communities can benefit from programs that highlight the importance of mental health awareness. Such initiatives can provide individuals with the tools to understand their emotions better and recognize that seeking help is a strength rather than a weakness. By normalizing conversations about mental health, we can create a culture where individuals feel safe to express their vulnerabilities, ultimately leading to healthier communities.

Moreover, the digital age has provided a unique platform for individuals to share their mental health journeys. Social media and online forums have become spaces where people can connect over shared experiences, offering support and validation. When individuals share their vulnerabilities online, they reach a broader audience, spreading awareness and building solidarity among those facing similar challenges. This digital community can serve as a lifeline, providing encouragement and resources to those who may feel alone in their struggles. The power of storytelling, especially in the digital realm, can be transformative, inspiring others to seek help and embrace their own vulnerabilities.

Therapeutic practices also emphasize the importance of vulnerability in healing. Many therapeutic approaches, including cognitive-behavioral therapy (CBT) and acceptance and commitment therapy (ACT), encourage individuals to confront their fears and emotions head-on. By creating a safe space for individuals to explore their vulnerabilities, therapists can guide them toward understanding and acceptance. This therapeutic relationship itself is built on vulnerability, as clients share their most intimate thoughts and feelings. The trust established in this dynamic reinforces the notion that vulnerability can lead to profound healing and transformation.

In addition to personal benefits, embracing vulnerability can have a broader societal impact. When individuals openly discuss their mental health challenges, they contribute to a collective understanding that mental health is a shared human experience. This normalization can help reduce stigma and foster empathy among those who may not have firsthand experience with mental health issues. By creating a culture of openness, we can encourage a more compassionate society, where individuals support one another through their struggles rather than shying away from difficult conversations.

Furthermore, vulnerability can enhance resilience in the face of adversity. When individuals acknowledge their challenges, they are better equipped to cope with difficult situations. This acknowledgment allows them to seek support and develop effective coping strategies. By facing their vulnerabilities, individuals can also cultivate a growth mindset, viewing challenges as opportunities for learning and personal development. This resilience is crucial, as it empowers individuals to navigate future obstacles with greater confidence and adaptability.

While embracing vulnerability is a powerful step toward healing, it is essential to approach it with care. Not everyone may be ready to share their experiences, and that's okay. Each individual's journey is unique and unfolds at its own pace. It's important to create a supportive environment that respects personal boundaries and encourages individuals to engage with their vulnerabilities when they feel safe to do so. Compassionate listening and understanding can help foster a safe space where vulnerability can be explored, without pressure or judgment.

In conclusion, recognizing and embracing strength in vulnerability surrounding mental health is a transformative process that can lead to deeper connections, personal growth, and societal change. By sharing our struggles, we not only lighten our own burdens but also empower others to do the same. As we continue to cultivate a culture of openness and acceptance, let us remember that vulnerability is not a sign of weakness but a testament to our shared humanity. By celebrating our vulnerabilities, we pave the way for healing, resilience, and a more compassionate world.

Chapter Nine:

Finding the Right Support System

Finding the right support system is crucial for anyone navigating the complexities of mental health. The journey of mental well-being can be daunting, and having a network of understanding individuals can make a significant difference. Support systems can come in various forms, including friends, family, therapists, support groups, and even online communities. Identifying the right combination of these resources can provide the emotional support, encouragement, and understanding needed to thrive.

One of the first steps in building a support system is recognizing the importance of open communication. Being able to express your feelings and experiences openly allows you to identify who in your life is willing and able to support you. This might involve having honest conversations with friends or family members about your mental health struggles and what kind of support you are seeking. It's essential to communicate your needs clearly, whether it's a listening ear, practical assistance, or simply companionship during tough times. This openness can pave the way for deeper connections and understanding.

Additionally, seeking professional help is a vital component of a strong support system. Mental health professionals, such as therapists, psychologists, and counselors, are trained to provide guidance and support tailored to individual needs. They can offer coping strategies, tools for managing symptoms, and a safe space to explore feelings. Finding the right therapist is a personal journey; it's important to seek someone with whom you feel comfortable, respected, and understood. This relationship can serve as a cornerstone of your support system, providing ongoing assistance as you navigate your mental health journey.

Peer support groups can also be an invaluable resource. These groups, often facilitated by trained individuals, bring together people who share similar experiences and challenges. The power of peer support lies in the shared understanding of mental health struggles. Participants can offer insights, share coping strategies, and provide validation in a non-judgmental environment. Engaging with a support group can foster a sense of belonging and reduce feelings of isolation, helping individuals realize that they are not alone in their experiences.

In addition to traditional support systems, online communities have emerged as a powerful tool for connection and support. Social media platforms, forums, and dedicated mental health websites allow individuals to share their experiences, seek advice, and find solace in the stories of others. These online spaces can be particularly beneficial for those who may feel uncomfortable discussing their mental health face-to-face or who live in areas with limited access to mental health resources. However, it's essential to approach online support with caution, ensuring that the communities you engage with are safe and supportive.

Family dynamics play a significant role in one's support system, and it's crucial to assess how your family interacts with mental health issues. Having family members who understand and support your mental health journey can be incredibly beneficial. If family dynamics are complicated or if there is a lack of understanding around mental health, it may be helpful to educate them on your experiences or even involve a therapist to facilitate conversations.

Building a supportive family environment can foster a sense of security and understanding, making it easier to navigate challenges.

When building a support system, it's also essential to consider the role of self-care. While external support is important, developing an internal support system through self-compassion and self-awareness can significantly enhance your resilience. Practicing self-care can involve engaging in activities that bring joy, relaxation, and fulfillment. Mindfulness, journaling, and physical activity are examples of practices that can help you connect with your feelings and foster a positive mindset. By prioritizing self-care, you reinforce your ability to cope with challenges, making your support system more effective.

As you build your support network, it's crucial to evaluate the quality of your relationships. Surrounding yourself with individuals who uplift and encourage you is essential for mental well-being. Conversely, relationships that drain energy or contribute to negative feelings can hinder your progress. Assessing your social circle and making conscious choices about who to spend time with can help cultivate a more supportive environment. Remember that it's okay to distance yourself from toxic relationships in favor of those that contribute positively to your mental health.

Moreover, it's essential to be proactive in seeking out support. It can be easy to fall into a pattern of waiting for others to reach out or offer help, but taking the initiative can lead to more fulfilling connections. Don't hesitate to seek out friends or loved ones when you're feeling low; reaching out can strengthen your bonds and create a sense of reciprocity in your relationships. Additionally, actively participating in community events, workshops, or classes can introduce you to new people who may become valuable additions to your support system.

Lastly, it's important to remember that finding the right support system is an ongoing process. As your mental health needs evolve, so too might your support network. Being open to change and willing to seek out new connections can enhance your resilience and sense of belonging. Whether through friendships, professional guidance, or community involvement, the right support system can provide the foundation for your mental health journey, helping you navigate challenges and celebrate successes along the way.

In conclusion, finding the right support system is a dynamic and essential aspect of maintaining mental health and well-being. Each individual's journey is unique, and the right support system may look different for everyone. The process involves a combination of self-discovery, communication, and a willingness to seek help from various sources. By recognizing and embracing the multifaceted nature of support, individuals can cultivate a network that fosters resilience, understanding, and healing.

One crucial element to consider in building a support system is the importance of trust. Trust is the foundation of any meaningful relationship, and it becomes even more vital when addressing sensitive topics like mental health. When seeking support, it's important to choose individuals who respect your boundaries, listen without judgment, and maintain confidentiality. This trust allows for open dialogue, enabling you to share your feelings and experiences more freely. When you feel safe with those around you, it can significantly enhance your ability to cope with challenges.

Additionally, diversity in your support system can enhance its effectiveness. Surrounding yourself with a range of perspectives and experiences can provide a more holistic approach to your mental health. Different people may offer various coping strategies, insights, and ways of understanding your situation. For example, while a therapist may provide professional guidance, a friend might offer camaraderie and lightheartedness, and a support group can provide shared experiences. This diversity ensures that you have multiple resources to draw upon during difficult times.

Another critical aspect of finding the right support system involves setting realistic expectations. It's essential to recognize that no single person can fulfill all your emotional needs. Friends and family may have their limitations, and mental health professionals may not always have immediate solutions. By understanding that support is a collaborative effort, you can approach your relationships with patience and compassion. This awareness can also help mitigate disappointment and frustration when others cannot provide the support you seek.

The process of seeking support can also serve as an opportunity for personal growth. Engaging with different individuals and communities can help you develop greater emotional intelligence, empathy, and communication skills. As you navigate these relationships, you may find yourself becoming more aware of your own needs, desires, and boundaries. This self-awareness can enhance your overall mental health and well-being, making you more equipped to support others in return. The reciprocal nature of support systems can create a network of care that benefits everyone involved.

As you build your support system, it's also vital to be mindful of the potential for burnout, both for yourself and for those providing support. Emotional labor can be taxing, and it's essential to recognize when you or your supporters need a break. Practicing self-care and encouraging your supporters to do the same can help prevent feelings of exhaustion and resentment. Openly discussing the need for boundaries and self-care within your support network can contribute to healthier and more sustainable relationships.

In addition to human connections, consider incorporating community resources into your support system. Local organizations, mental health hotlines, and online platforms can provide valuable information and assistance. These resources may offer workshops, educational materials, and opportunities for connection that can complement your personal relationships. Engaging with community resources can help you feel more connected and supported, particularly during times when you may feel isolated or overwhelmed.

As you continue to navigate your mental health journey, remember that seeking support is a sign of strength, not weakness. It takes courage to reach out, share your experiences, and ask for help. Embracing vulnerability in this way can lead to deeper connections and a more profound understanding of yourself and your needs. By acknowledging that you are deserving of support, you empower yourself to seek out the resources that will enhance your mental well-being.

Ultimately, finding the right support system is an evolving process that requires patience, openness, and self-compassion. The relationships you build, the resources you engage with, and the personal growth you experience will all contribute to your overall mental health. As you cultivate a network of support, you create a foundation that fosters resilience, connection, and healing. In this journey, remember that you are not alone; there are countless individuals and resources willing to walk alongside you as you navigate the complexities of mental health.

Chapter Ten:

Professional Help: Therapists and Counselors

Mental health has emerged as a critical aspect of overall well-being, leading to a growing recognition of the importance of professional help from therapists and counselors. These trained professionals play a vital role in supporting individuals grappling with various mental health issues, from anxiety and depression to trauma and relationship difficulties. By providing a safe and confidential space, therapists and counselors empower clients to explore their thoughts and feelings, facilitating personal growth and healing.

Therapists and counselors come from diverse educational backgrounds, often holding advanced degrees in psychology, social work, or counseling. Their training equips them with the skills necessary to understand complex emotional and psychological issues. Many also undergo rigorous clinical training, which includes supervised experience in therapeutic settings. This education and training ensure that they are well-prepared to navigate the intricacies of human behavior and mental health challenges.

One of the key features of therapy is the establishment of a therapeutic alliance between the client and the therapist. This relationship is built on trust, empathy, and respect, allowing clients to feel comfortable sharing their innermost thoughts and feelings. The effectiveness of therapy often hinges on this connection, as it enables clients to engage more fully in the therapeutic process. A strong therapeutic alliance can foster a sense of safety, encouraging clients to confront difficult emotions and experiences.

Therapists and counselors employ various therapeutic modalities and techniques tailored to the individual needs of their clients. Cognitive-behavioral therapy (CBT), for example, focuses on identifying and changing negative thought patterns and behaviors. In contrast, psychodynamic therapy delves into the unconscious mind to uncover underlying issues that may be influencing current behavior. Other approaches, such as mindfulness-based therapies, emphasize the importance of being present and accepting one's feelings without judgment. This diversity in therapeutic approaches allows clients to find a method that resonates with them.

In recent years, the stigma surrounding mental health has diminished, leading more individuals to seek professional help. This shift is crucial, as it encourages people to acknowledge their struggles and pursue treatment without fear of judgment. Increased awareness of mental health issues has also been fueled by social media and public campaigns, which highlight the importance of seeking help and normalize conversations about mental health.

Access to therapy has become more widespread, thanks in part to technological advancements. Teletherapy, or online therapy, has gained popularity, providing clients with greater flexibility and accessibility. This mode of therapy allows individuals to connect with therapists from the comfort of their homes, eliminating barriers such as transportation and geographical limitations. As a result, more people can access the support they need, regardless of their circumstances.

Despite the many benefits of therapy, some individuals may still hesitate to seek help due to misconceptions about mental health treatment. Common myths include the belief that therapy is only for those with severe mental illness or that it is a sign of weakness to seek help. In reality, therapy can be beneficial for anyone facing life's challenges, and seeking help signifies strength and a willingness to grow. Educating the public about the realities of therapy can help dispel these myths and encourage more individuals to pursue mental health support.

The role of therapists and counselors extends beyond individual therapy sessions. They often engage in community outreach and education, providing resources and information about mental health to the public. This can include workshops, support groups, and informational sessions that aim to raise awareness and promote mental well-being. By fostering a deeper understanding of mental health issues, therapists can contribute to a more supportive and informed community.

In addition to addressing immediate mental health concerns, therapy can also facilitate long-term personal development. Many clients find that through therapy, they gain valuable insights into their patterns of behavior, relationships, and coping strategies. This self-awareness can lead to more fulfilling lives, as individuals learn to navigate challenges with greater resilience. As clients develop healthier coping mechanisms, they often report improved relationships, increased self-esteem, and a clearer sense of purpose.

The journey of seeking professional help is often a transformative experience. For many, the initial step of reaching out to a therapist or counselor can feel daunting, yet it is a courageous move toward healing and self-discovery. As clients engage in therapy, they learn to confront their fears, process their emotions, and develop the tools necessary to cope with life's difficulties. The support and guidance of a trained professional can make a significant difference in one's mental health journey, ultimately leading to a more balanced and fulfilling life.

In conclusion, therapists and counselors play an essential role in the landscape of mental health. Their expertise, compassion, and commitment to helping others create a supportive environment where individuals can explore their mental health challenges. By fostering awareness, dispelling stigma, and providing access to treatment, these professionals contribute to a healthier society, where individuals are empowered to seek help and prioritize their mental well-being.

The evolution of mental health care and the role of therapists and counselors have become increasingly relevant in today's fast-paced and often stressful society. As people navigate the complexities of modern life, the demand for psychological support has surged. Therapists and counselors are equipped not only to address existing mental health issues but also to help individuals develop resilience against future challenges. Their expertise allows them to guide clients through periods of uncertainty and stress, fostering a sense of stability and perspective.

One of the significant advantages of therapy is its adaptability. Different life stages and circumstances call for different approaches, and therapists are trained to modify their strategies to meet the unique needs of their clients. For instance, children may benefit from play therapy, which uses games and creative activities to help them express their feelings. Adolescents may require a different approach that emphasizes building coping skills and navigating peer relationships. Adults often seek therapy for a range of issues, including stress management, work-life balance, and relationship challenges. This versatility ensures that therapy remains relevant for individuals of all ages.

Therapists also recognize the importance of culture and diversity in the therapeutic process. Different cultural backgrounds can significantly influence an individual's perspective on mental health, coping mechanisms, and willingness to seek help. Culturally competent therapists are trained to understand and respect these differences, creating an inclusive environment that affirms the client's identity. By integrating cultural sensitivity into their practice, these professionals can better support clients from various backgrounds, ultimately leading to more effective and personalized treatment.

In addition to one-on-one sessions, group therapy has emerged as a powerful tool for healing and connection. Group therapy brings together individuals facing similar challenges, allowing them to share their experiences and support one another. This collective approach fosters a sense of community and belonging, which can be particularly beneficial for those who feel isolated in their struggles. The shared insights and encouragement found in group settings often lead to significant breakthroughs and enhanced coping strategies, as participants learn from each other's journeys.

As mental health continues to gain recognition, the integration of therapy into holistic health practices is becoming more common. Many therapists now collaborate with other healthcare professionals, such as physicians, nutritionists, and fitness trainers, to provide a comprehensive approach to well-being. This integrative model acknowledges that mental health is interconnected with physical health, and addressing both aspects can lead to more effective outcomes. By working in tandem with other professionals, therapists can offer clients a more rounded perspective on their overall health.

The impact of therapy also extends to the workplace, where employee mental health has become a critical focus. Organizations are increasingly recognizing the importance of supporting their employees' mental well-being, leading to the introduction of employee assistance programs (EAPs) that provide access to counseling and mental health resources. By fostering a supportive work environment, companies can enhance employee satisfaction, reduce burnout, and improve overall productivity. Therapists can play a crucial role in this process, offering workshops and training that promote mental health awareness and resilience in the workplace.

The ongoing advancements in mental health research further enhance the effectiveness of therapy. As new findings emerge regarding brain function, trauma, and emotional regulation, therapists are better equipped to apply evidence-based practices in their work. This commitment to continual learning ensures that therapy remains a dynamic field, adapting to new knowledge and evolving with the changing needs of society. Clients benefit from this progressive approach, receiving treatments grounded in the latest scientific understanding.

Ultimately, the journey of seeking help from a therapist or counselor is deeply personal and can lead to profound changes in one's life. Many clients report feeling a renewed sense of hope and empowerment after engaging in therapy. The process of exploring thoughts and feelings, coupled with the guidance of a trained professional, can facilitate healing and growth that extends beyond the therapy room. Clients often find themselves equipped with new tools for managing stress, improving relationships, and approaching life's challenges with a positive mindset.

In summary, therapists and counselors are integral to the mental health landscape, providing essential support and guidance to individuals from all walks of life. Through their expertise, cultural competence, and commitment to ongoing education, they help clients navigate the complexities of mental health and personal growth. As society continues to embrace the importance of mental well-being, the role of these professionals will only become more vital, fostering a healthier, more resilient community.

Chapter Eleven:

Expressing Your Feelings

Expressing feelings is a fundamental aspect of maintaining mental health and well-being. It serves as a vital outlet for individuals to process their emotions, articulate their experiences, and communicate their needs. In a world that often encourages stoicism and emotional restraint, recognizing the importance of expressing feelings can be transformative. This practice not only fosters self-awareness but also helps individuals build resilience against the challenges they face in their lives.

One of the primary benefits of expressing feelings is the reduction of emotional burden. When individuals suppress their emotions, they can accumulate stress and anxiety, which may lead to physical and mental health issues. By openly sharing their feelings, whether through conversations with friends, journaling, or therapy, individuals can alleviate this internal pressure. This act of expression can lead to a sense of relief, as it allows people to confront their emotions rather than allowing them to fester in silence.

Moreover, expressing feelings fosters deeper connections in relationships. When individuals share their thoughts and emotions, it invites vulnerability and authenticity into their interactions. This openness not only strengthens existing relationships but also encourages others to share their feelings in return. Such exchanges create a supportive environment where individuals can feel understood, validated, and less isolated in their struggles. This sense of connection is particularly crucial during challenging times when emotional support is needed most.

Articulating feelings can also serve as a powerful tool for self-discovery. When individuals take the time to explore their emotions, they gain insights into their needs, desires, and triggers. This self-awareness can lead to healthier coping strategies and improved emotional regulation. By understanding the root causes of their feelings, individuals can make more informed decisions and take proactive steps toward their mental health. This journey of self-discovery can be empowering, as it encourages individuals to take ownership of their emotional well-being.

In the context of mental health, expressing feelings can be a form of therapy in itself. Many therapeutic practices emphasize the importance of verbalizing emotions as a pathway to healing. Techniques such as talk therapy, group therapy, and expressive writing provide individuals with structured ways to communicate their feelings and experiences. These practices not only facilitate healing but also promote the development of effective coping mechanisms and problem-solving skills. In this way, expressing feelings becomes a crucial component of the therapeutic process.

Additionally, expressing feelings can contribute to the destigmatization of mental health issues. When individuals openly share their struggles, it helps normalize conversations about mental health and emotional well-being. By challenging the societal norms that often discourage emotional expression, individuals can create a culture of openness and acceptance. This shift can empower others to seek help when needed, ultimately leading to a more supportive community where mental health is prioritized.

The act of expressing feelings can also have physiological benefits. Research has shown that sharing emotions can lead to a decrease in stress hormones and an increase in overall well-being. For instance, individuals who engage in expressive writing often report feeling less anxious and more optimistic. This connection between emotional expression and physical health underscores the importance of addressing mental health holistically. By recognizing the mind-body connection, individuals can take proactive steps to enhance their overall quality of life.

In moments of crisis or emotional distress, expressing feelings can be a lifeline. When individuals experience overwhelming emotions, sharing their struggles can prevent feelings of isolation and hopelessness. This is particularly important in situations where individuals may feel trapped or powerless. By reaching out to trusted friends, family members, or mental health professionals, individuals can find support and guidance during their most challenging moments. This sense of connection can be a source of strength, helping individuals navigate through their difficulties.

Furthermore, creative expression can be a powerful avenue for communicating feelings. Many individuals find solace in artistic pursuits, such as painting, music, or writing poetry, as they provide an alternative means of expression. Creativity allows individuals to explore complex emotions in a way that may be difficult to articulate verbally. Engaging in creative outlets can serve as a therapeutic process, enabling individuals to confront their feelings, reflect on their experiences, and ultimately find healing through artistic expression.

In conclusion, the importance of expressing feelings surrounding mental health cannot be overstated. It is a vital practice that fosters self-awareness, emotional relief, and stronger relationships. By openly sharing their thoughts and emotions, individuals can reduce the burden of unprocessed feelings, enhance their connections with others, and contribute to a culture of acceptance around mental health. Whether through conversation, creative expression, or therapeutic practices, the act of expressing feelings is a powerful tool for personal growth and mental well-being. Embracing this practice can lead to a more fulfilling and balanced life, where individuals feel empowered to navigate their emotional landscapes with resilience and courage.

Building on the importance of expressing feelings surrounding mental health, it is essential to recognize that emotional expression is not just a personal benefit; it also creates a ripple effect in society. When individuals are open about their emotions and mental health struggles, they contribute to a broader cultural shift that values vulnerability and authenticity. This openness encourages others to share their stories, leading to collective healing and understanding. As more people engage in conversations about mental health, societal stigma begins to diminish, ultimately fostering a healthier environment for everyone.

In educational settings, teaching students the value of expressing their feelings can have profound long-term effects. Programs that incorporate social-emotional learning emphasize the importance of emotional literacy, equipping students with the tools to identify, articulate, and manage their emotions. By fostering a culture of open expression from a young age, schools can help cultivate emotionally intelligent individuals who are better equipped to navigate the complexities of life. This foundational understanding can reduce issues such as bullying, anxiety, and depression among students, leading to healthier school environments.

The workplace, too, can benefit significantly from a culture that promotes emotional expression. Employers who encourage their employees to share their feelings and experiences create a more inclusive and supportive atmosphere. When employees feel safe to express their concerns or frustrations, it can enhance job satisfaction and overall productivity. Additionally, workplaces that prioritize mental health often see lower turnover rates and improved employee morale. By valuing emotional expression, organizations can foster a culture of mental well-being that benefits both individuals and the organization as a whole.

Therapists and mental health professionals play a crucial role in facilitating emotional expression. Through various therapeutic techniques, they create safe spaces for clients to explore their feelings without fear of judgment. Techniques such as active listening, reflective dialogue, and validation help clients articulate their emotions effectively. These professionals guide clients in understanding their feelings, empowering them to express themselves outside of therapy sessions. As clients learn to communicate their emotions, they often experience a transformation in their relationships and overall mental well-being.

Moreover, the digital age has provided new avenues for expressing feelings, particularly through social media and online platforms. While there are undoubtedly challenges associated with social media, it can also serve as a powerful tool for individuals to share their mental health journeys. Online communities provide spaces for individuals to connect with others who share similar experiences, fostering a sense of belonging and support. These platforms can empower individuals to voice their emotions, seek advice, and find solidarity in their struggles, reinforcing the idea that they are not alone.

Expressing feelings is also integral to the healing process for those who have experienced trauma. For many, recounting their traumatic experiences can be daunting, but sharing these feelings is often a critical step toward recovery. Therapies such as Narrative Exposure Therapy and Eye Movement Desensitization and Reprocessing (EMDR) emphasize the importance of processing and articulating traumatic memories. By expressing their feelings surrounding their trauma, individuals can begin to reframe their experiences and integrate them into their narrative, paving the way for healing and empowerment.

In addition to formal therapeutic settings, support groups can provide invaluable opportunities for emotional expression. These groups bring together individuals who share similar challenges, allowing for open dialogue and shared experiences. The act of voicing feelings in a group setting can help individuals feel validated and understood, reinforcing the idea that their emotions are legitimate. Support groups can help individuals develop new coping strategies and foster meaningful connections with others who are on similar journeys.

Practicing emotional expression can also lead to enhanced emotional regulation. When individuals learn to articulate their feelings, they gain a better understanding of their emotional triggers and responses. This awareness enables them to respond to situations more thoughtfully rather than reactively. As a result, individuals can develop healthier coping mechanisms, reducing the likelihood of emotional outbursts or internalized stress. This growth in emotional regulation can lead to more stable relationships and improved mental health overall.

In summary, the importance of expressing feelings surrounding mental health is multifaceted and far-reaching. From fostering deeper connections and building resilience to contributing to societal change, the act of articulating emotions plays a crucial role in individual and collective well-being. By creating supportive environments, whether in schools, workplaces, or communities, we can encourage emotional expression as a vital component of mental health. As we continue to prioritize open dialogue about feelings, we move toward a more compassionate and understanding society where mental health is recognized as a fundamental aspect of human experience. Embracing emotional expression empowers individuals to take control of their mental health journeys, ultimately leading to healthier, more fulfilling lives.

Chapter Twelve:

Talking to Friends and Family

Talking to friends and family during times of mental health challenges is of paramount importance. When individuals face mental health issues, the burden can often feel isolating and overwhelming. Engaging in conversations with trusted loved ones can alleviate this sense of isolation, providing emotional support and understanding. These interactions can help individuals feel less alone in their struggles, reminding them that they are part of a community that cares about their well-being.

The act of sharing feelings and experiences with friends and family can also facilitate emotional processing. Many individuals find that articulating their emotions allows them to gain clarity and insight into their mental health challenges. When they express what they are going through, they can better understand their feelings and identify patterns or triggers. This process of reflection can lead to greater self-awareness, enabling individuals to recognize their needs and seek appropriate help when necessary.

Moreover, friends and family often provide a unique perspective that can be invaluable during difficult times. Loved ones may recognize changes in behavior or mood that the individual may not be aware of, offering insights that can prompt further exploration of mental health. Their observations can serve as a gentle nudge toward seeking professional help or trying different coping strategies.

The support of trusted individuals can sometimes be the catalyst for someone to take the necessary steps toward recovery.

In addition to offering support, friends and family can help hold individuals accountable in their mental health journeys. When someone is struggling, it can be easy to fall into unhealthy habits or neglect self-care. By talking openly about their feelings, individuals can invite their loved ones to check in on them and encourage positive behaviors. This accountability can be a motivating factor in maintaining mental health practices and seeking help when needed, fostering a sense of responsibility toward one's well-being.

The benefits of talking to friends and family extend beyond emotional support; they can also provide practical assistance. Loved ones can help individuals navigate the complexities of mental health care, such as finding a therapist, scheduling appointments, or researching treatment options. Additionally, they can offer help in managing day-to-day responsibilities that may feel overwhelming during tough times. This practical support can make a significant difference in an individual's ability to focus on recovery.

Furthermore, conversations with friends and family can contribute to the destigmatization of mental health issues. When individuals openly discuss their struggles, it encourages a culture of acceptance and understanding. By normalizing these conversations, loved ones can help break down the barriers that often prevent people from seeking help. This shift in perspective can lead to a broader societal understanding of mental health, making it easier for others to share their experiences and seek support.

The emotional bond shared with friends and family can also serve as a protective factor against the negative impacts of mental health challenges. Research has shown that strong social support networks can lead to better mental health outcomes. When individuals feel loved and supported, they are more likely to cope effectively with stress and adversity. This sense of belonging can foster resilience, helping individuals navigate their mental health challenges with greater strength.

Additionally, talking to friends and family can promote positive coping strategies. Loved ones can share their own experiences and coping mechanisms, providing individuals with new tools and perspectives. These conversations can introduce individuals to healthy ways of managing stress, such as engaging in hobbies, physical activity, or mindfulness practices. By learning from the experiences of others, individuals can expand their repertoire of coping strategies, enhancing their ability to manage their mental health.

In times of crisis, the importance of reaching out to friends and family becomes even more pronounced. In moments of acute distress, having someone to talk to can be a lifeline. Friends and family can provide immediate support, helping individuals navigate overwhelming emotions and thoughts. Whether it's through a simple phone call, a text message, or spending time together, these interactions can make a significant difference in someone's ability to cope with a crisis.

Finally, it's essential to recognize that while talking to friends and family is crucial, it should complement, not replace, professional help. Mental health professionals possess the training and expertise to provide appropriate support and treatment for mental health issues. Encouraging individuals to seek professional help alongside their support network can create a comprehensive approach to mental health care, ensuring that they receive the best possible support.

In conclusion, talking to friends and family when facing mental health problems is a vital component of recovery and well-being. These conversations provide emotional support, practical assistance, and a sense of belonging that can significantly impact an individual's ability to cope. By fostering open dialogue about mental health, individuals can not only improve their own well-being but also contribute to a culture of acceptance and understanding. The combined support of loved ones and mental health professionals creates a powerful framework for healing, resilience, and growth. Embracing this support system can ultimately lead to a more fulfilling and balanced life.

Continuing the discussion on the importance of talking to friends and family while facing mental health challenges, it is vital to acknowledge the role of empathy in these conversations. When loved ones listen without judgment, they create a safe space for individuals to express their emotions freely. This empathetic listening can validate the person's feelings, making them feel heard and understood. Knowing that someone is genuinely interested in their well-being can have a profound impact on an individual's mental state, helping them feel more secure in sharing their experiences.

Additionally, discussing mental health issues with friends and family can foster a sense of community. It reminds individuals that they do not have to face their struggles in isolation. By creating an environment where mental health is openly discussed, families and friend groups can cultivate a culture of support that encourages everyone to prioritize their emotional well-being. This communal approach can help break the silence that often surrounds mental health issues, making it easier for others within the community to share their struggles as well.

Moreover, sharing mental health challenges with friends and family can enhance the quality of relationships. Vulnerability often leads to deeper connections, as individuals learn to lean on one another during difficult times. As friends and family members support one another, they build trust and intimacy, strengthening their bonds. This emotional closeness can lead to healthier relationships overall, as individuals feel more comfortable discussing not only their struggles but also their triumphs and joys.

Conversations about mental health can also serve as a platform for educating loved ones about the complexities of mental health issues. Many people may not fully understand what someone is experiencing, leading to misconceptions or unhelpful advice. By articulating their feelings and experiences, individuals can provide insight into their struggles, helping loved ones understand the nuances of mental health. This education can foster compassion and support, allowing friends and family to respond more effectively to someone in need.

The concept of "checking in" is another important aspect of maintaining open lines of communication about mental health. Regularly reaching out to friends and family can serve as a reminder that they are not alone in their struggles. Simple gestures, such as asking how someone is feeling or offering to spend time together, can convey love and support. These small acts can significantly impact an individual's mental health, reminding them that they are surrounded by a caring network of people.

In addition to emotional support, talking to friends and family can also provide individuals with practical advice and guidance. Loved ones who have faced similar challenges can share their coping strategies, offering valuable insights that may not have been considered. This exchange of ideas can facilitate personal growth and encourage individuals to explore new avenues for managing their mental health. By learning from each other's experiences, individuals can build a toolkit of strategies to help them navigate their own challenges.

Furthermore, discussing mental health with friends and family can help dispel the myths and stereotypes surrounding mental illness. Many individuals still harbor misconceptions about mental health, leading to stigma and discrimination. By openly sharing their experiences, individuals can challenge these stereotypes and promote a more accurate understanding of mental health issues. This advocacy can create a more supportive environment for those struggling, as it encourages acceptance and empathy rather than fear and misunderstanding.

It's also important to recognize that talking about mental health is not a one-time event but an ongoing process. Conversations should be encouraged regularly, as mental health can fluctuate over time. Friends and family members should feel comfortable revisiting the topic, checking in on each other's well-being, and discussing how they can continue to support one another. This ongoing dialogue can help create a lasting culture of openness and support that benefits everyone involved.

Another significant aspect of talking to friends and family about mental health is the potential for shared activities that promote well-being. Engaging in activities together, such as exercise, mindfulness practices, or even just spending time outdoors, can enhance emotional health. These shared experiences can foster a sense of camaraderie and provide positive distractions from mental health challenges. By participating in uplifting activities together, individuals can cultivate positive memories and reinforce their support systems.

In conclusion, the importance of talking to friends and family while navigating mental health challenges cannot be overstated. These conversations provide emotional support, deepen relationships, and foster a sense of community and understanding. By creating an environment where mental health is openly discussed, we can collectively work toward destigmatizing mental illness and promoting well-being. The bonds formed through these conversations can lead to lasting support networks that empower individuals to face their challenges with resilience and hope. Ultimately, the shared journey of navigating mental health together enriches the lives of everyone involved, paving the way for healing and growth.

Chapter Thirteen:

Writing as a Therapeutic Tool

Writing has long been recognized as a powerful form of self-expression, but it is also increasingly acknowledged as a therapeutic tool that can significantly enhance mental health. In its various forms, journaling, poetry, storytelling, and even structured writing exercises. Writing allows individuals to explore their thoughts and emotions in a safe and creative manner. This process can lead to greater self-awareness, emotional release, and ultimately, healing. The therapeutic benefits of writing are rooted in its ability to serve as a conduit for self-reflection, allowing individuals to confront their feelings and experiences without the fear of judgment.

One of the most accessible forms of therapeutic writing is journaling. Keeping a journal can provide a private space for individuals to articulate their thoughts and feelings, which can be particularly helpful during times of stress or emotional turmoil. When people write down their experiences, they often find clarity in their emotions, allowing them to process complex feelings they might otherwise struggle to confront. This form of self-exploration can lead to enhanced emotional regulation, as individuals learn to identify triggers and patterns in their behavior, ultimately fostering resilience.

Research supports the notion that expressive writing can have significant mental health benefits. Studies have shown that writing about traumatic or challenging experiences can lead to reductions in anxiety, depression, and even physical health symptoms. The act of writing serves as a form of emotional release, allowing individuals to externalize their pain and gain distance from their experiences. This cathartic process can facilitate a better understanding of one's emotions and experiences, promoting healing and personal growth.

Poetry and creative writing also offer unique therapeutic benefits. The artistic nature of poetry encourages individuals to play with language, explore metaphors, and express feelings in innovative ways. This creative outlet can be especially beneficial for those who may struggle to articulate their emotions through conventional means. Writing poetry allows for a deeper exploration of complex feelings, often leading to insights that might not emerge through straightforward narrative writing. The creative aspect of this form of writing can also foster a sense of joy and freedom, which is essential for mental well-being.

Storytelling, whether through fiction or personal narratives, can serve as a powerful tool for understanding one's life and experiences. By crafting narratives, individuals can reframe their experiences, finding meaning and coherence in their stories. This process of narrative construction not only helps in making sense of past events but also empowers individuals to envision their future. Storytelling can be particularly therapeutic in group settings, allowing individuals to connect with others and share their experiences in a supportive environment.

Writing can also serve as a means of fostering mindfulness. The act of writing encourages individuals to focus on the present moment, engaging with their thoughts and feelings without distraction. This mindfulness aspect can enhance emotional well-being by promoting a greater awareness of one's internal landscape. Through writing, individuals can cultivate a sense of grounding, helping them to manage anxiety and stress more effectively. The reflective nature of writing invites individuals to slow down and engage with their feelings, creating a meditative practice that can be both calming and insightful.

In addition to its individual benefits, writing can facilitate connection and community. Writing groups or workshops provide a supportive environment where individuals can share their work and experiences, fostering a sense of belonging. This communal aspect can be particularly beneficial for those who may feel isolated due to their mental health struggles. By sharing their writing, individuals can receive validation and support from others, which can be incredibly empowering. The act of listening and responding to others' stories can also deepen empathy and understanding within the group.

For those working with mental health professionals, writing can be integrated into therapeutic practices. Therapists often encourage clients to engage in writing exercises as a way to process emotions or explore specific themes related to their therapy. Techniques like "stream of consciousness" writing or focused prompts can help clients delve deeper into their thoughts and feelings, providing valuable material for discussion in therapy sessions. This collaborative approach can enhance the therapeutic relationship and promote a more profound understanding of the individual's experiences.

Moreover, the accessibility of writing as a therapeutic tool cannot be understated. Unlike other forms of therapy that may require professional guidance or resources, writing can be done anywhere and at any time. All one needs is a pen and paper or a digital device. This ease of access allows individuals to engage in self-therapy at their own pace, making it a flexible and adaptable practice for anyone seeking mental health support.

It is essential to recognize that while writing can be a powerful tool for healing, it is not a substitute for professional mental health care when needed. For some individuals, particularly those dealing with severe trauma or mental health disorders, writing may be most effective when combined with traditional therapeutic interventions. However, for many, writing offers a valuable complement to therapy, providing a means of self-exploration and emotional release that can enhance the overall therapeutic process.

In conclusion, writing stands out as a versatile and effective therapeutic tool with numerous mental health benefits. From journaling and poetry to storytelling and group writing, the act of writing allows individuals to explore their emotions, gain insight into their experiences, and foster a deeper understanding of themselves. Each form of writing offers unique advantages, catering to different preferences and emotional needs. As individuals engage with their thoughts through writing, they often discover new perspectives and pathways to healing. The versatility of writing makes it an invaluable resource in the pursuit of mental well-being.

One significant aspect of writing as a therapeutic tool is its role in emotional processing. When individuals write about their feelings, they create a narrative that can help them make sense of their emotions. This narrative allows for a clearer examination of feelings such as grief, anger, or anxiety, enabling individuals to confront and understand these emotions rather than suppress them. By articulating their experiences, individuals can develop a sense of control over their feelings, which can lead to a reduction in emotional distress.

Additionally, writing can serve as a form of self-affirmation. Through positive affirmations or reflections on past successes, individuals can counteract negative self-talk and build self-esteem. Writing about achievements, strengths, or moments of joy can foster a more positive self-image, which is particularly important for those struggling with mental health issues. This practice of self-affirmation through writing can help individuals cultivate resilience and a more optimistic outlook on life.

The practice of writing can also enhance problem-solving skills. When individuals articulate their thoughts on paper, they create a tangible representation of their challenges, which can facilitate clearer thinking and decision-making. This externalization of thoughts can lead to new insights or solutions that may not have been apparent when the thoughts remained internal. By breaking down complex problems through writing, individuals can approach their challenges with a renewed sense of clarity and purpose.

Moreover, writing can be a powerful tool for fostering gratitude. Keeping a gratitude journal, where individuals regularly note things they are thankful for, can shift focus from negative thoughts to positive experiences. This practice has been shown to enhance overall well-being and life satisfaction. By consistently reflecting on the positive aspects of their lives, individuals can cultivate a more hopeful and appreciative mindset, which can be particularly beneficial during difficult times.

Another important aspect of writing as a therapeutic tool is its ability to bridge the gap between the past and the present. Many individuals carry emotional burdens from their past experiences, and writing can provide a way to process these feelings. By reflecting on past events, individuals can gain insights into how these experiences shape their current behaviors and emotions. This reflective process can be instrumental in breaking negative cycles and fostering personal growth, allowing individuals to move forward with greater awareness and intention.

In educational and therapeutic settings, the integration of writing exercises can enhance the overall effectiveness of mental health support. For example, therapists may incorporate guided writing prompts that align with specific therapeutic goals, enabling clients to explore relevant themes more deeply. This structured approach can help clients articulate their feelings and experiences in a focused manner, making the therapeutic process more productive.

Writing can also serve as a springboard for discussions in therapy, allowing for more profound exploration of emotions and experiences.

In summary, writing is a multifaceted therapeutic tool that offers a wide range of mental health benefits. Its ability to facilitate emotional processing, enhance self-affirmation, improve problem-solving skills, foster gratitude, and bridge the gap between past and present makes it an invaluable resource for individuals seeking to improve their mental well-being. As more people recognize the power of writing, it is likely that its integration into therapeutic practices will continue to grow, helping individuals navigate their mental health journeys with greater insight and resilience.

Chapter Fourteen:

Creating a Positive and Supportive Environment

Creating a positive and supportive environment surrounding mental health is essential for fostering well-being and resilience in individuals and communities. This environment encompasses various elements, including open communication, access to resources, and a culture of empathy and understanding. When individuals feel supported in their mental health journey, they are more likely to seek help, engage in self-care, and develop healthy coping mechanisms. A positive environment not only benefits individuals but also strengthens the fabric of communities, promoting overall societal wellness.

One key aspect of a supportive mental health environment is the elimination of stigma. Stigma surrounding mental health issues often prevents individuals from seeking help or discussing their struggles openly. By promoting awareness and education about mental health, communities can challenge misconceptions and foster a culture of acceptance. Initiatives such as mental health awareness campaigns, workshops, and community discussions can help normalize conversations around mental health, encouraging individuals to share their experiences without fear of judgment.

In addition to combating stigma, a supportive environment should prioritize open communication. This means creating spaces where individuals feel safe to express their feelings and concerns. Whether in schools, workplaces, or at home, encouraging dialogue about mental health can help individuals feel more connected and understood. Active listening and validation of emotions are important components of this communication, as they demonstrate care and support. When individuals know they can openly discuss their mental health, they are more likely to seek help when needed.

Access to mental health resources is another critical factor in establishing a supportive environment. This includes not only professional mental health services but also community resources such as support groups, workshops, and educational materials. Ensuring that individuals are aware of and can easily access these resources can empower them to take charge of their mental health. Moreover, integrating mental health services into primary care settings can promote early intervention and reduce barriers to accessing help.

A positive and supportive environment also fosters resilience by encouraging individuals to engage in self-care and wellness practices. Communities can promote mental well-being by providing opportunities for physical activity, mindfulness, and social connection. Programs that encourage exercise, yoga, meditation, and creative arts can enhance mental health and overall well-being. By prioritizing self-care and wellness, individuals are more likely to develop healthy habits that can serve as protective factors against mental health issues.

Supportive environments are characterized by empathy and understanding. Cultivating a culture of compassion within families, schools, and workplaces can significantly impact individuals' mental health. When people feel valued and understood, they are more likely to thrive. Training programs that focus on emotional intelligence, conflict resolution, and active listening can help foster empathy in various settings. This approach not only benefits individuals experiencing mental health challenges but also enhances relationships and teamwork within communities.

In educational settings, creating a positive environment for mental health is particularly crucial. Schools play a pivotal role in shaping young people's attitudes and behaviors toward mental health. Implementing mental health education as part of the curriculum can equip students with the knowledge and skills to recognize and address their mental health needs. Additionally, schools can establish supportive systems, such as counseling services and peer support programs, that encourage students to seek help and support one another.

Workplaces also have a significant role in promoting mental health. Employers can create supportive environments by implementing policies that prioritize mental well-being, such as flexible work arrangements, mental health days, and employee assistance programs. Encouraging a healthy work-life balance and fostering a culture of support can lead to increased job satisfaction, productivity, and overall employee well-being. When employees feel that their mental health is valued, they are more likely to contribute positively to the workplace.

The role of community in creating a positive mental health environment cannot be overstated. Community organizations, local governments, and grassroots initiatives can work together to build mental health awareness and support systems. Community events, workshops, and resource fairs can connect individuals with mental health services and foster a sense of belonging. By cultivating a community that prioritizes mental health, individuals can find support and connection, which are vital for overall well-being.

Finally, creating a positive and supportive environment for mental health requires ongoing effort and commitment. It is essential to continually assess and adapt initiatives based on the needs of individuals and communities. Engaging diverse voices and perspectives in discussions about mental health can lead to more inclusive and effective solutions. By fostering a culture of continuous learning and improvement, communities can ensure that their mental health support systems remain relevant and effective.

In conclusion, the importance of creating a positive and supportive environment surrounding mental health cannot be overstated. By addressing stigma, promoting open communication, ensuring access to resources, and fostering empathy and resilience, communities can significantly enhance the mental well-being of their members. A supportive environment empowers individuals to seek help, engage in self-care, and thrive in their personal and professional lives. Ultimately, investing in mental health support not only benefits individuals but also strengthens communities, paving the way for a healthier and more compassionate society.

To further emphasize the significance of creating a positive and supportive environment for mental health, it is crucial to consider the role of leadership and policy-making. Leaders in various sectors, whether in education, healthcare, or corporate environments, have the power to influence and shape cultures that prioritize mental well-being. By advocating for mental health initiatives and modeling healthy behaviors, leaders can set the tone for their organizations and communities. Policies that promote mental health awareness, provide resources, and create safe spaces for open discussions can lead to a profound change in how mental health is perceived and addressed.

Moreover, incorporating mental health training into professional development programs can enhance the skills of those in leadership positions. Training in mental health first aid, for instance, equips leaders and colleagues with the knowledge to recognize signs of mental distress and respond appropriately. This not only benefits the individuals directly affected but also cultivates a supportive atmosphere where everyone feels empowered to contribute positively to the mental health landscape. By prioritizing mental health training, organizations can create a ripple effect that reaches all levels of the workforce.

Family dynamics also play a pivotal role in establishing a supportive environment for mental health. Families are often the first line of support for individuals facing mental health challenges. Encouraging open communication within families about emotions, mental health issues, and coping strategies can create a nurturing environment where individuals feel safe to express their feelings. Family members should be educated about mental health to better understand the challenges faced by their loved ones. When families actively engage in discussions about mental well-being, they foster a culture of support that can significantly impact an individual's ability to cope with mental health challenges.

Furthermore, the integration of mental health initiatives into community events can enhance public awareness and engagement. Festivals, health fairs, and community workshops that focus on mental health can provide valuable information and resources while fostering a sense of unity. These events can serve as platforms for individuals to share their experiences, learn coping strategies, and connect with local mental health services. By normalizing mental health discussions in community settings, individuals are more likely to seek help and support when needed.

Another essential aspect of a supportive environment is the role of technology. In today's digital age, leveraging technology can help bridge gaps in mental health access and support. Online resources, teletherapy, and mental health apps provide individuals with tools and support systems that are easily accessible. These digital platforms can help reduce barriers to seeking help, especially for those who may feel uncomfortable discussing their mental health in person. By embracing technology, communities can reach a broader audience and provide valuable resources at individuals' fingertips.

Moreover, peer support plays a significant role in creating a positive mental health environment. Peer support groups provide individuals with the opportunity to connect with others who have similar experiences, fostering a sense of belonging and understanding. These groups can be instrumental in reducing feelings of isolation and promoting shared healing journeys. Training individuals to become peer support specialists can further enhance this environment, as they can offer valuable insights and encouragement based on their lived experiences.

In educational contexts, involving parents and guardians in mental health initiatives is vital. Schools can host workshops that educate parents about the importance of mental health, how to recognize signs of distress in their children, and ways to foster resilience at home. By engaging families in the conversation about mental health, schools can create a more comprehensive support system that extends beyond the classroom. This collaboration between educators and families can lead to a stronger community that prioritizes the well-being of its youth.

Additionally, fostering a sense of community through volunteer opportunities can significantly impact mental health. Engaging individuals in community service not only benefits those in need but also promotes a sense of purpose and connection among volunteers. Research has shown that helping others can boost mental well-being, reduce feelings of isolation, and create a sense of belonging. By encouraging volunteerism and community involvement, individuals can find fulfillment and support through shared experiences, further strengthening the social fabric of the community.

In summary, the importance of creating a positive and supportive environment for mental health encompasses various elements, including leadership, family dynamics, community engagement, technology, peer support, and volunteerism. By addressing these aspects, communities can foster an atmosphere that prioritizes mental well-being, encourages open dialogue, and provides resources for those in need. When individuals feel supported and understood, they are more likely to thrive and contribute positively to their communities. Ultimately, a collective commitment to mental health creates a ripple effect that enhances the quality of life for everyone involved, paving the way for a more compassionate and resilient society.

Chapter Fifteen:

Identifying Trustworthy Individuals

Identifying trustworthy individuals in the realm of mental health is crucial for fostering a support system that can significantly influence one's journey toward wellness. Trustworthy individuals can take various forms, including friends, family members, mental health professionals, and community support figures. The presence of these individuals allows for open communication, which is essential for expressing feelings, sharing experiences, and seeking guidance during challenging times. This open dialogue is a cornerstone of mental health support, as it helps individuals feel understood and less isolated in their struggles.

Trustworthy individuals serve as a safe space for sharing vulnerabilities. Mental health issues can often lead to feelings of shame or embarrassment, making it difficult for individuals to express their emotions openly. When surrounded by people who are empathetic, non-judgmental, and supportive, individuals are more likely to articulate their thoughts and feelings. This environment encourages honesty and transparency, allowing for healthier discussions about mental health challenges and potential solutions.

Moreover, the role of trustworthy individuals extends to providing accurate information about mental health resources. With the prevalence of misinformation and stigma surrounding mental health, having individuals who can guide you toward reliable resources is invaluable. These individuals can help identify qualified mental health professionals, programs, or support groups that cater to specific needs, ensuring that individuals receive the appropriate care and support necessary for their circumstances.

Additionally, trustworthy individuals can act as advocates, helping to navigate the often complex mental health system. Individuals may feel overwhelmed when seeking help, especially if they are dealing with the stigma associated with mental health issues. A supportive person can accompany them to appointments, assist in making informed decisions, and provide encouragement throughout the process. This advocacy can empower individuals, making them feel more confident in their journey to recovery.

The emotional support provided by trustworthy individuals can also enhance resilience. Mental health challenges can lead to feelings of hopelessness and despair, but having a solid support network can mitigate these feelings. Trustworthy individuals can offer encouragement, reinforce positive coping strategies, and remind individuals of their strengths. This support ultimately fosters resilience, enabling individuals to face their mental health challenges with greater determination and hope.

In times of crisis, trustworthy individuals become even more critical. Mental health crises can be intense and disorienting, making it difficult for individuals to think clearly or make rational decisions. Having someone who is reliable and knowledgeable can provide immediate support, whether that means offering a listening ear, helping to de-escalate a situation, or connecting the individual with emergency services. This kind of immediate intervention can make a significant difference in the outcome of a crisis.

The importance of identifying trustworthy individuals also relates to the broader social context of mental health. When individuals surround themselves with supportive people, they contribute to a culture that prioritizes mental well-being. This culture can challenge societal stigma and promote understanding and acceptance of mental health issues. As more people engage in discussions about mental health and share their experiences, the normalization of these conversations helps create an environment where seeking help is encouraged rather than discouraged.

Additionally, building relationships with trustworthy individuals allows for the sharing of effective coping strategies and resources. Each person's mental health journey is unique, but learning from others' experiences can provide valuable insights. Trustworthy individuals can share techniques that have worked for them, whether through self-care practices, mindfulness exercises, or therapeutic approaches. This exchange of information can empower individuals to take an active role in their mental health management.

Furthermore, identifying trustworthy individuals can lead to enhanced emotional intelligence within a community. When individuals engage with those who are empathetic and emotionally aware, they develop their own emotional skills. This growth can lead to better communication, deeper connections, and a greater understanding of mental health issues within the community. As emotional intelligence increases, it can create a ripple effect, encouraging others to become more compassionate and supportive.

In conclusion, the importance of identifying trustworthy individuals surrounding mental health cannot be overstated. These individuals provide a foundation of support, understanding, and advocacy that is essential for navigating the complexities of mental health challenges. Their presence not only promotes individual healing but also contributes to a more compassionate and informed society. By fostering relationships with trustworthy individuals, individuals can create a network that enhances resilience, encourages open dialogue, and ultimately leads to improved mental well-being for everyone involved.

Identifying trustworthy individuals in the realm of mental health is essential for creating a robust support system that significantly impacts an individual's journey toward recovery and wellness. These trustworthy figures can include friends, family members, mental health professionals, and community mentors. Their presence fosters an environment where open communication can thrive, allowing individuals to express their feelings, share their experiences, and seek guidance during difficult times. This open dialogue is critical, as it helps to alleviate feelings of isolation and provides a sense of belonging, which is invaluable for anyone grappling with mental health challenges.

Trustworthy individuals provide a safe space for people to share their vulnerabilities. Mental health issues often come with feelings of shame or fear of judgment, making it difficult for individuals to articulate their struggles. When surrounded by empathetic and non-judgmental individuals, they are more likely to share their thoughts and feelings. This supportive environment encourages honesty and transparency, which are essential for engaging in healthier discussions about mental health challenges. The act of sharing can be therapeutic in itself, helping individuals feel understood and less burdened by their struggles.

In addition to emotional support, trustworthy individuals play a crucial role in guiding people toward accurate mental health resources. With the prevalence of misinformation and stigma surrounding mental health, it is vital to have reliable sources of information at one's disposal. Trustworthy individuals can help identify qualified mental health professionals, community programs, or support groups tailored to specific needs. By ensuring that individuals have access to the right resources, these figures contribute to a more informed approach to mental health care, which can lead to better outcomes.

Trustworthy individuals also act as advocates within the often complex mental health system. Seeking help can feel daunting, particularly when one is already dealing with the stigma associated with mental health issues. A supportive person can accompany individuals to appointments, help them understand their treatment options, and encourage them throughout the process. This advocacy is empowering, making individuals feel more confident in their decisions regarding their mental health and facilitating a stronger commitment to their recovery journey.

The emotional support provided by trustworthy individuals can enhance resilience. Mental health challenges can lead to feelings of hopelessness and despair, but having a solid support network can provide a buffer against these negative emotions. Trustworthy individuals can offer encouragement, remind individuals of their strengths, and reinforce positive coping strategies. This kind of support fosters resilience and equips individuals with the tools they need to face their mental health challenges with determination and hope.

During times of crisis, the importance of trustworthy individuals becomes even more pronounced. Mental health crises can be overwhelming and disorienting, making it difficult to think clearly. Reliable and knowledgeable individuals can provide immediate support, whether through active listening, helping to de-escalate a situation, or connecting the individual with emergency resources. This immediate intervention can significantly impact the outcome of a crisis, highlighting the critical role that trustworthy individuals play in times of need.

Beyond individual benefits, identifying trustworthy individuals contributes to a broader cultural shift regarding mental health. When people surround themselves with supportive figures, they help create a culture that prioritizes mental well-being and challenges societal stigma. As individuals engage in open discussions about mental health and share their experiences, they contribute to normalizing these conversations, making it more acceptable for others to seek help without fear of judgment.

Building relationships with trustworthy individuals can also facilitate the sharing of effective coping strategies and resources. Each person's mental health journey is unique, but learning from others' experiences can provide valuable insights and alternatives for managing mental health. Trustworthy individuals can share techniques that have proven effective for them, such as mindfulness practices or therapeutic approaches. This exchange of information empowers individuals to take an active role in their mental health management, creating a collaborative atmosphere where everyone can learn and grow.

In summary, the importance of identifying trustworthy individuals surrounding mental health is multifaceted and profound. These individuals provide vital emotional support, guidance, and advocacy, helping to navigate the complexities of mental health challenges. Their presence not only promotes individual healing but also contributes to a more compassionate and informed society. By fostering relationships with trustworthy individuals, individuals can create a network that enhances resilience, encourages open dialogue, and ultimately leads to improved mental well-being for everyone involved. The collective impact of these relationships can create a ripple effect, nurturing a community that values mental health and well-being.

Chapter Sixteen:

Establishing Boundaries for Your Well-being
Establishing boundaries is a fundamental aspect of maintaining mental health and overall well-being. In our increasingly interconnected world, where the lines between personal and professional life often blur, the importance of setting clear boundaries cannot be overstated. Boundaries act as a protective barrier, allowing individuals to navigate their emotional landscapes without becoming overwhelmed or depleted by external pressures. By defining what is acceptable and what is not, individuals can cultivate a sense of safety and control over their lives.

One of the primary benefits of establishing boundaries is the promotion of self-awareness. When individuals take the time to assess their needs and limits, they gain a clearer understanding of their emotional and mental states. This self-awareness fosters healthier relationships with others, as individuals can articulate their needs and expectations more effectively. The ability to communicate one's boundaries not only benefits oneself but also enhances the dynamics of interpersonal relationships, leading to greater empathy and understanding between parties.

Mental health often suffers when boundaries are not established. Without clear limits, individuals may find themselves overcommitting to obligations, whether at work or in personal life. This overextension can lead to burnout, anxiety, and feelings of resentment. By setting boundaries, individuals can prioritize their well-being and allocate their time and energy to activities and relationships that genuinely nurture them. This prioritization is essential for maintaining mental clarity and emotional stability.

Moreover, boundaries serve as an essential tool for managing stress. Life can be inherently stressful, and external demands can quickly accumulate, leaving individuals feeling trapped and overwhelmed. By setting boundaries, individuals create a structured environment where they can manage their stressors more effectively. This might involve saying no to additional responsibilities, limiting exposure to negative influences, or carving out time for self-care. Such practices not only mitigate stress but also empower individuals to take charge of their mental health.

Establishing boundaries also fosters resilience. When individuals learn to recognize their limits and uphold them, they develop a stronger sense of self. This self-assertiveness is crucial in facing life's challenges, as it enables individuals to respond to difficulties from a place of strength rather than vulnerability. Resilience is built on the understanding that one's needs are valid and worthy of respect, which is exactly what boundaries help to reinforce.

In relationships, boundaries are vital for ensuring mutual respect. Healthy relationships are built on a foundation of understanding and consideration for each other's limits. When individuals clearly communicate their boundaries, it allows for more authentic interactions and reduces the likelihood of misunderstandings or conflicts. Establishing boundaries helps individuals advocate for themselves while also being sensitive to the needs of others, creating a balanced dynamic that fosters trust and respect.

Additionally, the act of setting boundaries can enhance personal growth. It encourages individuals to reflect on their values, priorities, and what truly matters to them. By identifying and enforcing boundaries, individuals can create an environment that supports their goals and aspirations. This intentional approach to life helps individuals thrive, as they engage in activities and relationships that align with their core values, ultimately contributing to a more fulfilling existence.

Furthermore, boundaries play a crucial role in maintaining mental health during challenging times. Life is full of unexpected events and stressors, and having established boundaries can provide a crucial support system. When faced with adversity, individuals who have clear boundaries are better equipped to protect their mental health, as they know when to step back, seek support, or disengage from unhealthy situations. This proactive approach to mental health allows individuals to preserve their emotional resources and navigate difficulties with greater ease.

In the professional realm, boundaries are equally important. Many individuals grapple with work-life balance, often feeling pressured to respond to emails after hours or take on additional tasks beyond their capacity. Establishing boundaries in the workplace can prevent burnout and enhance productivity. By clearly delineating work hours and personal time, individuals can create an environment where they can recharge and maintain their mental well-being, leading to improved job satisfaction and performance.

Ultimately, the establishment of boundaries is an act of self-care and self-respect. It sends a powerful message to oneself and to others that one's mental health matters. By prioritizing boundaries, individuals can create a healthier relationship with themselves and others, fostering an environment conducive to growth, happiness, and emotional well-being. In a world where demands are ever-increasing, setting and maintaining boundaries is not just beneficial; it is essential for sustaining mental health and overall life satisfaction.

In conclusion, the importance of establishing boundaries for mental health and well-being can hardly be overstated. They provide the necessary structure and protection individuals need to navigate their personal and professional lives effectively. By promoting self-awareness, managing stress, fostering resilience, and enhancing relationships, boundaries serve as a foundational element in the journey toward mental wellness. Embracing the practice of setting boundaries is not merely a choice; it is a vital investment in one's health and happiness.

Establishing boundaries is a crucial ingredient in the recipe for maintaining mental health and overall well-being. In an age characterized by constant connectivity and overlapping responsibilities, having clear boundaries allows individuals to navigate their personal and professional lives with greater ease. Boundaries act as a protective barrier, enabling individuals to safeguard their emotional and mental states from the demands and pressures that can lead to stress and burnout. By defining what is acceptable behavior and what is not, individuals can cultivate a sense of safety and control over their lives.

One significant advantage of establishing boundaries is the promotion of self-awareness. Engaging in the practice of defining one's limits requires introspection and reflection on personal needs. This self-awareness fosters healthier relationships, as individuals become more adept at articulating their needs and expectations to others. When people understand their own boundaries, they can communicate them clearly, reducing the likelihood of misunderstandings and creating more supportive and respectful interactions with friends, family, and colleagues.

Mental health is often compromised in the absence of clear boundaries. Without limits, individuals can find themselves overwhelmed by commitments, leading to feelings of anxiety and exhaustion. Overcommitting can result in a cycle of burnout, where mental and emotional resources are depleted, leaving individuals feeling resentful and trapped. By establishing boundaries, individuals can prioritize their well-being, allowing them to focus on activities and relationships that genuinely nurture them. This ability to say no or to limit exposure to negative influences is essential for maintaining mental clarity and emotional stability.

Boundaries also serve as a powerful tool for managing stress. Life is inherently full of stressors, and external demands can quickly pile up, leading to feelings of being overwhelmed. By creating clear boundaries, individuals can better manage these stressors, providing themselves with the necessary space to breathe and regroup. Setting limits on how much time and energy to invest in various areas of life—such as work, social obligations, and self-care—enables individuals to protect their mental health and maintain a sense of balance, ultimately leading to a healthier lifestyle.

Additionally, establishing boundaries fosters resilience. When individuals recognize their limits and uphold them, they develop a more robust sense of self. This self-assertiveness is crucial when facing life's challenges, as it allows individuals to respond to difficulties from a position of strength rather than vulnerability. By understanding that their needs and feelings are valid, individuals can cultivate resilience and navigate challenges with greater confidence and poise. Boundaries become a source of empowerment, reinforcing the idea that taking care of oneself is not only acceptable but necessary.

In personal relationships, boundaries are vital for promoting mutual respect and understanding. Healthy relationships thrive on a foundation of open communication and consideration for each other's limits. When individuals express their boundaries, it creates an environment where both parties can feel safe and respected. This clarity reduces the potential for conflicts and misunderstandings, allowing for more authentic and meaningful connections. By establishing boundaries, individuals advocate for themselves and foster a balanced dynamic that encourages trust and collaboration.

Moreover, the act of setting boundaries can significantly enhance personal growth. When individuals take the time to reflect on their values and priorities, they can make conscious decisions about how to allocate their time and energy. Boundaries encourage individuals to engage in activities and relationships that align with their core values, promoting a sense of fulfillment and purpose. This intentional approach to life not only supports mental health but also enables individuals to thrive and reach their full potential.

In challenging times, having established boundaries is particularly important for maintaining mental health. Life can throw unexpected stressors our way, and individuals with clear boundaries are better equipped to handle these difficulties. They know when to step back, seek support, or disengage from unhealthy situations. This proactive approach to mental health allows individuals to preserve their emotional resources and navigate obstacles with greater ease, ultimately leading to a more resilient mindset.

In the professional arena, boundaries play an equally critical role. Many individuals struggle with work-life balance, often feeling pressured to respond to emails at all hours or take on extra responsibilities that can lead to burnout. Establishing boundaries in the workplace, such as setting specific work hours and respecting personal time, can prevent burnout and enhance productivity. By maintaining a clear distinction between work and personal life, individuals can recharge and sustain their mental well-being, resulting in improved job satisfaction and overall performance.

In conclusion, the importance of establishing boundaries for mental health and well-being is profound. They provide essential structure and protection, allowing individuals to navigate the complexities of life more effectively. By promoting self-awareness, managing stress, fostering resilience, and enhancing relationships, boundaries serve as a foundational element in the pursuit of mental wellness. Embracing the practice of setting boundaries is not merely a beneficial choice; it is a vital investment in one's health and happiness, paving the way for a more balanced and fulfilling life.

Chapter Seventeen:

Mindfulness and Meditation

Mindfulness and meditation have gained significant attention in recent years as essential practices for enhancing mental health and well-being. These techniques encourage individuals to cultivate a state of awareness and presence, allowing them to connect with their thoughts, feelings, and surroundings in a non-judgmental manner. By fostering this awareness, mindfulness and meditation can help individuals manage stress, reduce anxiety, and improve overall emotional regulation. As people increasingly recognize the importance of mental well-being, integrating mindfulness practices into daily routines has become a vital component of holistic health.

At the core of mindfulness is the practice of being fully present in the moment. This awareness encourages individuals to observe their thoughts and feelings without becoming overwhelmed by them. By acknowledging their emotions without judgment, individuals can create distance from negative thought patterns that contribute to anxiety and depression. This process of observation allows for a greater understanding of one's emotional landscape, enabling individuals to respond to their feelings with clarity and compassion rather than reacting impulsively.

Meditation, a practice often associated with mindfulness, offers a structured way to cultivate this awareness. Through various techniques, such as focused attention, loving-kindness, or body scans, individuals can train their minds to remain centered and calm.

Regular meditation practice has been shown to decrease symptoms of anxiety and depression by promoting relaxation and reducing the body's stress response. This physiological change can lead to profound improvements in mental health, as individuals learn to manage their stress more effectively and develop a greater sense of emotional resilience.

The benefits of mindfulness and meditation extend beyond immediate stress relief; they also promote long-term mental health. Research has shown that consistent practice can lead to structural changes in the brain, particularly in areas associated with emotional regulation and resilience. For instance, regular mindfulness practice can increase the thickness of the prefrontal cortex, which is responsible for higher-order thinking and decision-making. This neuroplasticity highlights the potential for individuals to reshape their mental habits and create a more balanced emotional landscape over time.

Mindfulness and meditation are also powerful tools for enhancing self-compassion. Many individuals struggle with self-criticism, often exacerbating feelings of inadequacy and anxiety. Through mindfulness practices, individuals learn to approach themselves with kindness and understanding. This shift in perspective can be transformative, as it allows individuals to break free from negative self-talk and cultivate a more positive self-image. By fostering self-compassion, mindfulness and meditation contribute to improved mental health and overall life satisfaction.

Moreover, these practices can enhance emotional intelligence by encouraging individuals to become more attuned to their emotions and the emotions of others. Mindfulness promotes active listening and empathy, allowing individuals to engage more meaningfully in their relationships. This increased emotional intelligence can lead to healthier interpersonal dynamics, as individuals learn to communicate more effectively and respond to others' needs with greater sensitivity. This enhancement of social connections is essential for mental well-being, as strong relationships are a key factor in emotional health.

Incorporating mindfulness and meditation into daily life can also serve as a preventive measure against mental health issues. By equipping individuals with the tools to manage stress and enhance emotional regulation, these practices create a buffer against the onset of anxiety and depression. Regular engagement in mindfulness can promote a greater sense of control over one's thoughts and feelings, which is particularly beneficial during challenging times. This proactive approach to mental health empowers individuals to take charge of their well-being and cultivate resilience.

The accessibility of mindfulness and meditation further contributes to their importance in mental health. With the rise of technology, there are countless resources available, including apps, online courses, and guided meditations, making these practices easier to adopt. This accessibility has enabled individuals from diverse backgrounds and lifestyles to engage with mindfulness and meditation, fostering a widespread culture of mental health awareness. The democratization of these practices allows for a more inclusive approach to mental wellness.

Mindfulness and meditation also promote a greater sense of gratitude and appreciation for life. By encouraging individuals to focus on the present moment, these practices help cultivate a mindset of gratitude, allowing individuals to recognize and celebrate the positive aspects of their lives. This shift in focus can lead to increased happiness and life satisfaction, as individuals learn to savor their experiences rather than getting caught up in worries about the future or regrets about the past. This enhanced perspective can significantly improve overall mental health.

In conclusion, the importance of mindfulness and meditation in promoting mental health cannot be overstated. These practices empower individuals to cultivate awareness, emotional regulation, and self-compassion, ultimately leading to a more balanced emotional state. By encouraging a greater understanding of one's thoughts and feelings, mindfulness and meditation provide essential tools for managing stress, fostering resilience, and enhancing overall well-being. As society continues to prioritize mental health, integrating mindfulness and meditation into daily life will remain a crucial component of holistic health, enabling individuals to lead more fulfilling and emotionally balanced lives.

Mindfulness and meditation have emerged as vital practices in the pursuit of mental health and well-being, gaining widespread recognition for their ability to enhance emotional regulation and reduce stress. At the heart of mindfulness is the practice of being fully present in the moment, which encourages individuals to observe their thoughts and feelings without passing judgment. This non-judgmental awareness allows people to connect with their emotional states more deeply, promoting a greater understanding of their inner experiences. By fostering this awareness, mindfulness can help individuals manage stress, alleviate anxiety, and cultivate a greater sense of emotional resilience.

The practice of meditation, often associated with mindfulness, provides a structured approach to developing this awareness. Through various techniques, such as focused attention, loving-kindness, or body scans, individuals can train their minds to remain centered and calm. Research has shown that regular meditation practice can lead to significant reductions in anxiety and depression symptoms. By promoting relaxation and reducing the body's stress response, meditation creates a physiological shift that can result in lasting improvements in mental health. This ability to manage stress effectively is especially crucial in our fast-paced, modern world.

One of the most profound benefits of mindfulness and meditation is their potential to enhance self-compassion. Many individuals struggle with harsh self-criticism, which can exacerbate feelings of inadequacy and anxiety. Mindfulness practices encourage an attitude of kindness and understanding toward oneself, allowing individuals to break free from negative self-talk. This shift in perspective can be transformative, fostering a more positive self-image and promoting emotional well-being. By cultivating self-compassion, individuals are better equipped to navigate the ups and downs of life with grace and resilience.

In addition to enhancing self-compassion, mindfulness and meditation can improve emotional intelligence. These practices encourage individuals to become more attuned to their own emotions as well as the emotions of others. By promoting active listening and empathy, mindfulness facilitates more meaningful interactions and deeper connections in relationships. This increased emotional intelligence not only enhances interpersonal dynamics but also contributes to overall mental health. Strong social connections are a key factor in emotional well-being, and mindfulness can significantly enrich these relationships.

Incorporating mindfulness and meditation into daily life can also serve as a preventive measure against mental health issues. By equipping individuals with tools to manage stress and enhance emotional regulation, these practices act as a buffer against the onset of anxiety and depression. Regular engagement in mindfulness helps individuals gain a sense of control over their thoughts and feelings, empowering them to respond to challenges with greater confidence. This proactive approach to mental health is essential for fostering resilience and promoting a sense of well-being in the face of life's difficulties.

The accessibility of mindfulness and meditation further underscores their importance in promoting mental health. With the proliferation of technology, a wealth of resources,such as apps, online courses, and guided meditations, are readily available, making these practices easier to adopt. This accessibility allows individuals from diverse backgrounds and lifestyles to engage with mindfulness and meditation, fostering a culture of mental health awareness. By democratizing these practices, more people can benefit from the mental health advantages they offer, contributing to a collective shift toward prioritizing emotional well-being.

In conclusion, the significance of mindfulness and meditation in enhancing mental health is profound. These practices empower individuals to cultivate awareness, emotional regulation, and self-compassion, leading to a more balanced emotional state. By encouraging a deeper understanding of one's thoughts and feelings, mindfulness and meditation provide essential tools for managing stress and fostering resilience. As society increasingly prioritizes mental health, integrating these practices into daily life will remain a crucial component of holistic health, enabling individuals to lead more fulfilling and emotionally balanced lives.

Chapter Eighteen:

Journaling Your Thoughts

Journaling is a powerful tool that can significantly impact mental health by providing an outlet for self-expression and emotional processing. In a world where stress and anxiety often feel overwhelming, the act of putting pen to paper allows individuals to articulate their thoughts and feelings in a structured way. This practice can serve as a cathartic release, enabling individuals to confront their emotions rather than suppress them. By externalizing thoughts, journaling helps reduce the intensity of negative feelings, making it easier to manage stress and anxiety in everyday life.

One of the primary benefits of journaling is its ability to promote self-reflection. As individuals write about their experiences, they gain insight into their thoughts and behaviors. This process fosters greater awareness of patterns in one's emotional responses, helping to identify triggers for stress or anxiety. By understanding these patterns, individuals can take proactive steps to address them, leading to improved emotional regulation. This self-awareness can also help individuals cultivate a more compassionate understanding of themselves, reducing the likelihood of harsh self-criticism.

Journaling can also serve as a means of organizing thoughts during chaotic or overwhelming times. When faced with stressors, individuals often experience a whirlwind of thoughts and emotions that can be difficult to untangle. Writing provides a structured way to sort through these feelings, allowing individuals to clarify their thoughts and prioritize their concerns. This organization can lead to a greater sense of control and empowerment, as individuals recognize that they can manage their stressors more effectively through careful analysis and reflection.

Additionally, journaling encourages emotional release by providing a safe space for individuals to express their innermost thoughts. This act of writing can be especially beneficial for those who may struggle to communicate their feelings verbally. By allowing oneself to write freely without judgment, individuals can explore and confront difficult emotions such as sadness, anger, or frustration. This unfiltered expression can help individuals process their feelings and ultimately find resolution, contributing to a sense of relief and emotional balance.

Incorporating gratitude journaling into one's practice can further enhance the mental health benefits of writing. Focusing on positive experiences and expressing gratitude can shift attention away from stress and negativity, fostering a more optimistic mindset. Research has shown that practicing gratitude can lead to improved emotional well-being, increased resilience, and reduced symptoms of anxiety and depression. By regularly reflecting on what one is thankful for, individuals can cultivate a more positive outlook, which can help buffer against stress.

Moreover, journaling can be a valuable tool for goal-setting and personal growth. By documenting aspirations, challenges, and achievements, individuals can track their progress and reflect on their journeys. This process can provide motivation and encouragement, as individuals recognize their growth over time. Setting goals and documenting steps toward achieving them can also help individuals feel more grounded and focused, reducing feelings of aimlessness that often accompany stress.

The act of journaling can also serve as a mindfulness practice, helping individuals stay present and engaged with their thoughts and feelings. By dedicating time to reflect and write, individuals create a mindful space for themselves, away from the distractions of daily life. This intentional engagement allows for a deeper connection to one's emotions and experiences, fostering a sense of calm and clarity. In this way, journaling not only helps release stress but also promotes mindfulness, which is essential for overall mental health.

Journaling can also support emotional healing during difficult life transitions or traumatic experiences. Writing about one's thoughts and feelings can facilitate the processing of grief, loss, or trauma, allowing individuals to make sense of their experiences. This reflective practice can be a significant step toward healing, as it provides a means to confront painful emotions in a safe and controlled manner. Over time, this process can lead to greater acceptance and understanding, ultimately contributing to emotional resilience.

Furthermore, journaling can enhance creativity and problem-solving skills. Engaging in free writing can unlock new ideas and perspectives, allowing individuals to explore solutions to challenges they may be facing. This creative outlet can be particularly beneficial when dealing with stress, as it encourages individuals to think outside the box and approach problems from different angles. By fostering creativity, journaling not only aids in stress relief but also enhances cognitive flexibility, which is essential for navigating life's challenges.

In conclusion, the importance of journaling in relation to mental health is profound. By providing an outlet for self-expression, promoting self-reflection, and encouraging emotional release, journaling serves as a valuable tool for managing stress and enhancing overall well-being. The practice offers individuals a safe space to confront their thoughts and feelings, leading to greater emotional awareness and resilience. As an accessible and flexible tool, journaling can empower individuals to take charge of their mental health, fostering a more balanced and fulfilling life. Embracing the practice of journaling can be a transformative step toward achieving emotional clarity and peace of mind in a complex and often stressful world.

Journaling stands out as a powerful tool for enhancing mental health, offering individuals a unique avenue for self-expression and emotional processing. In a world filled with stress and anxiety, the act of writing allows individuals to articulate their thoughts and feelings in a structured way. This practice serves as a cathartic release, enabling people to confront their emotions rather than suppress them. By externalizing thoughts onto paper, journaling helps reduce the intensity of negative feelings, making it easier to manage stress effectively in daily life.

One of the primary benefits of journaling is its capacity to foster self-reflection. As individuals write about their experiences, they gain valuable insights into their thoughts and behaviors. This process enhances awareness of emotional patterns, helping to identify triggers for stress or anxiety. With a clearer understanding of these patterns, individuals can take proactive steps to address them, leading to improved emotional regulation. This self-awareness diminishes the likelihood of harsh self-criticism, promoting a more compassionate understanding of oneself.

Moreover, journaling provides a means of organizing thoughts during chaotic moments. When faced with overwhelming stressors, individuals often experience a whirlwind of emotions that can be difficult to untangle. Writing offers a structured way to sort through these feelings, enabling individuals to clarify their concerns and prioritize their worries. This organization fosters a greater sense of control and empowerment, allowing individuals to manage their stressors more effectively through careful analysis and reflection.

Another significant advantage of journaling is its ability to facilitate emotional release. It creates a safe space for individuals to express their innermost thoughts without fear of judgment. This freedom to write openly allows individuals to explore and confront difficult emotions, such as sadness or anger. By articulating these feelings on paper, individuals can process their experiences and find resolution, leading to a sense of relief and emotional balance. This unfiltered expression is crucial for mental well-being, as it allows individuals to acknowledge and confront rather than avoid their feelings.

Incorporating gratitude journaling into one's practice can further enhance the mental health benefits of writing. By focusing on positive experiences and expressing gratitude, individuals can shift their attention away from stress and negativity. Research has shown that practicing gratitude can lead to improved emotional well-being and resilience, as well as reduced symptoms of anxiety and depression. Regularly reflecting on what one is thankful for fosters a more positive outlook, creating a buffer against stress and enhancing overall mental health.

Journaling also serves as a valuable tool for goal-setting and personal growth. By documenting aspirations, challenges, and achievements, individuals can track their progress and reflect on their journeys. This process not only provides motivation but also encourages individuals to recognize their growth over time. Setting goals and documenting steps toward achieving them can instill a sense of purpose and direction, reducing feelings of aimlessness that often accompany stress.

In conclusion, the importance of journaling in relation to mental health is profound. By offering an outlet for self-expression, promoting self-reflection, and facilitating emotional release, journaling serves as an essential tool for managing stress and enhancing overall well-being. This accessible and flexible practice empowers individuals to confront their thoughts and feelings, leading to greater emotional awareness and resilience. Embracing journaling can be a transformative step toward achieving clarity and peace of mind in an often chaotic world, ultimately fostering a more balanced and fulfilling life.

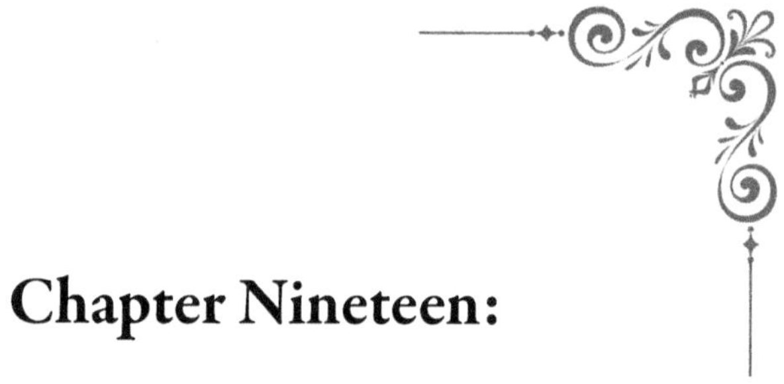

Chapter Nineteen:

Physical Activity and Its Benefits

Physical activity is not only essential for maintaining physical health but also plays a critical role in promoting mental well-being. Numerous studies have highlighted the connection between exercise and mental health, demonstrating that regular physical activity can significantly reduce symptoms of anxiety, depression, and stress. This relationship can be attributed to various physiological and psychological mechanisms that are activated when we engage in physical movement.

One of the primary ways physical activity benefits mental health is through the release of endorphins, often referred to as "feel-good" hormones. When we exercise, our bodies produce these natural chemicals that interact with the receptors in our brain, leading to feelings of euphoria and pain relief. This phenomenon, commonly known as the "runner's high," provides an immediate boost to mood and can help alleviate feelings of sadness or anxiety. The more consistent the physical activity, the more pronounced these effects can become, creating a positive feedback loop that encourages further engagement in exercise.

Additionally, physical activity promotes better sleep, which is essential for mental health. Regular exercise can help individuals fall asleep faster and deepen their sleep, leading to improved overall sleep quality. Sleep is crucial for cognitive functions such as memory, concentration, and emotional regulation. Poor sleep can exacerbate mental health issues, creating a vicious cycle. By incorporating physical activity into one's routine, individuals can improve their sleep patterns, which in turn can enhance their mental resilience and emotional stability.

Engaging in physical activity can also serve as a powerful form of stress relief. Exercise reduces levels of the body's stress hormones, such as cortisol, while simultaneously stimulating the production of neurotransmitters like serotonin and dopamine, which are crucial for mood regulation. By providing a healthy outlet for stress and anxiety, physical activity equips individuals with the tools to handle life's challenges more effectively. This can be particularly beneficial in high-pressure situations, where the ability to manage stress can significantly impact overall mental health.

Social interaction is another significant benefit of physical activity, particularly in group settings. Activities such as team sports, group fitness classes, or even walking clubs can foster a sense of community and belonging. This social component helps combat feelings of isolation and loneliness, which are often linked to mental health issues. Building relationships through shared physical activities can offer emotional support, camaraderie, and a sense of purpose, all of which are vital for maintaining good mental health.

Moreover, physical activity can enhance self-esteem and body image. As individuals become more active and start to see improvements in their physical abilities and overall fitness, they often experience a boost in confidence. This newfound sense of achievement can translate into other areas of life, encouraging individuals to set and pursue personal goals. A positive self-image is closely tied to mental health, and physical activity can be a powerful catalyst for promoting a healthier perception of oneself.

Incorporating physical activity into daily life can also foster a greater sense of mindfulness and present-moment awareness. Many forms of exercise, such as yoga, tai chi, or even mindful walking, encourage individuals to focus on their breath, body movements, and surroundings. This practice of mindfulness can help reduce rumination, a common symptom of anxiety and depression, allowing individuals to cultivate a more balanced mental state. By being present in the moment, people can learn to appreciate the small joys of life, which can enhance overall well-being.

The type of physical activity does not necessarily need to be intense or time-consuming. Even moderate activities such as walking, gardening, or dancing can yield significant mental health benefits. The key is consistency and finding an activity that one enjoys, as this increases the likelihood of adherence to a regular exercise routine. The versatility of physical activity allows individuals to choose options that align with their preferences and lifestyles, making it more accessible to a broader audience.

Furthermore, physical activity can serve as a form of therapy for those dealing with specific mental health issues. Many therapeutic programs now incorporate exercise as a complementary treatment alongside traditional therapies, such as cognitive-behavioral therapy (CBT). This holistic approach recognizes the interconnectedness of physical and mental health, allowing individuals to address their challenges from multiple angles. As a result, exercise can become a valuable tool in the recovery and management of mental health conditions.

In summary, the benefits of physical activity for mental health are profound and multifaceted. From the biochemical effects of endorphin release to the social support gained through group activities, the positive impacts of exercise are far-reaching. By understanding and harnessing these benefits, individuals can enhance their mental resilience, improve their mood, and cultivate a more fulfilling life. As society becomes increasingly aware of the importance of mental health, incorporating physical activity into daily routines should be a priority for everyone, regardless of age or fitness level. The path to better mental health can indeed begin with a single step.

Engaging in physical activity is a vital component of promoting mental well-being, offering a range of psychological benefits in addition to its physical advantages. As research continues to unveil the complexities of this relationship, it becomes increasingly evident that regular exercise can help alleviate symptoms associated with anxiety, depression, and stress. This connection arises from a combination of biological responses and psychological effects that occur during physical exertion.

One of the most notable benefits of exercise is the elevation of endorphin levels, which are chemicals produced by the brain that contribute to feelings of happiness and satisfaction. When individuals engage in physical activities, their bodies generate these hormones, leading to an experience often referred to as the "runner's high." This euphoric feeling can significantly diminish negative emotions, fostering a more positive outlook. With consistent participation in exercise, the effects on mood can become even more pronounced, reinforcing the desire to remain physically active.

In addition to enhancing mood, physical activity plays a significant role in improving sleep patterns. Regular exercise has been linked to quicker sleep onset and deeper, more restorative slumber. Quality rest is essential for optimal cognitive function, including processes like memory retention, problem-solving, and emotional regulation. Conversely, inadequate sleep can worsen mental health conditions, perpetuating a cycle of distress. By incorporating regular movement into their lives, individuals can enhance their sleep quality, which in turn bolsters emotional resilience.

Physical activity also acts as an effective method for managing stress. Exercise lowers levels of stress hormones such as cortisol and stimulates the release of neurotransmitters like serotonin and dopamine, which are crucial for emotional balance. This constructive outlet helps individuals cope with everyday pressures, equipping them with strategies to face challenges more effectively. The ability to manage stress has a profound impact on overall mental health, particularly during difficult times.

Moreover, participating in physical activities often fosters social connections, especially in communal or team settings. Engaging in group sports, fitness classes, or walking clubs can create a sense of belonging and camaraderie among participants. These social interactions can alleviate feelings of loneliness and isolation, which are common contributors to mental health struggles. Building supportive relationships through shared activities enhances emotional well-being and provides a network of encouragement and motivation.

Furthermore, regular engagement in exercise can enhance self-esteem and promote a positive body image. As individuals become more active and experience improvements in their physical capabilities, they often gain confidence in their abilities. This newfound self-assurance can extend beyond physical fitness, inspiring individuals to pursue personal goals in various aspects of their lives. A healthier self-image is closely linked to improved mental health, and physical activity serves as a key driver in fostering this transformation.

Incorporating movement into daily routines can also cultivate mindfulness and present-moment awareness. Practices such as yoga, tai chi, and mindful walking encourage individuals to focus on their breathing, body movements, and surroundings. This emphasis on mindfulness can help reduce negative thought patterns, which are often associated with anxiety and depression, allowing for a more balanced mental state. By embracing the present, individuals can find joy in everyday moments, enhancing their overall sense of well-being.

Lastly, exercise serves as a valuable component in therapeutic approaches for addressing specific mental health challenges. Many treatment programs now integrate physical activity alongside traditional therapies like cognitive-behavioral therapy (CBT). This comprehensive approach recognizes the interplay between physical and mental health, allowing individuals to address their concerns from multiple dimensions. By incorporating movement into their recovery journey, people can experience enhanced outcomes and a more well-rounded approach to managing their mental health.

Chapter Twenty:

The Power of Hobbies and Interests

Hobbies and interests hold a unique power in our lives, serving as outlets for creativity, relaxation, and personal growth. In an increasingly fast-paced world, where stress and responsibilities often dominate our daily routines, engaging in hobbies provides a necessary escape. These activities allow individuals to step outside the pressures of work, family obligations, and societal expectations, creating a space for self-expression. Whether it's painting, gardening, playing a musical instrument, or even knitting, hobbies can offer a sense of fulfillment that many people find lacking in their professional lives.

Moreover, hobbies are instrumental in fostering social connections. Participating in group activities, such as sports, book clubs, or community classes, brings together like-minded individuals who share similar passions. These social interactions can lead to friendships that might not have formed otherwise, providing a supportive network that enriches our lives. In a world where loneliness and isolation are increasingly prevalent, hobbies can serve as a vital bridge, uniting people from diverse backgrounds and fostering a sense of community.

Additionally, hobbies can enhance mental well-being. Engaging in activities we love triggers the release of dopamine, often referred to as the "feel-good" neurotransmitter. This natural boost can alleviate symptoms of anxiety and depression, uplifting our mood and providing emotional stability. Mindfulness practices, such as yoga or meditation, are also considered hobbies that can help individuals center themselves and cultivate a greater awareness of their thoughts and feelings, promoting a healthier mental state.

The benefits of hobbies extend beyond emotional health; they also stimulate cognitive function and boost creativity. Learning a new skill, whether it's cooking a new recipe or mastering a new language, challenges the brain and enhances our cognitive abilities. This cognitive engagement can improve memory, problem-solving skills, and overall mental agility. Furthermore, creative hobbies, like writing or crafting, allow individuals to explore their imagination, leading to innovative thinking both in personal and professional spheres.

Hobbies can also serve as a powerful tool for personal development. They often push us out of our comfort zones, encouraging risk-taking and experimentation. For instance, someone who takes up public speaking might initially feel intimidated, but through practice, they gain confidence and improve their communication skills. This growth can translate into various aspects of life, including career advancement and interpersonal relationships, as individuals learn to embrace challenges and overcome fears.

Furthermore, hobbies can cultivate a sense of accomplishment and purpose. Completing a project, whether it's finishing a book, completing a painting, or growing a vegetable garden, provides tangible evidence of our efforts. This sense of achievement boosts self-esteem and reinforces the idea that we can set and reach personal goals. Such experiences are crucial in building resilience, as they remind us of our capabilities and strengths, encouraging us to take on new challenges in other areas of our lives.

In today's digital age, hobbies can also serve as a means of self-discovery. Many individuals turn to online platforms to explore new interests, from photography to coding. This exploration can lead to the discovery of hidden talents or passions that might otherwise remain dormant. The ability to connect with global communities around shared interests further enriches this experience, allowing for collaborative learning and inspiration across borders.

Moreover, engaging in hobbies can provide an opportunity to disconnect from technology and the constant barrage of information. In a society where screens dominate our attention, dedicating time to a hobby can help reduce screen time and encourage more meaningful, tangible experiences. This digital detox allows for greater mindfulness and presence, fostering a deeper connection with ourselves and the world around us.

Hobbies can also teach valuable life skills that are transferable to other areas. For instance, gardening not only fosters patience as individuals wait for their plants to grow but also encourages responsibility and nurturing. Similarly, team sports can impart lessons in collaboration, leadership, and teamwork. These skills can enhance both personal and professional relationships, equipping individuals with the tools they need to navigate various life situations effectively.

Finally, the power of hobbies lies in their ability to remind us of the importance of play and leisure in our lives. In a culture that often glorifies productivity, hobbies serve as a vital reminder that taking time for ourselves is not just beneficial but essential. They challenge the notion that our worth is tied solely to our work output, encouraging a more balanced approach to life. By embracing hobbies and interests, we reclaim our time, our joy, and ultimately, our sense of self.

In essence, the power of hobbies and interests goes far beyond mere pastime activities. They enrich our lives, foster connections, enhance well-being, and contribute to personal growth. By prioritizing our passions, we not only cultivate happiness but also create a life filled with purpose and meaning. Whether through artistic expression, physical activity, or intellectual pursuits, the journey into our interests is one of the most rewarding paths we can take.

Hobbies and interests serve as powerful tools that enhance our lives in numerous ways, providing an essential balance to the demands of daily living. In a world characterized by relentless schedules and high expectations, engaging in hobbies creates a sanctuary where individuals can escape the pressures of work and personal obligations. These activities, whether painting, gardening, or playing a musical instrument, offer a form of self-expression that brings joy and satisfaction. They enable individuals to tap into their creativity and passions, leading to a more fulfilling and balanced life.

One of the most profound benefits of hobbies is their ability to foster social connections. Group activities such as team sports, book clubs, or community classes create opportunities for individuals to meet others with similar interests. These shared experiences can lead to meaningful friendships and a sense of belonging. In an age where feelings of isolation and loneliness are increasingly common, hobbies provide a vital link to others, allowing for the development of supportive networks that enhance our overall well-being.

Moreover, the mental health benefits of hobbies are significant. Engaging in enjoyable activities releases dopamine, a neurotransmitter associated with pleasure and reward. This release can alleviate symptoms of anxiety and depression, contributing to a more positive mood. Mindfulness practices, such as yoga or meditation, also fall under the umbrella of hobbies and can help individuals cultivate greater awareness of their thoughts and feelings. This heightened mindfulness promotes emotional balance and resilience, essential components of mental well-being.

Cognitive stimulation is another key advantage of pursuing hobbies. Learning new skills, whether it's mastering a musical instrument or picking up a new language, challenges the brain and enhances cognitive function. This mental engagement can improve memory, sharpen problem-solving skills, and foster overall mental agility. Creative hobbies, such as writing or crafting, encourage imaginative thinking, which can lead to innovative solutions in both personal and professional contexts.

Hobbies also play a significant role in personal development. They encourage individuals to step outside their comfort zones, fostering a spirit of risk-taking and experimentation. For instance, a person who takes up public speaking may initially feel apprehensive, but with practice, they gain confidence and improve their communication skills. This growth not only enhances personal capabilities but also translates into various aspects of life, including career advancement and improved interpersonal relationships.

In addition, engaging in hobbies cultivates a sense of accomplishment and purpose. Completing a project, whether it's finishing a painting, writing a novel, or successfully growing a vegetable garden, provides tangible proof of effort and dedication. This sense of achievement boosts self-esteem and reinforces the idea that individuals can set and achieve personal goals. Such experiences are crucial for building resilience, serving as reminders of our strengths and capabilities in the face of challenges.

Hobbies also offer a pathway for self-discovery, particularly in today's digital age. Many individuals turn to online platforms to explore new interests, from photography to coding. This exploration can lead to the discovery of hidden talents and passions that may have remained dormant. The ability to connect with global communities around shared interests further enriches this experience, allowing for collaborative learning and inspiration across cultural boundaries.

Moreover, engaging in hobbies encourages individuals to disconnect from technology and the constant influx of information. In a society dominated by screens and digital distractions, dedicating time to a hobby can serve as a much-needed break from technology. This digital detox fosters mindfulness and presence, allowing individuals to reconnect with themselves and their surroundings. It creates an opportunity to engage with the physical world, promoting a deeper appreciation for life.

Hobbies also impart valuable life skills that are transferable to various aspects of life. For example, gardening teaches patience and responsibility, while team sports underscore the importance of collaboration and leadership. These skills enhance personal and professional relationships, equipping individuals with the tools they need to navigate different life situations effectively. The lessons learned through hobbies can have far-reaching impacts, shaping how we approach challenges and interact with others.

Ultimately, the power of hobbies lies in their ability to remind us of the importance of play and leisure in our lives. In a culture that often prioritizes productivity above all else, hobbies serve as a vital reminder that taking time for ourselves is essential for our overall well-being. By embracing our passions and interests, we reclaim our time and joy, enriching our lives with meaning and fulfillment. Engaging in hobbies is not merely a pastime; it is a journey of self-exploration and growth that leads to a more balanced and satisfying life.

Chapter Twenty One:

Volunteering and Helping Others

Volunteering and helping others have long been recognized as powerful tools for enhancing mental health and well-being. Engaging in volunteer work not only benefits the community but also fosters personal growth, emotional resilience, and a sense of purpose. The act of giving back creates a positive feedback loop that can significantly improve one's mental health while addressing the needs of others.

One of the most profound benefits of volunteering is the sense of purpose it instills in individuals. Many people struggle with feelings of aimlessness or lack of direction in their lives. When individuals dedicate their time and energy to helping others, they often discover a new sense of meaning. This newfound purpose can drive motivation, boost self-esteem, and enhance overall life satisfaction. Engaging in meaningful activities allows volunteers to connect their skills and passions with the needs of their communities, leading to a fulfilling experience.

Moreover, volunteering fosters social connections, which are fundamental to mental health. Many individuals experience loneliness or isolation, particularly in today's fast-paced, technology-driven world. By volunteering, individuals have the opportunity to meet new people, forge friendships, and build a sense of community. These social interactions can reduce feelings of loneliness and promote a sense of belonging, which is essential for emotional well-being. The shared experiences of working towards a common goal can strengthen bonds and create lasting relationships.

Additionally, volunteering can serve as a powerful stress reliever. Engaging in altruistic activities shifts the focus away from personal problems and challenges. When individuals immerse themselves in the needs of others, they often experience a sense of joy and fulfillment that can alleviate feelings of anxiety and sadness. The act of helping others can also release endorphins, the body's natural feel-good hormones, contributing to an overall uplift in mood. This positive emotional shift can be a critical component in managing stress and improving mental health.

Volunteering also provides opportunities for skill development and personal growth. Many volunteer roles offer training and experiences that can enhance one's skill set, from communication and leadership to problem-solving and teamwork. This newfound competence can boost self-confidence and self-worth, which are vital aspects of mental health. As individuals gain new skills and overcome challenges through volunteering, they can build resilience, making it easier to cope with life's difficulties.

Furthermore, volunteering can offer a healthy distraction from personal struggles. When individuals focus their energy on helping others, they may find relief from their own worries and challenges. This redirection of energy can be particularly beneficial for those dealing with mental health issues, as it encourages a more positive and constructive mindset. By engaging in volunteer work, individuals can cultivate a sense of gratitude and perspective, recognizing that their struggles are part of a broader human experience.

In addition to the personal benefits, volunteering helps to create a positive impact on society. Individuals who volunteer contribute to the well-being of their communities, addressing various social, economic, and environmental challenges. This sense of contribution can enhance feelings of civic responsibility and pride, leading to greater community cohesion. When individuals see the tangible effects of their efforts, it can reinforce their commitment to helping others and improve their overall mental health.

Another significant advantage of volunteering is the opportunity for physical activity. Many volunteer roles involve physical tasks, whether it's working in a community garden, participating in cleanup events, or assisting in shelters. Physical activity has been proven to have numerous mental health benefits, including reducing symptoms of anxiety and depression. By incorporating movement into their volunteering efforts, individuals can enhance their mental health while making a positive contribution to their communities.

Volunteering can also provide a unique perspective on life. Individuals often encounter diverse populations and challenging situations that may differ from their own experiences. This exposure can foster empathy and understanding, leading to personal growth and a broader worldview. As volunteers learn about the struggles and triumphs of others, they may find their own challenges seem more manageable, promoting resilience and emotional strength.

Moreover, volunteering can instill a sense of gratitude and appreciation for one's own life circumstances. By witnessing the challenges faced by others, individuals may develop a greater sense of gratitude for their own opportunities and resources. This shift in perspective can lead to increased happiness and contentment, as individuals learn to appreciate the positives in their lives. Gratitude has been linked to improved mental health, making this aspect of volunteering particularly valuable.

In conclusion, the benefits of volunteering and helping others extend far beyond the immediate impact on those in need. Engaging in volunteer work can enhance mental health by instilling a sense of purpose, fostering social connections, relieving stress, promoting personal growth, and providing a healthy distraction. As individuals contribute to their communities, they not only uplift others but also cultivate their own emotional resilience and well-being. In a world that often emphasizes individualism, the act of giving back serves as a powerful reminder of our interconnectedness and the profound impact we can have on one another's lives.

Volunteering and helping others play a crucial role in enhancing mental health and well-being. Engaging in volunteer work goes beyond simply providing assistance to those in need; it fosters personal growth, emotional resilience, and a profound sense of purpose. The act of giving back creates a positive feedback loop, where the benefits of altruism extend to the volunteer, leading to improved mental health while simultaneously addressing the needs of the community.

One of the most significant advantages of volunteering is the sense of purpose it instills in individuals. Many people face feelings of aimlessness or lack of direction, which can contribute to mental health challenges. When individuals dedicate their time and energy to helping others, they often discover a renewed sense of meaning in their lives. This newfound purpose can drive motivation, enhance self-esteem, and contribute to overall life satisfaction. Engaging in meaningful activities allows volunteers to connect their skills and passions with the needs of their communities, resulting in a deeply fulfilling experience.

Volunteering also fosters social connections, which are essential for maintaining mental health. In an age where loneliness and isolation are increasingly common, volunteering provides opportunities to meet new people and forge meaningful relationships. Engaging in shared experiences while working towards a common goal can create a strong sense of community and belonging. These social interactions are vital for combating feelings of loneliness, which can significantly impact emotional well-being.

Additionally, volunteering serves as a powerful stress reliever. When individuals immerse themselves in the needs of others, they often find relief from their own problems. The act of helping can spark joy and fulfillment, alleviating feelings of anxiety and sadness. Moreover, volunteering can lead to the release of endorphins, the body's natural feel-good hormones, which contribute to an overall uplift in mood. This positive emotional shift can be especially beneficial for individuals managing stress or mental health issues, as it encourages a more optimistic and constructive mindset.

Moreover, volunteering provides opportunities for skill development and personal growth. Many volunteer roles offer training and experiences that enhance communication, leadership, and teamwork skills. This newfound competence can boost self-confidence and self-worth, both of which are vital for mental health. As individuals gain new skills and overcome challenges through volunteering, they build resilience, making it easier to cope with life's difficulties and uncertainties.

Another important aspect of volunteering is the healthy distraction it offers from personal struggles. By focusing their energy on helping others, individuals may find relief from their own worries. This redirection can be particularly beneficial for those dealing with mental health challenges, as it encourages a shift in focus and perspective. Engaging in volunteer work allows individuals to cultivate gratitude and recognize that their struggles are part of a broader human experience, ultimately enhancing their emotional resilience.

In addition to personal benefits, volunteering creates a positive impact on society. Volunteers contribute to addressing various social, economic, and environmental challenges within their communities. This sense of contribution fosters civic responsibility and pride, leading to greater community cohesion. When individuals witness the tangible effects of their efforts, it reinforces their commitment to helping others, further enhancing their mental health and sense of belonging.

Engaging in volunteer activities also promotes physical activity, which is vital for mental well-being. Many volunteer roles involve physical tasks like gardening, cleanup events, or assisting in shelters. Physical activity has been proven to reduce symptoms of anxiety and depression, thereby improving overall mental health. By incorporating movement into their volunteer efforts, individuals can enhance their emotional well-being while making a meaningful contribution to their communities.

Lastly, volunteering can provide a unique perspective on life. Interacting with diverse populations and challenging situations fosters empathy and understanding, leading to personal growth. As volunteers learn about the struggles and triumphs of others, they often find that their own challenges seem more manageable. This shift in perspective promotes resilience and emotional strength, enabling individuals to navigate their lives with greater ease and confidence. By recognizing the interconnectedness of human experiences, volunteers can develop a profound appreciation for their own lives, ultimately contributing to their overall mental health.

Chapter Twenty Two:

Engaging in Community Activities

Engaging in community activities surrounding mental health is vital for fostering a supportive environment that promotes well-being and resilience. Mental health issues affect individuals and communities alike, and addressing these challenges collectively can lead to more effective solutions and a greater understanding of mental health. Community initiatives can reduce stigma, provide resources, and create safe spaces for open discussions about mental health, ultimately benefiting individuals and society as a whole.

One of the primary benefits of engaging in community activities related to mental health is the reduction of stigma. Many individuals who struggle with mental health issues face societal misconceptions and discrimination, which can deter them from seeking help. Community initiatives that focus on mental health education and awareness can challenge these stereotypes, promoting a more compassionate understanding of mental health challenges. By fostering open conversations, communities can help to normalize discussions around mental health, making it easier for individuals to seek support without fear of judgment.

Community activities surrounding mental health also provide essential resources and support networks. Many people may not have access to mental health services due to various barriers, such as cost, location, or lack of information. By organizing community events such as workshops, support groups, and mental health fairs, communities can connect individuals with vital resources. These initiatives can also help people learn about available services, coping strategies, and how to support others in their mental health journeys.

Moreover, engaging in community activities promotes social connections, which are essential for emotional well-being. Isolation and loneliness are common factors that contribute to mental health issues. Community events can help individuals build relationships, create friendships, and form support networks. When people come together to discuss mental health, they often realize they are not alone in their struggles, fostering a sense of belonging and community. This connectedness is crucial for enhancing resilience and providing emotional support during difficult times.

Participation in community activities can also empower individuals to take charge of their mental health. Through workshops and educational programs, participants can learn coping strategies, stress management techniques, and the importance of self-care. This knowledge enables individuals to recognize the signs of mental health issues, both in themselves and in others, and encourages proactive approaches to mental well-being. Empowering community members with information fosters a culture of support and resilience, equipping them to navigate challenges more effectively.

In addition to providing support for individuals, community activities surrounding mental health can engage families and caregivers. Mental health challenges can be isolating not just for individuals but also for their loved ones. Community initiatives can offer resources and support specifically tailored to families and caregivers, helping them better understand mental health conditions and how to provide effective support. By involving the entire family unit, communities can create a more comprehensive support system that fosters healing and understanding.

Furthermore, community activities can contribute to policy change and advocacy efforts surrounding mental health. When communities come together to raise awareness and advocate for mental health resources, they can influence local and national policies. Collective voices can demand better access to mental health services, funding for community programs, and improved mental health education in schools. By actively participating in advocacy efforts, individuals can drive meaningful change that benefits the entire community.

Engaging in community activities also allows for the celebration of mental health awareness days and events, which can have a significant impact on public perception. Events such as Mental Health Awareness Month or World Mental Health Day provide opportunities for communities to come together, share stories, and promote understanding. These occasions can serve as powerful platforms for raising awareness and encouraging individuals to prioritize their mental health. By participating in such events, communities can demonstrate their commitment to mental well-being and create a culture that values mental health.

Artistic and creative community activities can also play a pivotal role in promoting mental health. Programs that incorporate art, music, or other forms of creative expression can provide individuals with a healthy outlet for their emotions. Creative activities can foster self-expression and help individuals process their feelings, enhancing their overall mental well-being. Community art projects, workshops, or performances can also serve as a means of raising awareness and promoting conversations about mental health in an engaging and accessible way.

In conclusion, engaging in community activities surrounding mental health is essential for creating a supportive, informed, and connected environment. By reducing stigma, providing resources, and fostering social connections, communities can significantly impact individuals' mental health and well-being. Through education, empowerment, advocacy, and creative expression, communities can create a culture that prioritizes mental health and supports those in need. As we work together to address mental health challenges, we can build a more compassionate and resilient society that values the well-being of all its members.

Engaging in community activities surrounding mental health is crucial for fostering a supportive environment that enhances well-being and resilience. Mental health issues affect not only individuals but also the broader community, and addressing these challenges collectively can lead to more effective solutions. Community initiatives can help reduce stigma, provide essential resources, and create safe spaces for open discussions about mental health. Ultimately, these efforts benefit individuals and society as a whole, promoting a culture of understanding and support.

One of the most significant advantages of community initiatives focused on mental health is the reduction of stigma. Individuals struggling with mental health issues often face societal misconceptions and discrimination, which can deter them from seeking help. By promoting mental health education and awareness, community activities can challenge these stereotypes and foster a more compassionate understanding of mental health challenges. Open conversations about mental health can help normalize these discussions, making it easier for individuals to seek support without fear of judgment.

Community activities also provide vital resources and support networks. Many people encounter barriers to accessing mental health services, such as cost, location, or lack of information. Organizing community events like workshops, support groups, and mental health fairs can connect individuals with essential resources. These initiatives not only provide information about available services but also empower individuals to learn coping strategies and ways to support others in their mental health journeys.

Additionally, engaging in community activities promotes social connections, which are critical for emotional well-being. Isolation and loneliness can contribute to mental health issues, making it essential for individuals to build relationships and create friendships. Community events that focus on mental health allow participants to connect with one another, fostering a sense of belonging. When individuals come together to discuss their experiences, they often realize they are not alone in their struggles, which enhances resilience and provides emotional support.

Engagement in community activities can also empower individuals to take charge of their mental health. Through workshops and educational programs, participants learn about coping strategies, stress management techniques, and the importance of self-care. This knowledge enables individuals to recognize the signs of mental health issues in themselves and others, encouraging proactive approaches to well-being. By equipping community members with information, we foster a culture of support and resilience, empowering them to navigate challenges more effectively.

Furthermore, community activities can engage families and caregivers, providing them with vital resources and support. Mental health challenges can be isolating not only for individuals but also for their loved ones. Initiatives that involve families can help them better understand mental health conditions and how to provide effective support. By involving the entire family unit, communities can create a comprehensive support system that fosters healing and understanding, reinforcing the importance of mental health for all.

In conclusion, engaging in community activities surrounding mental health is essential for creating a supportive and informed environment. By reducing stigma, providing resources, and fostering connections, communities can significantly impact individuals' mental health and well-being. Through education, empowerment, and family engagement, communities can create a culture that prioritizes mental health. As we work together to address mental health challenges, we can build a more compassionate and resilient society that values the well-being of every member.

Chapter Twenty Three:

Understanding Your Values and Beliefs
Unity in values and beliefs plays a crucial role in supporting mental health, both on an individual and societal level. When individuals align their actions with their core values, they experience a sense of coherence and purpose, which is essential for mental well-being. This alignment fosters a stable sense of identity, enabling people to navigate life's challenges with resilience. In a world filled with constant change and uncertainty, having a solid foundation based on shared values can provide individuals with a sense of direction and clarity.

Moreover, when communities embrace unity in values and beliefs, they create a supportive environment that nurtures mental health. This sense of belonging can significantly reduce feelings of isolation and loneliness, which are often precursors to mental health issues. Communities that uphold shared values, such as empathy, compassion, and respect, foster connections among their members, encouraging open dialogue about mental health challenges. This openness can lead to early intervention and support, which are critical in managing mental health issues effectively.

Incorporating unity in values and beliefs into mental health discussions can help destigmatize these issues. When people come together around shared beliefs, they create a safe space for vulnerability and authenticity. This collective understanding diminishes the fear of judgment, encouraging individuals to seek help when needed. By normalizing conversations about mental health within a framework of shared values, communities can break down barriers and promote a culture of understanding and support.

Furthermore, unity in values can enhance the effectiveness of mental health initiatives. Programs designed to improve mental health outcomes benefit from community buy-in, which is more easily achieved when values align. When individuals believe in the goals and objectives of mental health programs, they are more likely to participate actively, leading to better outcomes. A unified approach ensures that mental health initiatives resonate with the community's values, making them more relevant and impactful.

At the individual level, aligning one's actions with personal values can lead to increased life satisfaction. People who engage in activities that reflect their beliefs often report higher levels of happiness and fulfillment. This congruence between values and actions fosters a sense of authenticity, which is crucial for mental health. When individuals act in ways that are true to their beliefs, they cultivate self-esteem and resilience, equipping them to handle life's adversities more effectively.

Moreover, unity in values and beliefs can serve as a protective factor against mental health challenges. Individuals who share a sense of purpose and commitment to their values are more likely to exhibit resilience in the face of stress. This collective strength can be especially important during times of crisis, as it allows individuals to draw on the support of their community. With a solid foundation of shared beliefs, individuals can find comfort and solace in knowing they are not alone in their struggles.

In the workplace, unity in values and beliefs is equally vital for supporting employee mental health. Organizations that prioritize shared values create a positive work culture that fosters employee engagement and satisfaction. When employees feel aligned with their organization's mission and values, they are more likely to experience job satisfaction and commitment. This alignment not only enhances individual mental health but also contributes to a more productive and harmonious workplace environment.

Additionally, the concept of unity in values can extend to families, which are often the first line of support for individuals facing mental health challenges. Families that uphold shared beliefs and values create a nurturing environment where open communication thrives. This supportive atmosphere encourages family members to express their feelings and seek help when necessary. When families operate from a foundation of unity, they can better navigate the complexities of mental health together, fostering resilience and understanding.

To cultivate unity in values and beliefs, education and awareness are paramount. Initiatives that promote mental health literacy can help individuals understand the importance of aligning their values with their actions. By fostering an environment where conversations about values are encouraged, individuals can reflect on their beliefs and how they impact their mental health. This self-reflection is a critical step toward creating a more unified community that prioritizes mental well-being.

As we strive for unity in values and beliefs, it is essential to recognize the diversity of perspectives within communities. Embracing this diversity while finding common ground can lead to a richer understanding of mental health. By engaging in inclusive dialogues that respect different beliefs and experiences, communities can create a more supportive environment for all individuals. This inclusivity not only strengthens the community but also enhances collective mental health outcomes.

In conclusion, the importance of unity in values and beliefs cannot be overstated when it comes to supporting mental health. Both individuals and communities benefit from a shared foundation that fosters connection, understanding, and resilience. By prioritizing unity in discussions about mental health, we can create supportive environments that empower individuals to seek help, embrace their authenticity, and navigate challenges with confidence. As we work toward a more unified approach, we must recognize the transformative power of shared values in promoting mental well-being for all.

Unity in values and beliefs plays a foundational role in supporting mental health at both individual and community levels. When people align their actions with their core values, they often experience a sense of coherence and purpose. This alignment fosters a stable identity, which is crucial for mental well-being. In a rapidly changing world, having a solid foundation based on shared values provides individuals with direction and clarity, helping them navigate life's challenges with greater resilience.

Communities that embrace unity in values create supportive environments that nurture mental health. A strong sense of belonging can significantly reduce feelings of isolation and loneliness. Common precursors to mental health issues. When communities uphold shared values such as empathy, compassion, and respect, they encourage open dialogue about mental health challenges. This openness facilitates early intervention and support, making it easier for individuals to seek help when they need it.

Moreover, promoting unity in values can help destigmatize mental health issues. When individuals come together around shared beliefs, they create safe spaces for vulnerability and authenticity. This collective understanding reduces the fear of judgment, making it easier for people to discuss their mental health challenges and seek help. Normalizing conversations about mental health within a framework of shared values fosters a culture of understanding and support, which is essential for community well-being.

At the practical level, unity in values enhances the effectiveness of mental health initiatives. Programs aimed at improving mental health outcomes benefit from community buy-in, which is more likely when values align. When individuals believe in the goals of mental health programs, they are more inclined to participate actively, leading to better outcomes. A unified approach ensures that mental health initiatives resonate with the community's values, making them more relevant and impactful.

On an individual level, acting in accordance with personal values can significantly enhance life satisfaction. People who engage in activities aligned with their beliefs often report higher levels of happiness and fulfillment. This congruence fosters authenticity, which is essential for mental health. When individuals live in ways that reflect their values, they cultivate self-esteem and resilience, equipping themselves to handle life's adversities more effectively.

In challenging times, unity in values serves as a protective factor against mental health challenges. Individuals who share a sense of purpose and commitment to their values are more likely to exhibit resilience in the face of stress. This collective strength proves invaluable during crises, as individuals can draw on the support of their community. A solid foundation of shared beliefs allows individuals to find comfort in knowing that they are not alone in their struggles.

In the workplace, unity in values also significantly impacts employee mental health. Organizations that prioritize shared values often foster positive work cultures, leading to enhanced employee engagement and satisfaction. When employees feel aligned with their organization's mission and values, they are more likely to experience job satisfaction and commitment. This alignment contributes to a more productive and harmonious workplace, benefiting both employees and the organization as a whole.

Families represent another critical space where unity in values can bolster mental health. Families that uphold shared beliefs create nurturing environments that encourage open communication. This supportive atmosphere allows family members to express their feelings and seek help without fear of judgment. By operating from a foundation of unity, families can better navigate the complexities of mental health challenges together, fostering resilience and understanding among their members.

To cultivate unity in values and beliefs, education and awareness are paramount. Initiatives that promote mental health literacy can help individuals understand the significance of aligning their values with their actions. By encouraging conversations about values, individuals can reflect on their beliefs and their impact on mental health. This self-reflection is essential for creating a more unified community that prioritizes mental well-being. Ultimately, the transformative power of shared values can lead to a more supportive society, enhancing mental health outcomes for everyone involved.

Chapter Twenty Four:

Setting Small, Achievable Goals

Setting small, achievable goals is a powerful strategy for supporting mental health. In a world that often feels overwhelming, breaking down larger aspirations into manageable tasks can significantly alleviate stress and anxiety. This approach helps individuals regain a sense of control over their lives, fostering a positive mindset. When goals are realistic and attainable, the likelihood of success increases, which can boost self-esteem and overall mental well-being.

One of the most significant benefits of setting small goals is the immediate sense of accomplishment they provide. Completing even minor tasks can lead to a rush of positive feelings, reinforcing the idea that progress is possible. This sense of achievement can create a positive feedback loop, encouraging individuals to continue setting and accomplishing more goals. Even the simplest tasks can serve as stepping stones toward larger ambitions, making the journey feel less daunting.

Small goals also help to combat feelings of overwhelm. When faced with a significant challenge, it's easy to feel paralyzed by the enormity of the task ahead. By breaking it down into smaller, actionable steps, individuals can focus on one thing at a time. This method not only makes the task more manageable but also allows for a clearer path forward. Each small success can help individuals gain momentum, gradually building their confidence to tackle more significant challenges.

Moreover, small, achievable goals facilitate better time management. Individuals can prioritize their tasks and allocate their time more effectively when they have a clear set of smaller objectives. This structured approach can reduce procrastination and enhance productivity, contributing to a sense of accomplishment. Feeling productive can be immensely satisfying and can positively impact mental health, as individuals perceive that they are making progress in their lives.

Setting small goals can also promote mindfulness. When individuals focus on achieving one specific task at a time, they are encouraged to be present in the moment. This practice can help reduce anxiety and stress, as it allows individuals to concentrate on what they can control right now, rather than worrying about the past or future. Mindfulness, in turn, can lead to increased emotional regulation and improved mental health.

Another significant advantage of small goals is their adaptability. Life is unpredictable, and circumstances can change quickly. Small, achievable goals can be adjusted as needed, allowing individuals to remain flexible in their approach. This adaptability can alleviate feelings of frustration or defeat when things don't go as planned. Instead of feeling overwhelmed, individuals can pivot their focus and adjust their goals, maintaining a sense of progress in their lives.

Additionally, setting small goals encourages individuals to practice self-compassion. When people establish realistic objectives, they are less likely to set themselves up for failure. Recognizing that it's okay to take small steps fosters a kinder internal dialogue. This self-compassion is vital for mental health, as it helps individuals develop a more forgiving relationship with themselves, reducing feelings of guilt or shame associated with perceived inadequacies.

Incorporating small goals into daily routines can also create a sense of structure. Establishing a routine that includes small, achievable tasks can provide individuals with a sense of normalcy and stability, especially during challenging times. This structure can be particularly beneficial for those dealing with anxiety or depression, as it creates a framework for daily life and helps individuals feel more grounded.

Furthermore, small goals can enhance social connections. Sharing personal goals with friends, family, or support groups can lead to increased accountability and encouragement. When individuals have a support system that understands their objectives, they are more likely to stay motivated and committed to their goals. This social aspect can be especially beneficial for mental health, as it fosters a sense of belonging and community.

Celebrating small achievements is another critical component of this process. Taking the time to acknowledge and celebrate even minor successes reinforces the positive impact that goal-setting can have on mental health. This practice encourages individuals to take pride in their accomplishments, no matter how small. Celebrations can be as simple as treating oneself to a favorite activity or sharing successes with loved ones, reinforcing the notion that progress deserves recognition.

Small, achievable goals can also serve as valuable tools for building resilience. When individuals face setbacks, having established small objectives allows them to refocus their efforts and adapt their strategies. This resilience is crucial for mental health, as it helps individuals develop coping mechanisms and maintain a positive outlook, even in the face of adversity. The ability to bounce back from challenges is a significant predictor of overall well-being.

Moreover, setting small goals can help individuals clarify their values and priorities. As they work through their objectives, they may discover what truly matters to them, leading to a more authentic and fulfilling life. This clarity can enhance motivation, as individuals become more aware of their desires and aspirations. Aligning goals with personal values is essential for a sense of purpose, which is a vital aspect of mental health.

In addition, small goals can promote a growth mindset. When individuals view challenges as opportunities for growth rather than as insurmountable obstacles, they cultivate resilience and adaptability. This mindset shift is crucial for mental health, as it encourages individuals to embrace learning and development rather than fear Incorporating small, achievable goals into one's daily routine can significantly enhance mental health by fostering a sense of accomplishment and purpose. When individuals break down larger objectives into smaller tasks, they create a clear pathway to success. This approach not only makes daunting tasks feel manageable but also allows individuals to celebrate their progress along the way. Each small success reinforces the belief that they can achieve their aspirations, leading to increased motivation and a more positive outlook on life.

The act of setting small goals can also serve as a form of self-care. By prioritizing manageable tasks, individuals can ensure that they are not overloading themselves, which is crucial for maintaining mental well-being. This practice encourages individuals to listen to their needs and respect their limits, which is particularly important for those dealing with stress, anxiety, or depression. By taking a balanced approach to goal-setting, individuals can create a healthier relationship with productivity and achievement.

Furthermore, small goals can provide a sense of agency and control in one's life. In times of uncertainty or distress, it's easy to feel powerless; however, focusing on what can be accomplished in the immediate future restores a sense of empowerment. This regained agency is essential for mental health, as it fosters resilience and the belief that individuals can influence their circumstances. When people feel in control of their actions, they are better equipped to handle life's challenges.

Another important aspect of small goal-setting is its capacity to reduce procrastination. Large tasks often feel overwhelming, leading individuals to delay taking action. By breaking these tasks into smaller, specific goals, the pressure is alleviated, making it easier to start. This gradual approach can significantly reduce the tendency to procrastinate, allowing individuals to experience the satisfaction of completing tasks and boosting their overall productivity. In turn, this enhanced productivity can lead to improved mental health as individuals experience a sense of achievement and fulfillment.

Setting small, achievable goals also encourages a focus on the process rather than solely on outcomes. This emphasis on the journey allows individuals to appreciate their efforts, skills, and growth along the way. By acknowledging the importance of the steps taken toward a goal, individuals can cultivate a more positive and accepting mindset. This shift in focus can lead to increased self-compassion, as individuals learn to value their efforts regardless of the final result, fostering a healthier relationship with success and failure.

Moreover, establishing small goals can enhance social connections and support systems. Sharing personal objectives with friends or family creates opportunities for encouragement and accountability. This social interaction is vital for mental health, as it reinforces a sense of belonging and community. When individuals feel supported in their pursuits, they are more likely to stay committed to their goals and celebrate their achievements together, further enhancing their mental well-being.

In conclusion, setting small, achievable goals is a highly effective strategy for supporting mental health. By breaking down larger objectives into manageable tasks, individuals can experience immediate feelings of accomplishment, regain a sense of control, and foster resilience. This approach not only promotes mindfulness and self-care but also enhances social connections and self-compassion. Ultimately, the practice of setting small goals empowers individuals to navigate their lives with greater purpose and positivity, contributing to overall mental well-being.

Chapter Twenty Five:

The Importance of Daily Routines
Establishing a daily routine is essential for maintaining mental health and well-being. Routines provide structure and predictability, which can be especially beneficial during times of uncertainty or stress. When individuals have a consistent framework for their day, it allows them to feel more grounded and in control. This stability can help alleviate anxiety and foster a sense of security, contributing positively to overall mental health.

A well-structured daily routine can also enhance productivity. By allocating specific times for various tasks, whether work-related, personal, or leisure, individuals can create a clear roadmap for their day. This organization can reduce feelings of overwhelm and procrastination, as people know what to expect and when to focus on specific activities. As tasks are completed, the sense of accomplishment can further boost self-esteem and motivation, reinforcing a positive mindset.

Moreover, a daily routine can promote healthy habits. Incorporating elements such as regular exercise, balanced meals, and adequate sleep into a routine can significantly impact mental health. Physical health is closely linked to mental well-being, and a structured routine that prioritizes these aspects can enhance mood, energy levels, and overall resilience. When individuals make conscious choices about their daily activities, they are more likely to engage in behaviors that support their mental health.

In addition to promoting healthy habits, a daily routine provides opportunities for self-care. Setting aside time for activities that bring joy and relaxation, such as reading, meditation, or hobbies, can help individuals recharge and reduce stress. By intentionally including self-care in their routines, individuals can prioritize their mental health and cultivate a greater sense of well-being. This practice not only helps to alleviate stress but also fosters a deeper connection with oneself.

A consistent routine also facilitates better time management. When individuals have a clear plan for their day, they can allocate time more effectively, ensuring that important tasks and activities are completed. This efficiency reduces the likelihood of feeling rushed or overwhelmed, which can contribute to anxiety. In turn, this improved time management can lead to more leisure time, allowing individuals to engage in activities they enjoy and further enhance their mental health.

Furthermore, routines can help individuals develop a sense of purpose. Establishing daily goals, no matter how small, can provide motivation and direction. This sense of purpose is crucial for mental well-being, as it encourages individuals to engage in meaningful activities and work toward personal aspirations. When individuals have clear objectives to pursue each day, they are more likely to experience feelings of fulfillment and satisfaction.

The social aspect of daily routines also plays a vital role in mental health. Engaging in regular activities with family, friends, or colleagues can strengthen social connections and foster a sense of belonging. Whether it's sharing meals, participating in group exercises, or attending social events, these interactions are essential for emotional support. A routine that incorporates social engagement can reduce feelings of loneliness and isolation, which are significant risk factors for mental health issues.

Consistency in routines can also promote better sleep hygiene. Establishing regular sleep and wake times helps regulate the body's internal clock, leading to improved sleep quality. Adequate sleep is crucial for mental health, as it impacts mood, cognitive function, and emotional regulation. When individuals prioritize sleep within their daily routines, they are more likely to feel rested and better equipped to handle life's challenges.

In times of crisis or change, maintaining a daily routine can provide a sense of normalcy. During stressful periods, adhering to a familiar structure can be comforting and grounding. It allows individuals to focus on the things they can control, reducing feelings of helplessness and anxiety. A consistent routine can serve as an anchor, helping individuals navigate through difficult times while maintaining their mental health.

Moreover, the act of reflecting on daily routines can lead to personal growth. Taking the time to evaluate what is working and what may need adjustment can foster self-awareness. Individuals can identify patterns in their behaviors, recognize triggers for stress or anxiety, and make necessary changes to better support their mental health. This reflective practice encourages individuals to take an active role in shaping their routines in ways that align with their mental health needs.

Incorporating mindfulness into daily routines can further enhance their benefits for mental health. Mindfulness practices, such as meditation, deep breathing, or intentional moments of gratitude, can be seamlessly integrated into a routine. These practices promote relaxation and self-awareness, helping individuals manage stress more effectively. By making mindfulness a regular part of their day, individuals can cultivate a more positive mindset and improve their emotional well-being.

Lastly, the importance of flexibility within a daily routine cannot be overlooked. While consistency is key, it's also essential to remain adaptable. Life can be unpredictable, and allowing room for spontaneous changes or adjustments can help individuals feel more in control. This balance between structure and flexibility ensures that routines remain supportive rather than restrictive, ultimately fostering a healthier relationship with daily life and mental health.

In conclusion, establishing a daily routine is a fundamental aspect of maintaining mental health. From providing structure and enhancing productivity to promoting healthy habits and fostering social connections.

Establishing a daily routine is crucial for maintaining mental health and overall well-being. A well-structured routine provides individuals with a sense of stability and predictability, which can be particularly beneficial during stressful periods or times of uncertainty. When people have a consistent framework for their daily activities, they often feel more grounded and in control of their lives. This sense of security can significantly alleviate anxiety and contribute positively to mental health, helping individuals navigate the challenges they face with greater resilience.

One of the primary benefits of a daily routine is its ability to enhance productivity. By allocating specific times for tasks, whether they be work-related, personal, or recreational, individuals create a clear roadmap for their day. This organization reduces feelings of overwhelm and procrastination, as people know what to expect and when to focus on certain activities. Completing tasks as planned can lead to a sense of accomplishment, which boosts self-esteem and motivation, reinforcing a more positive mindset overall.

In addition to improving productivity, a daily routine encourages the development of healthy habits. Incorporating elements such as regular physical activity, balanced meals, and sufficient sleep into a routine can have a profound impact on mental health. The relationship between physical and mental well-being is well-documented, and when individuals prioritize these aspects of their lives through a structured routine, they often experience enhanced mood, higher energy levels, and improved resilience against stressors.

Moreover, a daily routine provides essential opportunities for self-care. Setting aside time for activities that are enjoyable and relaxing, such as reading, practicing mindfulness, or engaging in hobbies, allows individuals to recharge and reduce stress. By intentionally including self-care practices in their routines, individuals prioritize their mental health and cultivate a greater sense of well-being. This focus on self-care not only mitigates stress but also fosters a deeper connection with oneself, promoting emotional stability.

A consistent routine also aids in better time management, allowing individuals to allocate their time more effectively. With a clear plan for the day, individuals can ensure that important tasks and activities are completed without feeling rushed or overwhelmed. This improvement in time management can lead to increased leisure time, enabling individuals to participate in activities they enjoy, further enhancing their mental health. The ability to balance responsibilities with personal enjoyment is vital for maintaining a healthy mindset.

Furthermore, establishing daily goals within a routine can provide a sense of purpose and direction. When individuals set clear objectives for themselves, even if they are small, they are more likely to engage in meaningful activities and work toward personal aspirations. This sense of purpose is crucial for mental well-being, as it encourages individuals to find fulfillment in their daily lives. The act of pursuing achievable goals fosters a sense of achievement and satisfaction, contributing to a positive outlook on life.

The social aspect of daily routines is another important factor in supporting mental health. Engaging in regular activities with family, friends, or colleagues strengthens social connections and fosters a sense of belonging. Whether it's sharing meals, participating in group exercises, or attending social gatherings, these interactions are essential for emotional support. A routine that incorporates social engagement can help reduce feelings of loneliness and isolation, which are significant risk factors for mental health issues.

Maintaining a daily routine can also provide a sense of normalcy during times of crisis or change. When unexpected challenges arise, adhering to a familiar structure can be comforting and grounding. It allows individuals to focus on what they can control, helping to reduce feelings of helplessness and anxiety. A consistent routine can serve as an anchor, allowing individuals to navigate difficult times while prioritizing their mental health.

Finally, while consistency is key, flexibility within a daily routine is equally important. Life is unpredictable, and maintaining the ability to adapt to new circumstances can help individuals feel more in control. This balance between structure and flexibility ensures that routines remain supportive rather than restrictive. By allowing for spontaneous changes or adjustments, individuals can foster a healthier relationship with their daily lives and better support their mental health. In conclusion, the importance of a daily routine cannot be overstated, as it plays a vital role in enhancing mental well-being and overall quality of life.

Chapter Twenty Six:

Recognizing Cognitive Distortions

Recognizing cognitive distortions is an essential skill for supporting mental health and emotional well-being. Cognitive distortions are irrational or exaggerated thought patterns that can negatively influence how individuals perceive themselves, their surroundings, and their experiences. Understanding these distortions is a crucial step toward developing healthier thinking habits and improving mental health outcomes. By identifying and challenging these negative thoughts, individuals can cultivate a more balanced and realistic perspective on their lives.

One common cognitive distortion is all-or-nothing thinking, which leads individuals to view situations in black-and-white terms. For example, someone may believe that if they do not achieve perfection in a task, they have failed entirely. This type of thinking can create unnecessary pressure and anxiety, hindering one's ability to appreciate progress and accomplishments. By recognizing this distortion, individuals can learn to embrace a more nuanced viewpoint, acknowledging that there is often a spectrum of outcomes rather than absolute success or failure.

Another prevalent cognitive distortion is overgeneralization, which involves drawing broad conclusions based on a single event. For instance, if a person experiences rejection in one aspect of their life, they may conclude that they will always be rejected in future endeavors. This type of distorted thinking can lead to feelings of hopelessness and despair. By recognizing overgeneralization, individuals can challenge these negative beliefs and focus on specific instances rather than allowing one experience to define their entire self-worth.

Catastrophizing is yet another common cognitive distortion, where individuals anticipate the worst possible outcomes in a given situation. This type of thinking can lead to excessive anxiety and stress, as individuals become consumed by worst-case scenarios. For example, someone may worry that making a mistake at work will lead to losing their job. By learning to recognize and reframe catastrophic thoughts, individuals can develop a more balanced perspective, focusing on realistic outcomes rather than imagined disasters.

Personalization is another cognitive distortion that can significantly impact mental health. This distortion occurs when individuals take responsibility for events outside their control, leading them to feel excessive guilt or shame. For instance, a parent may blame themselves for their child's struggles, believing that they are a failure as a caregiver. By recognizing this distortion, individuals can learn to separate their actions from the outcomes of others, fostering a healthier sense of self and reducing feelings of guilt.

Recognizing cognitive distortions can also improve interpersonal relationships. Distorted thinking can lead to misinterpretations of others' actions or intentions, resulting in unnecessary conflicts and misunderstandings. For example, someone may assume that a friend is upset with them without any evidence, causing tension in the relationship. By identifying these distortions, individuals can communicate more openly and effectively, fostering healthier connections with others and enhancing their emotional well-being.

Mindfulness practices can be beneficial in recognizing and addressing cognitive distortions. By cultivating present-moment awareness, individuals can become more attuned to their thoughts and feelings, allowing them to identify distorted thinking patterns as they arise. Mindfulness encourages individuals to observe their thoughts without judgment, creating space for self-reflection and challenging negative beliefs. This practice can lead to greater emotional regulation and resilience in the face of stress.

Cognitive-behavioral therapy (CBT) is another effective approach for recognizing and reframing cognitive distortions. CBT focuses on identifying negative thought patterns and replacing them with more balanced, rational beliefs. Through structured exercises and guided reflection, individuals learn to challenge their cognitive distortions and develop healthier thinking habits. This therapeutic approach has been shown to be effective in treating various mental health conditions, including anxiety and depression.

Journaling is a practical tool that can aid individuals in recognizing cognitive distortions. By writing down thoughts and feelings, individuals can gain insight into their mental processes and identify patterns of distorted thinking. Journaling provides a safe space for self-exploration, allowing individuals to reflect on their experiences and challenge negative beliefs. Over time, this practice can lead to increased self-awareness and improved mental health.

Support from friends, family, or mental health professionals can also play a crucial role in recognizing cognitive distortions. Discussing thoughts and feelings with trusted individuals can provide valuable perspective and validation. Others may help identify patterns of distorted thinking that individuals may not see in themselves. This social support can foster a sense of community and understanding, reinforcing the idea that everyone struggles with negative thoughts at times.

In conclusion, recognizing cognitive distortions is a vital component of supporting mental health. By identifying and challenging these irrational thought patterns, individuals can cultivate a more balanced perspective on their lives. Techniques such as mindfulness, cognitive-behavioral therapy, and journaling can aid in this process, promoting greater self-awareness and emotional resilience. Ultimately, learning to recognize and reframe cognitive distortions empowers individuals to take control of their mental health and enhance their overall well-being.

Recognizing cognitive distortions is not just about identifying negative thought patterns; it's about developing a toolkit for emotional regulation and self-compassion. When individuals become aware of their cognitive distortions, they can approach their thoughts with curiosity rather than judgment. This shift in perspective allows them to understand that everyone experiences distorted thinking at times, and it does not define their worth or capabilities. Emphasizing self-compassion is vital, as it alleviates the pressure to be perfect and fosters a more forgiving attitude toward oneself during challenging times.

Another important aspect of recognizing cognitive distortions is learning how to reframe negative thoughts. Reframing involves taking a negative thought and altering its context to create a more balanced and constructive view. For instance, if someone thinks, "I always mess things up," they can reframe it to, "I've made mistakes before, but I also learn from them and improve." This cognitive restructuring empowers individuals to replace harmful beliefs with more realistic and positive affirmations, ultimately contributing to improved self-esteem and mental health.

Engaging in regular self-reflection can further enhance the ability to recognize cognitive distortions. Setting aside time each day to consider one's thoughts and feelings can help individuals identify patterns of negativity that may otherwise go unnoticed. Through self-reflection, individuals can ask themselves critical questions: "Is this thought based on facts or assumptions?" or "What evidence do I have to support this belief?" By doing so, they can cultivate a more rational mindset that acknowledges the complexity of their experiences.

Incorporating positive affirmations into daily routines can also support the recognition and challenge of cognitive distortions. Positive affirmations are statements that reinforce self-worth and encourage a positive self-image. By regularly affirming one's strengths and accomplishments, individuals can counteract the effects of cognitive distortions that promote self-doubt or negativity. This practice encourages a shift in mindset, allowing individuals to focus on their positive qualities and capabilities rather than their perceived shortcomings.

Seeking professional help from a mental health therapist can be highly beneficial for individuals struggling with persistent cognitive distortions. Therapists trained in cognitive-behavioral therapy (CBT) can provide personalized strategies and support for recognizing and reframing negative thoughts. They can guide individuals through the process of challenging cognitive distortions with evidence-based techniques, helping them develop healthier thinking patterns. Therapy can also create a safe space for individuals to explore their thoughts without fear of judgment, fostering deeper self-understanding.

Education about common cognitive distortions can empower individuals to recognize these patterns in themselves and others. Understanding that distortions like mind reading, where individuals assume they know what others are thinking, or labeling, where they assign negative labels to themselves or others, can promote empathy and understanding. When people are educated about these distortions, they can better navigate their interactions and avoid misunderstandings that stem from distorted perceptions.

Support groups or peer-led discussions can also provide valuable opportunities for individuals to share their experiences with cognitive distortions. Hearing from others who face similar challenges can create a sense of belonging and validation. These groups can facilitate open conversations about distorted thinking, allowing individuals to learn from each other's coping strategies and gain new insights into their thought processes. The shared experience fosters a sense of community and reinforces the idea that no one is alone in their struggles.

Gratitude practices can also play a role in counteracting cognitive distortions. Regularly expressing gratitude can shift focus away from negative thought patterns and toward positive aspects of life. By intentionally reflecting on what they appreciate, whether it's supportive relationships, personal achievements, or simple joys, individuals can cultivate a more positive mental landscape. This practice can help counterbalance the effects of cognitive distortions, promoting a more optimistic outlook.

Finally, the importance of patience and persistence cannot be overstated when it comes to recognizing and challenging cognitive distortions. Changing ingrained thought patterns takes time and consistent effort. Individuals may find themselves slipping back into old habits, but it's essential to approach these setbacks with kindness rather than self-criticism. Acknowledging that progress is not linear allows individuals to stay committed to their journey of mental health improvement, ultimately leading to a more resilient and positive mindset.

In conclusion, recognizing cognitive distortions is a fundamental skill that can significantly enhance mental health. By developing awareness of negative thought patterns, reframing those thoughts, and incorporating supportive practices, individuals can create a more balanced and fulfilling perspective on their lives. The journey toward recognizing and overcoming cognitive distortions is ongoing, but with patience, self-compassion, and the right tools, individuals can foster healthier thinking habits and improve their overall emotional well-being.

Chapter Twenty Seven:

Practicing Positive Affirmations

Practicing positive affirmations has become a popular technique for enhancing mental health and well-being. Positive affirmations are simple, positive statements that individuals repeat to themselves to challenge negative thoughts and self-doubts. This practice can empower individuals, reshape their thought patterns, and cultivate a more positive self-image. The benefits of incorporating positive affirmations into daily life are numerous, and they can lead to significant improvements in mental health.

One of the most immediate benefits of practicing positive affirmations is reduced stress and anxiety. By focusing on uplifting and positive statements, individuals can shift their mindset away from stress-inducing thoughts. For example, affirmations such as "I am capable of handling whatever challenges come my way" can help combat feelings of overwhelm and anxiety. This realignment of thoughts allows individuals to approach stressful situations with a calmer mindset, ultimately reducing the physiological effects of stress.

Positive affirmations also play a crucial role in boosting self-esteem and self-confidence. Many individuals struggle with negative self-talk and feelings of inadequacy, which can hinder personal and professional growth. By regularly repeating affirmations like "I am worthy of love and respect" or "I believe in my abilities," individuals can gradually dismantle these negative beliefs. Over time, this practice fosters a more positive self-image and encourages individuals to take on new challenges with confidence.

In addition to enhancing self-esteem, positive affirmations promote resilience. Resilience is the ability to bounce back from setbacks and navigate adversity effectively. When individuals embed positive affirmations into their daily routine, they cultivate a mindset that embraces challenges as opportunities for growth. Affirmations such as "I learn from my mistakes" or "Every setback is a setup for a comeback" encourage individuals to view obstacles through a lens of possibility rather than defeat.

Another benefit of positive affirmations is their ability to improve overall mood and emotional well-being. Engaging in this practice can create a more optimistic outlook on life. Research has shown that individuals who regularly utilize positive affirmations report higher levels of happiness and satisfaction. By consciously focusing on positive attributes and experiences, individuals can train their minds to recognize and appreciate the good in their lives, leading to improved emotional health.

Positive affirmations can also enhance motivation and goal achievement. When individuals articulate their aspirations through affirmations, they create a sense of purpose and direction. For example, repeating affirmations like "I am focused, and I am making progress toward my goals" reinforces commitment and determination. This practice can serve as a powerful reminder of one's ambitions, helping individuals stay motivated and engaged in their pursuits.

The practice of positive affirmations can also foster a sense of gratitude and appreciation. By focusing on positive statements, individuals can train themselves to recognize the aspects of their lives that they are thankful for. Affirmations such as "I am grateful for the love and support in my life" can help individuals cultivate a mindset of appreciation. This shift in perspective can reduce feelings of envy or dissatisfaction, enhancing overall mental well-being.

Furthermore, positive affirmations can improve interpersonal relationships. When individuals feel more confident and positive about themselves, they are more likely to engage with others in a constructive manner. Affirmations such as "I communicate openly and honestly" can promote healthier interactions and enhance emotional connections. As individuals develop a more positive self-image, they often find themselves attracting supportive relationships that reinforce their affirming beliefs.

Incorporating positive affirmations into daily routines can also improve focus and concentration. In a world filled with distractions, maintaining clarity of thought is essential. Affirmations like "I am focused and present in each moment" can help individuals center their thoughts and minimize distractions. This heightened focus can lead to improved productivity and the ability to engage more fully in tasks, whether in personal or professional settings.

The flexibility of positive affirmations makes them accessible to everyone, regardless of their circumstances. Individuals can tailor their affirmations to suit their unique needs and goals, making the practice highly personalized and effective. Whether someone is working on self-love, career aspirations, or overcoming anxiety, they can create affirmations that resonate with them. This adaptability ensures that positive affirmations can be integrated into anyone's life, providing a valuable mental health tool.

Moreover, the practice of positive affirmations can be enhanced through visualization techniques. When individuals combine affirmations with visualization, imagining themselves embodying the qualities or achievements they affirm, they can deepen the impact of the practice. For example, visualizing oneself confidently presenting in front of an audience while repeating affirmations about competence can reinforce those beliefs and reduce performance anxiety. This combined approach amplifies the benefits of positive affirmations, making them even more powerful.

Lastly, the cumulative effects of practicing positive affirmations can lead to lasting changes in mental health and overall outlook on life. As individuals repeat positive statements over time, the brain begins to rewire itself, forming new neural pathways that support positive thinking. This long-term commitment can lead to a profound transformation in how individuals perceive themselves and their circumstances. By fostering a positive mindset, individuals can experience greater resilience, improved emotional regulation, and a heightened ability to cope with life's challenges. This transformation reinforces the idea that mental health is not merely the absence of distress but rather the presence of a positive, proactive approach to life.

One of the remarkable aspects of positive affirmations is their ability to create a self-fulfilling prophecy. When individuals consistently affirm their worth, capabilities, and potential, they begin to act in ways that align with these beliefs. For instance, someone who regularly states, "I am a valuable team member," may find themselves contributing more actively in group settings, leading to greater acknowledgment and appreciation from peers. This shift in behavior not only reinforces the affirmation but also cultivates a cycle of positive reinforcement that further solidifies self-beliefs.

Additionally, the communal aspect of affirmations can enhance mental health when practiced in groups or shared settings. Engaging in positive affirmations within a supportive community, such as a therapy group or a workshop, can amplify the effects. Group members can encourage each other, share personal affirmations, and create a collective atmosphere of positivity and support. This community reinforcement can be especially beneficial for individuals who may struggle to affirm themselves in solitude, providing a sense of belonging and mutual encouragement.

Practicing positive affirmations can also serve as a form of self-care. In today's fast-paced world, it is common for individuals to neglect their mental health amidst various responsibilities and pressures. Incorporating affirmations into a self-care routine—such as during morning rituals or before bedtime—can provide dedicated time for self-reflection and positivity. This intentional practice allows individuals to prioritize their mental health and emotional well-being, reinforcing the notion that self-care is not just about physical health but also about nurturing a positive mindset.

Furthermore, the integration of positive affirmations into mindfulness practices can enhance their effectiveness. Mindfulness encourages individuals to be present in the moment and aware of their thoughts and feelings. When combined with affirmations, mindfulness can create a powerful experience of self-acceptance and positivity. For example, while practicing mindfulness meditation, individuals can repeat affirmations that resonate with their current state, such as "I am at peace with my journey." This synergy promotes a deeper connection to one's thoughts and emotions, fostering acceptance and inner peace.

The effects of positive affirmations extend beyond personal well-being; they can also influence how individuals navigate their professional environments. In workplaces where stress and competition can take a toll on mental health, positive affirmations can help create a more supportive and collaborative atmosphere. Employees who practice affirmations like "I contribute positively to my team" or "I embrace challenges as opportunities for growth" can foster a culture of encouragement and cooperation. This shift can lead to improved teamwork, enhanced morale, and decreased workplace anxiety.

Moreover, positive affirmations can aid in the recovery process for those dealing with mental health challenges. For individuals experiencing depression, anxiety, or trauma, negative self-talk can be pervasive and debilitating. Positive affirmations serve as a counterbalance to these harmful thoughts, providing a pathway toward healing. Mental health professionals often recommend affirmations as part of therapeutic interventions, helping clients to gradually rewire their thinking patterns and adopt a more compassionate and empowering self-dialogue.

As individuals become more adept at using positive affirmations, they can also learn to incorporate them into everyday situations. For example, when facing a challenging task or decision, a person might remind themselves with affirmations such as "I trust my instincts" or "I am capable of making the right choice." This application of affirmations in real-time can enhance decision-making processes and reduce feelings of doubt or anxiety. By embedding affirmations into daily life, individuals cultivate a habit of self-empowerment that can be applied in various contexts.

The practice of positive affirmations can also lead to enhanced emotional intelligence. As individuals become more aware of their thoughts and feelings through affirmations, they develop a deeper understanding of their emotional responses. This self-awareness allows for better emotional regulation, as individuals can recognize when negative thoughts arise and consciously replace them with affirmations. Improved emotional intelligence not only benefits personal well-being but also enhances interpersonal relationships, as individuals become more attuned to the emotions of others.

Lastly, the long-term commitment to practicing positive affirmations can contribute to a more profound sense of purpose and fulfillment in life. When individuals consistently affirm their values, aspirations, and strengths, they align their actions with their beliefs. This alignment fosters a greater sense of authenticity and purpose, leading to a more meaningful and satisfying life. By cultivating a mindset rooted in positivity and self-empowerment, individuals can navigate the complexities of life with greater resilience and an unwavering sense of hope.

In conclusion, the benefits of practicing positive affirmations for mental health are extensive and multifaceted. From reducing stress and anxiety to enhancing self-esteem, resilience, and emotional intelligence, affirmations offer a powerful tool for personal growth and healing. By integrating positive affirmations into daily routines, individuals can create a lasting impact on their mental well-being.

Chapter Twenty Eight:

Reframing Your Perspective
Reframing your perspective is a powerful cognitive skill that can significantly enhance mental health and overall well-being. This practice involves shifting the way one perceives a situation, often changing a negative or limiting viewpoint into a more positive or constructive one. By reframing thoughts, individuals can transform challenges into opportunities for growth and resilience, ultimately leading to improved mental health. Understanding the importance of this practice can empower individuals to take control of their thought processes and emotional responses.

One of the primary benefits of reframing is its ability to reduce feelings of hopelessness and helplessness. When faced with difficult situations, it can be easy to succumb to negative thinking patterns that amplify distress. For example, someone who loses a job may initially view this as a catastrophic event. However, by reframing the situation to see it as an opportunity for new beginnings or a chance to pursue a long-held passion, that individual can shift their emotional response from despair to optimism. This shift can lead to proactive behaviors, such as networking or furthering education, that can ultimately result in positive outcomes.

Reframing also plays a crucial role in managing stress and anxiety. Negative thought patterns often exacerbate stress by creating a cycle of worry and fear. For instance, if someone is anxious about public speaking, they might focus on the potential for failure and embarrassment. By reframing this fear into a perspective that emphasizes growth and learning, such as viewing each speaking opportunity as a chance to improve communication skills, individuals can reduce anxiety and approach the situation with greater confidence. This change in perspective helps to break the cycle of negative thinking and fosters a more resilient mindset.

Furthermore, reframing can enhance emotional regulation. Individuals often experience overwhelming emotions in response to stressful situations, leading to impulsive reactions that may not serve their best interests. By consciously reframing their thoughts, individuals can create space between a situation and their emotional response. For example, instead of reacting with anger when faced with criticism, one might reframe the feedback as an opportunity for personal development. This shift allows individuals to respond thoughtfully rather than reactively, promoting healthier emotional responses and interactions.

The importance of reframing extends to interpersonal relationships as well. Misunderstandings and conflicts often arise from differing perspectives, leading to hurt feelings and resentment. By practicing reframing, individuals can gain a more empathetic understanding of others' viewpoints. For example, if a friend seems distant, one might initially interpret this as a lack of care or interest. However, reframing the situation to consider potential external stressors in the friend's life can foster compassion and improve communication. This practice not only enhances relationships but also contributes to a sense of connectedness and support.

Reframing is also a key strategy in cultivating a growth mindset, a belief that abilities and intelligence can be developed through effort and learning. Embracing a growth mindset allows individuals to view challenges as opportunities for growth rather than insurmountable obstacles. For instance, a student who struggles with a subject may initially see their difficulties as evidence of inadequacy.

However, by reframing these challenges as a natural part of the learning process, the student can approach their studies with determination and resilience. This perspective fosters perseverance, leading to improved performance and self-esteem.

Moreover, reframing can enhance problem-solving skills. When individuals are entrenched in negative thinking, they may become overwhelmed and unable to see viable solutions to their problems. By reframing the situation, they can create a mental space for creativity and exploration of alternatives. For example, someone facing a financial setback might initially feel defeated. However, by reframing the scenario to view it as a challenge that requires innovative solutions, they may develop a budget, explore new income opportunities, or seek financial advice. This proactive approach encourages individuals to take charge of their circumstances rather than feel victimized by them.

The practice of reframing can also contribute to greater resilience in the face of adversity. Resilience is the ability to bounce back from setbacks and maintain a positive outlook despite challenges. By reframing negative experiences as opportunities for learning and growth, individuals can cultivate a more resilient mindset. For instance, someone who experiences a personal loss may initially feel overwhelmed by grief. However, by reframing the experience to honor the positive memories and lessons learned from that relationship, they can find meaning and purpose in their grief, fostering healing and resilience over time.

Incorporating reframing into daily life can also foster a sense of empowerment. When individuals recognize their ability to change their perspectives, they gain a greater sense of control over their emotional responses and mental health. This empowerment can lead to increased self-efficacy, which is the belief in one's ability to accomplish tasks and achieve goals. For instance, someone struggling with self-doubt may choose to reframe their self-talk from "I'm not good enough" to "I am capable of growth and improvement." This shift not only promotes self-confidence but also encourages individuals to take actionable steps toward their goals.

Additionally, reframing can play a critical role in fostering gratitude, which is a powerful antidote to negative emotions. When individuals focus on what is lacking in their lives, feelings of dissatisfaction and unhappiness can flourish. By consciously reframing their perspective to focus on what they have, such as supportive relationships, personal strengths, or even small joys in everyday life. Individuals can cultivate a sense of gratitude. This practice not only enhances overall well-being but also shifts attention away from negative thought patterns, promoting a more positive and fulfilling outlook on life.

Another important aspect of reframing is its potential to help individuals navigate life transitions and changes. Life is often filled with unexpected twists and turns, and changes can evoke feelings of uncertainty and fear. For example, moving to a new city or starting a new job can be daunting. However, by reframing these transitions as opportunities for exploration and personal growth, individuals can approach them with excitement rather than dread. This perspective allows for a more adaptable mindset, enabling individuals to embrace change as a natural part of life rather than something to be feared.

The practice of reframing is also invaluable in the context of mental health treatment and therapy. Many therapeutic approaches emphasize the importance of cognitive restructuring, where clients learn to identify and challenge negative thought patterns. Through reframing, individuals can gain insight into their thought processes and develop healthier perspectives. Therapists often guide clients in this practice, helping them to reframe distressing thoughts into more balanced and constructive ones. This therapeutic technique can lead to significant improvements in mood and overall mental health.

Moreover, reframing can serve as a preventive measure against mental health issues. By cultivating the habit of reframing negative thoughts into positive ones, individuals can build emotional resilience before challenges arise. This proactive approach can equip individuals with the mental tools needed to handle future stressors more effectively. For instance, someone who regularly practices reframing may find themselves better prepared to cope with the stress of a demanding work project or a personal crisis, as they have already developed a mindset that views challenges as opportunities.

In addition to personal benefits, reframing can also have a profound impact on communities and relationships. When individuals engage in reframing, they not only improve their own mental health but also create a more positive environment for those around them. For example, a leader who embodies a reframed perspective during times of crisis can inspire their team to adopt the same mindset. This collective shift in perspective can foster camaraderie, collaboration, and support, ultimately enhancing the community's resilience and morale.

It is also important to acknowledge that reframing does not mean ignoring or downplaying genuine feelings of distress or sadness. Instead, it involves acknowledging those feelings while choosing to focus on a broader perspective that includes potential positives or lessons. This balanced approach allows individuals to validate their emotions while also empowering them to move forward constructively. For instance, someone grieving a loss may feel overwhelming sorrow; however, reframing this experience to recognize the love and joy shared can facilitate healing and acceptance.

Another key element of reframing is its potential to foster a sense of purpose. When individuals encounter setbacks, it can be easy to lose sight of their goals and aspirations. By reframing challenges as stepping stones toward personal growth and achievement, individuals can reconnect with their sense of purpose. For example, someone facing a health challenge might choose to view their journey as an opportunity to learn more about health and wellness, motivating them to make positive lifestyle changes. This renewed sense of purpose can enhance motivation and commitment to personal goals.

Incorporating reframing into daily routines can be a transformative practice. Simple techniques, such as journaling or using positive affirmations, can help individuals cultivate a reframed perspective. By taking time each day to reflect on experiences and consciously choose to focus on the positive, individuals can reinforce this mindset over time. For example, keeping a gratitude journal where one lists things they are thankful for can encourage a reframed outlook, shifting attention from difficulties to the abundance present in life.

Ultimately, the importance of reframing one's perspective cannot be overstated. It is a versatile tool that can enhance mental health, foster resilience, improve relationships, and cultivate a sense of purpose. As individuals learn to reframe their thoughts and experiences, they gain the power to transform challenges into opportunities for growth. In a world that often presents obstacles, the ability to reframe can serve as a guiding light, leading to a more fulfilling and balanced life. Embracing this practice not only benefits individuals but also contributes to a more positive and supportive community, reinforcing the interconnectedness of mental health and well-being.

Chapter Twenty Nine:

Understanding Mental Health Medications

Mental health medications play a crucial role in the treatment of various mental health disorders, including depression, anxiety, bipolar disorder, and schizophrenia. These medications can help alleviate symptoms, improve quality of life, and enable individuals to function more effectively in their daily lives. However, understanding how these medications work, their potential side effects, and the importance of adherence to prescribed regimens is essential for both patients and their families.

Mental health medications can be broadly classified into several categories, including antidepressants, antipsychotics, mood stabilizers, and anxiolytics. Antidepressants, such as selective serotonin reuptake inhibitors (SSRIs) and serotonin-norepinephrine reuptake inhibitors (SNRIs), are commonly prescribed for depression and anxiety disorders. Antipsychotics, both typical and atypical, are used primarily to manage symptoms of schizophrenia and bipolar disorder. Mood stabilizers, such as lithium, are critical for individuals experiencing manic episodes, while anxiolytics, like benzodiazepines, are often prescribed for short-term relief of anxiety symptoms.

Understanding the mechanism of action of these medications is vital. Antidepressants typically work by altering neurotransmitter levels in the brain, specifically serotonin and norepinephrine, which are linked to mood regulation. Antipsychotics can block dopamine receptors, helping to reduce psychotic symptoms. Mood stabilizers help to balance mood swings by influencing various neurotransmitters. A clear comprehension of how these medications function can empower patients to engage actively in their treatment.

While mental health medications can be effective, they also come with potential side effects. Common side effects may include weight gain, drowsiness, dry mouth, and sexual dysfunction. More serious risks, such as increased suicidal thoughts in certain age groups, particularly in young adults, must be carefully monitored. Patients should be informed about potential side effects and encouraged to report any adverse reactions to their healthcare provider promptly.

Adherence to prescribed medication regimens is critical for effective treatment outcomes. Many patients may experience a range of emotions, including stigma and fear, which can lead to non-compliance. Additionally, some individuals may feel better and mistakenly believe they no longer need medication. However, discontinuing medications without medical guidance can result in relapse or worsening of symptoms. Educating patients about the importance of sticking to their treatment plan can help mitigate these issues.

Healthcare providers play a vital role in managing mental health medications. They are responsible for prescribing the appropriate medications, monitoring progress, and adjusting dosages as necessary. Open communication between patients and providers is essential; patients should feel comfortable discussing their experiences with medications, including any side effects or concerns. Regular follow-ups can help ensure that the treatment plan remains effective and that any issues are addressed promptly.

Each individual's response to mental health medications can vary significantly. Factors such as genetics, co-occurring medical conditions, and personal history can influence how a person responds to a particular medication. As a result, mental health treatment should be personalized. Providers may need to try different medications or combinations to find the most effective treatment for each person, emphasizing the importance of patience and persistence in the process.

While medications are a vital aspect of treating mental health disorders, they are often most effective when combined with non-pharmacological interventions. Psychotherapy, lifestyle modifications, and support groups can provide additional support and coping strategies. Cognitive-behavioral therapy (CBT), for example, can help patients develop skills to manage their symptoms effectively, while regular exercise and a healthy diet can contribute to overall well-being.

Stigma surrounding mental health and the use of medications can create barriers to treatment. Many individuals may hesitate to seek help or adhere to medication regimens due to societal misconceptions. Education and advocacy play crucial roles in reducing stigma and promoting acceptance of mental health issues and their treatment. By fostering an environment of understanding and support, we can encourage more individuals to seek the help they need.

Mental health is a lifelong journey for many individuals, and long-term management of mental health disorders often includes ongoing medication. Regular check-ins with healthcare providers and adjustments to treatment plans are essential for maintaining stability. Patients should also be encouraged to set realistic goals and monitor their progress over time. This proactive approach can help individuals stay engaged in their treatment and maintain their mental health.

Understanding mental health medications is an essential component of effective treatment for those experiencing mental health disorders. By educating patients and their families about the types of medications available, their mechanisms of action, potential side effects, and the importance of adherence, we can empower individuals to take charge of their mental health. Ultimately, a comprehensive approach that combines medication, therapy, and support can lead to more successful outcomes.

Mental health medications are an essential component of the treatment landscape for various mental health disorders, including depression, anxiety, bipolar disorder, and schizophrenia. These medications can significantly alleviate symptoms, enhance daily functioning, and improve overall quality of life. Understanding the complexities surrounding these medications, such as their categories, mechanisms of action, potential side effects, and the importance of adherence to prescribed regimens—is crucial for patients, families, and healthcare providers alike.

Mental health medications can be categorized into several main groups: antidepressants, antipsychotics, mood stabilizers, and anxiolytics. Antidepressants, often prescribed for depression and anxiety, include selective serotonin reuptake inhibitors (SSRIs) and serotonin-norepinephrine reuptake inhibitors (SNRIs). Antipsychotics are primarily used to manage symptoms of schizophrenia and bipolar disorder, and they can be classified as either typical or atypical. Mood stabilizers, such as lithium, are important for individuals experiencing mood swings, while anxiolytics, like benzodiazepines, provide short-term relief for anxiety symptoms. Each category serves a unique purpose and is tailored to address specific symptoms and disorders.

The effectiveness of mental health medications often hinges on their mechanisms of action. Antidepressants work by modifying neurotransmitter levels in the brain, particularly serotonin and norepinephrine, which are vital for mood regulation. Antipsychotics function by blocking dopamine receptors, which can help mitigate psychotic symptoms like delusions and hallucinations. Mood stabilizers work by balancing neurotransmitter activity, thus helping to regulate mood swings. A clear understanding of how these medications work can empower patients to better engage in their treatment and manage their expectations regarding outcomes.

While mental health medications can be beneficial, they can also lead to side effects, which may range from mild to severe. Common side effects include weight gain, fatigue, dry mouth, and sexual dysfunction, which can impact a patient's quality of life. More serious risks, such as increased suicidal thoughts, are particularly concerning, especially among younger populations. It is crucial for patients to receive comprehensive information about potential side effects, enabling them to make informed decisions and to report any adverse reactions to their healthcare providers promptly.

Adherence to prescribed medication regimens is vital for achieving the desired treatment outcomes. Many patients may grapple with feelings of stigma associated with mental health issues, leading to reluctance in following through with their treatment plans. Additionally, some individuals may stop taking medications once they start feeling better, mistakenly believing they no longer need them. This can lead to relapse or worsening symptoms. Educating patients about the importance of consistent medication adherence can help mitigate these risks and foster a more positive treatment experience.

Healthcare providers are essential in the management of mental health medications. They are responsible for accurately diagnosing conditions, prescribing appropriate medications, and monitoring the patient's progress. Establishing open communication between patients and providers is critical, patients should feel comfortable discussing their experiences, including any side effects or concerns they may have. Regular follow-ups allow healthcare providers to adjust treatment plans as necessary, ensuring that patients receive the most effective care possible.

Mental health treatment is highly individualized, as each person's response to medications can vary significantly. Factors such as genetics, co-occurring medical conditions, and personal history can affect how an individual responds to a particular medication. Therefore, mental health treatment often requires a personalized approach, where providers may need to explore different medications or combinations to identify the most effective treatment plan. This process requires patience and persistence, as finding the right medication can sometimes take time.

While medications are a vital aspect of treating mental health disorders, they often work best when combined with non-pharmacological interventions. Therapeutic approaches, such as cognitive-behavioral therapy (CBT), can equip patients with coping strategies and skills to manage their symptoms effectively. Lifestyle changes, including regular exercise, a balanced diet, and mindfulness practices, can also contribute significantly to overall well-being. By incorporating both medication and therapy, patients can achieve more comprehensive and effective treatment outcomes.

The stigma surrounding mental health and the use of medications can create significant barriers to treatment. Many individuals may hesitate to seek help or adhere to their prescribed regimens due to societal misconceptions about mental illness. Education and advocacy are crucial in reducing stigma and promoting understanding of mental health issues and their treatment. By fostering an environment of acceptance and support, we can encourage more individuals to seek the help they need and feel empowered to manage their mental health.

Understanding mental health medications is a fundamental aspect of effective treatment for those facing mental health disorders. By providing education about the types of medications available, their mechanisms of action, potential side effects, and the importance of adherence, we can empower individuals to take.

Chapter Thirty:

Working with Healthcare Providers

Working with healthcare providers to support mental health is essential in promoting overall well-being and ensuring that individuals receive comprehensive care. Mental health is a crucial component of overall health, yet it often goes overlooked in medical settings. Healthcare providers play a vital role in identifying, diagnosing, and managing mental health issues, making their collaboration with patients essential for effective treatment.

One of the primary reasons for working with healthcare providers is the expertise they bring to the table. Mental health professionals, including psychologists, psychiatrists, and licensed counselors, possess specialized knowledge and training in mental health disorders. This expertise allows them to conduct thorough assessments, formulate accurate diagnoses, and develop tailored treatment plans that address each individual's unique needs. By collaborating with these professionals, patients can benefit from evidence-based interventions that are more likely to yield positive outcomes.

Moreover, healthcare providers can help destigmatize mental health issues. Many individuals still harbor misconceptions about mental illness, which can prevent them from seeking help. By openly discussing mental health in a clinical setting, healthcare providers can normalize these conversations and encourage patients to address their mental health needs. This shift in perspective is crucial in fostering a culture of acceptance and support, enabling individuals to seek the help they need without fear of judgment.

The integration of mental health services into primary care is another critical aspect of working with healthcare providers. Many people seek help for physical ailments but may not recognize the connection between their physical and mental health. By incorporating mental health screenings and services within primary care settings, healthcare providers can identify issues early on and facilitate timely interventions. This integrated approach ensures that patients receive holistic care that addresses both their physical and mental well-being.

In addition to direct treatment, healthcare providers can also offer valuable resources and referrals. Many individuals may feel overwhelmed by the prospect of finding a mental health professional or navigating the mental healthcare system. Healthcare providers can guide patients to appropriate resources, including therapy options, support groups, and community services. This support can be instrumental in helping individuals take the first steps toward improving their mental health.

Collaboration among healthcare providers is essential for comprehensive mental health care. Integrated care models, where primary care providers work alongside mental health specialists, can create a more cohesive treatment experience for patients. This collaboration allows for better communication, shared decision-making, and a more coordinated approach to care, ultimately leading to improved health outcomes.

Furthermore, healthcare providers can play a pivotal role in educating patients about mental health. Many individuals may not fully understand their mental health conditions or the treatment options available to them. By providing education and information, healthcare providers can empower patients to take an active role in their treatment. This empowerment can lead to increased adherence to treatment plans and better overall mental health management.

The importance of early intervention cannot be overstated when it comes to mental health. Healthcare providers are often the first point of contact for individuals experiencing mental health concerns. By identifying issues early and implementing appropriate interventions, providers can help prevent the escalation of mental health problems, reducing the risk of crisis situations, hospitalization, or long-term disability.

Moreover, the support of healthcare providers can extend beyond traditional treatment modalities. Many healthcare providers are now incorporating holistic approaches to mental health care, including lifestyle modifications, stress management techniques, and mindfulness practices. These complementary strategies can enhance the effectiveness of conventional treatments and promote overall mental well-being.

Additionally, the COVID-19 pandemic has underscored the importance of mental health support from healthcare providers. The pandemic has had profound effects on mental health, leading to increased anxiety, depression, and social isolation for many individuals. Healthcare providers have been instrumental in addressing these challenges, offering telehealth services, mental health screenings, and resources to help individuals cope during these difficult times.

Another essential aspect of working with healthcare providers is the emphasis on ongoing support and follow-up care. Mental health treatment is often a long-term process, and individuals may require consistent support to achieve and maintain their mental wellness. Healthcare providers can facilitate this ongoing care by scheduling regular check-ins, monitoring progress, and adjusting treatment plans as necessary.

Finally, advocating for mental health services within healthcare systems is crucial. Healthcare providers can play a significant role in emphasizing the need for mental health resources, increasing funding for mental health services, and promoting policies that prioritize mental health care. By championing these issues, healthcare providers can contribute to a healthcare system that recognizes and addresses the importance of mental health alongside physical health.

In conclusion, working with healthcare providers to support mental health is vital for individuals seeking comprehensive care. Their expertise, resources, and commitment to integrated care can help destigmatize mental health issues, facilitate early intervention, and promote overall well-being. By fostering collaboration and advocating for mental health services, healthcare providers can significantly impact the lives of individuals navigating mental health challenges.

Working with healthcare providers to support mental health is essential for fostering a holistic approach to well-being. Mental health is often intertwined with physical health, and when healthcare providers address both aspects, they can offer a more comprehensive treatment experience. This integrated approach not only enhances the effectiveness of treatment but also helps patients understand the interconnectedness of their mental and physical health.

Healthcare providers play a critical role in destigmatizing mental health issues. Many individuals may feel reluctant to seek help due to societal misconceptions about mental illness. By normalizing discussions around mental health within clinical settings, providers can create an environment where patients feel safe and supported in addressing their concerns. This cultural shift is vital for encouraging individuals to seek assistance without fear of judgment.

Early intervention is another significant benefit of working with healthcare providers. Many mental health conditions can escalate if left untreated, leading to more severe consequences. Healthcare providers, especially in primary care settings, are often the first point of contact for individuals experiencing symptoms of mental health issues. By recognizing these symptoms early and implementing appropriate interventions, providers can help prevent the worsening of these conditions and promote better long-term outcomes.

Education is a powerful tool in mental health care, and healthcare providers are uniquely positioned to offer it. Many patients may not fully understand their mental health conditions or the various treatment options available to them. By providing clear information and education, healthcare providers empower patients to take an active role in their treatment journey. This empowerment can lead to greater adherence to treatment plans and a more proactive approach to managing mental health.

The COVID-19 pandemic has further highlighted the importance of mental health support from healthcare providers. The crisis has resulted in increased levels of anxiety, depression, and social isolation for many individuals. In this challenging context, healthcare providers have adapted by offering telehealth services and mental health resources, making it easier for patients to access care. This shift underscores the necessity of having accessible mental health support embedded within healthcare systems.

Ongoing support and follow-up care are crucial components of effective mental health treatment. Mental health is often a long-term journey, requiring consistent monitoring and adjustment of treatment plans. Healthcare providers can facilitate this ongoing care by scheduling regular check-ins and ensuring that patients feel supported throughout their treatment process. This continuity of care is essential for helping individuals achieve and maintain their mental wellness.

Finally, advocating for mental health resources within healthcare systems is vital for creating a more supportive environment for mental health care. Healthcare providers can influence policy changes and promote the importance of mental health services, ensuring that these resources are prioritized alongside physical health care. By championing mental health initiatives, providers can contribute to a healthcare landscape that recognizes and addresses the full spectrum of health needs for individuals.

Chapter Thirty One:

When to Reassess Your Treatment Plan

Reassessing your treatment plan for mental health is a crucial part of ensuring that you receive the most effective and appropriate care. Mental health is dynamic, and what works for one person may not work for another or may change over time. Knowing when to reassess your treatment plan can lead to better outcomes and a more tailored approach to your mental well-being.

One of the most significant indicators that it's time to reassess your treatment plan is a lack of progress. If you have been following your treatment regimen for a set period and are not noticing any improvements, it may be time to discuss this with your healthcare provider. It's essential to recognize that mental health treatment can take time, but if you feel stagnant, a reassessment could be beneficial to explore alternative strategies or therapies.

Another indicator for reassessing your treatment plan is the emergence of new symptoms or changes in your condition. Mental health is not static; it can fluctuate based on various factors, including stressors in your life, changes in your environment, or even physical health changes. If you find yourself experiencing new symptoms or a worsening of existing ones, it's important to communicate this with your healthcare provider to determine whether your treatment plan needs adjustment.

Life changes can also signal the need for a reassessment of your treatment plan. Significant events such as a job change, the end of a relationship, or the loss of a loved one can have a profound impact on your mental health. These changes may necessitate a reevaluation of your current strategies to ensure that they remain effective in the context of your new circumstances. Being proactive in addressing these changes can help you maintain your mental health.

Moreover, if you are experiencing side effects from medications, it may be time to reassess your treatment plan. Some individuals may tolerate medications well, while others may struggle with side effects that impact their quality of life. If you find that side effects are interfering with your daily functioning or overall well-being, it's crucial to discuss these concerns with your healthcare provider. They may suggest modifications to your dosage or alternative medications to better suit your needs.

Therapeutic rapport is another factor to consider when thinking about reassessing your treatment plan. If you feel that your relationship with your therapist or healthcare provider is not as productive as it should be, it may be time to reevaluate. A strong therapeutic alliance is essential for effective treatment, and feelings of discomfort or disconnect can hinder progress. If this is the case, consider discussing your feelings with your provider or exploring alternative therapeutic options.

Additionally, significant changes in your lifestyle or routines can warrant a reassessment of your treatment plan. For instance, if you have started a new job with increased responsibilities, moved to a new city, or experienced changes in your support system, these factors can affect your mental health. It's essential to recognize how these changes may influence your treatment and to collaborate with your healthcare provider to adjust your plan accordingly.

Self-reflection can also play a vital role in determining when to reassess your treatment plan. Regularly evaluating your feelings, coping mechanisms, and overall mental health can provide insight into the effectiveness of your current strategies. If you notice that certain coping skills or therapeutic interventions no longer resonate with you, it may be time to have an open conversation with your provider about what may work better for you.

Another aspect to consider is whether your goals for treatment have evolved. As you progress in your mental health journey, your objectives may change. For example, if you initially sought treatment for anxiety but have now identified issues related to self-esteem or relationships, it's important to discuss these new goals with your provider. Reassessing your treatment plan in light of your evolving goals can help ensure that your care remains relevant and effective.

If you feel a sense of frustration or hopelessness regarding your treatment, this can also be a significant sign that it's time for a reassessment. Feeling stuck or disheartened can indicate that the current approach is not aligned with your needs. Openly communicating these feelings with your healthcare provider can lead to a re-evaluation of your treatment path and the exploration of new strategies that may provide a fresh perspective.

Support systems are another critical area to assess when considering a treatment plan reassessment. If your support system has changed, whether through loss, relocation, or changes in relationships, this can significantly influence your mental health. A strong support network is essential for sustaining mental well-being, and identifying gaps in support can lead to discussions on how to address these changes within your treatment plan.

Finally, regular check-ins with your healthcare provider are vital for ensuring that your treatment remains effective. Scheduling periodic evaluations allows for ongoing dialogue about your progress, any concerns that arise, and the overall effectiveness of your treatment plan. These check-ins can help create a collaborative environment where adjustments can be made as necessary, ultimately leading to improved mental health outcomes.

In conclusion, reassessing your treatment plan for mental health is an ongoing process that is essential for ensuring effective care. By recognizing the signs that indicate the need for a reassessment, you can engage in a more proactive approach to your mental health care. This process involves open communication with your healthcare provider, self-reflection, and a willingness to adapt your treatment plan to better suit your evolving needs.

Moreover, being an active participant in your mental health journey is crucial. You should feel empowered to voice any concerns or observations you have regarding your treatment. Your insights are valuable, and healthcare providers appreciate when patients take an active role in their care. This collaborative relationship can lead to more personalized treatment strategies that align with your preferences and lifestyle.

It's also important to consider the role of therapy modalities in your treatment. Different therapeutic approaches may be more suitable at different times in your life. For instance, cognitive-behavioral therapy (CBT) might be beneficial for managing anxiety, while other modalities like dialectical behavior therapy (DBT) could be more appropriate if you are dealing with emotional regulation issues. If you feel that your current therapy approach isn't yielding the desired results, discussing alternative methods with your provider can be beneficial.

Additionally, lifestyle factors should not be overlooked when considering a reassessment of your treatment plan. Changes in diet, exercise, sleep patterns, and stress management can significantly impact mental health. If you have made lifestyle changes, such as starting a new exercise routine or altering your diet, these should be discussed with your healthcare provider. They may offer insights into how these changes can be integrated into your treatment plan or suggest additional strategies to enhance your overall well-being.

Support groups can also serve as valuable resources during your mental health journey. If you find that the support you receive from friends and family is insufficient or if you are feeling isolated, exploring group therapy or support groups can provide a sense of community. Engaging with others who share similar experiences can offer new perspectives, coping strategies, and emotional support, making it an important consideration when reassessing your treatment plan.

Furthermore, you should also recognize that reassessment is not a sign of failure; rather, it is an essential part of the healing process. Mental health treatment is often nonlinear, and what works at one stage may need adjustment later on. Embracing this flexibility allows for growth and adaptation, ultimately leading to a more effective treatment plan. Remember that mental health is a journey, and it's perfectly normal for that journey to take unexpected turns.

The frequency of reassessment can vary depending on individual circumstances. Some may benefit from more regular check-ins, while others may find that less frequent reassessments are sufficient. Establishing a timeline with your healthcare provider can help ensure that you're consistently evaluating your treatment plan in a way that works for you. This proactive approach can help catch any potential issues early and keep your treatment aligned with your needs.

In some cases, external factors such as changes in healthcare policies or insurance coverage can necessitate a reassessment of your mental health treatment plan. If you are faced with new limitations or options for care, it is essential to discuss these changes with your provider. They can help you navigate these circumstances and find solutions that maintain the quality of your care.

Finally, never underestimate the importance of self-compassion during your mental health journey. Reassessing your treatment plan can sometimes feel daunting or overwhelming, especially if you are grappling with challenging emotions. It's important to approach this process with kindness toward yourself, recognizing that seeking the best possible care is a sign of strength. By taking the time to evaluate and adjust your treatment plan when necessary, you are taking an active role in your mental health and well-being.

In summary, knowing when to reassess your treatment plan for mental health is a vital skill for maintaining effective care. By being vigilant about signs that indicate the need for change, such as lack of progress, new symptoms, life changes, or dissatisfaction with current strategies, you can work collaboratively with your healthcare provider to create a treatment plan that truly meets your needs. Remember, mental health is a journey, and it is entirely appropriate to adjust your path as you move forward.

Chapter Thirty Two:

Crisis Hotlines and Text Lines

Crisis hotlines and text lines play a vital role in the mental health landscape, providing immediate support to individuals in distress. In moments of crisis, such as when someone is feeling overwhelmed, suicidal, or experiencing severe anxiety, the availability of trained professionals to listen and respond can be life-saving. These services ensure that help is just a call or text away, offering a lifeline for those who may feel isolated or hopeless.

One of the most significant advantages of crisis hotlines and text lines is their accessibility. Unlike traditional mental health services that may require appointments, insurance, or transportation, these services are often available 24/7 and can be accessed from anywhere. This immediacy is crucial, as mental health crises can arise unexpectedly, and having a resource available at any time can make a substantial difference.

Moreover, the anonymity provided by text lines and hotlines can encourage individuals to seek help. Many people may feel ashamed or embarrassed about discussing their mental health struggles face-to-face or even over the phone. Texting, in particular, allows individuals to communicate in a way that feels safe and private. This anonymity can be especially important for marginalized communities, who may face additional stigma regarding mental health issues.

Crisis hotlines and text lines also serve as an entry point to further mental health resources. When individuals reach out for help, trained professionals can assess their needs and provide appropriate referrals to local services, such as therapy or support groups. This guidance can be instrumental in navigating the often overwhelming mental health system, making it easier for individuals to find ongoing support.

The training that hotline and text line counselors receive is also essential. These professionals are equipped to handle a wide range of issues, from suicidal thoughts to substance abuse and relationship problems. Their expertise allows them to de-escalate crises, provide coping strategies, and help individuals work through their emotions in a supportive environment. This level of care can be critical for someone in a moment of vulnerability.

In addition to individual support, crisis hotlines and text lines also contribute to broader public health goals. By providing immediate help and resources, these services can reduce the risk of emergency room visits and hospitalizations related to mental health crises. This not only benefits individuals but also alleviates some of the burden on healthcare systems, allowing resources to be allocated more effectively.

Crisis hotlines and text lines also play a significant role in education and awareness. Many of these services engage in outreach efforts to inform the public about mental health issues, reducing stigma and encouraging more people to seek help when needed. By raising awareness of available resources, these services can empower individuals to take charge of their mental health and promote a culture of openness and support.

Furthermore, the effectiveness of crisis hotlines is supported by research. Studies have shown that individuals who call or text crisis services report feeling less distressed and more hopeful after their interactions. This positive impact underscores the importance of having accessible mental health resources that people can turn to in their time of need.

Another crucial aspect of crisis hotlines and text lines is their ability to cater to specific populations. Many services offer specialized support for various groups, including veterans, LGBTQ+ individuals, and survivors of domestic violence. By tailoring their services to meet the unique needs of these populations, crisis hotlines can provide more relevant and effective assistance.

The rise of technology has also enhanced the reach and effectiveness of crisis hotlines and text lines. Mobile apps and online chat services have made it easier for individuals to access help discreetly and conveniently. This technological integration is particularly beneficial for younger generations who may prefer texting or online communication over phone calls.

Community involvement is another essential element of crisis hotlines and text lines. Many of these services rely on volunteers who are passionate about mental health advocacy. This grassroots approach not only strengthens community ties but also helps to create a supportive environment where individuals feel comfortable seeking help. Volunteers often share their own experiences, fostering a sense of understanding and empathy.

The importance of crisis hotlines and text lines cannot be overstated. They provide essential support, accessibility, and education regarding mental health issues. As we continue to recognize the significance of mental well-being in our society, it is crucial to advocate for these services, ensuring they remain funded and available for all who need them. By supporting crisis hotlines and text lines, we take a step toward a healthier, more connected society where individuals feel empowered to seek help and support one another.

Crisis hotlines and text lines serve as critical resources in the realm of mental health, offering immediate support and assistance to individuals facing distressing situations. The importance of these services cannot be overstated, as they provide a lifeline during moments of crisis when individuals may feel overwhelmed, anxious, or even suicidal. Having access to trained professionals who can listen and respond quickly can be crucial in guiding someone through their darkest moments.

One significant advantage of crisis hotlines and text lines is their accessibility. These services are often available 24/7, which means that individuals can reach out for help at any time, regardless of the hour. This immediacy is essential, as mental health crises do not adhere to a schedule. Unlike traditional mental health services that may require appointments and can often involve long wait times, hotlines and text lines provide instant access to support.

Anonymity is another vital feature of these services. Many people are hesitant to seek help due to the stigma surrounding mental health issues. The option to communicate anonymously via text or phone can encourage those who may feel embarrassed or ashamed to reach out. This is especially crucial for marginalized communities, who may face additional barriers when discussing their mental health struggles openly.

Crisis hotlines and text lines also serve as a gateway to further mental health resources. When individuals reach out for help, the trained counselors can assess their needs and provide referrals to local services, such as therapy or community support groups. This guidance can be instrumental in navigating the mental health landscape, making the process of seeking ongoing support less daunting.

The training that crisis hotline and text line counselors undergo is essential for effective service delivery. These professionals are equipped to handle a variety of crises, from suicidal ideation to substance abuse and emotional distress. Their expertise enables them to de-escalate situations, offer coping strategies, and provide a safe space for individuals to express their feelings. This immediate, compassionate response can significantly impact someone in a vulnerable state.

Beyond individual support, crisis hotlines and text lines contribute to public health by potentially reducing the burden on emergency services. By providing immediate assistance to individuals in crisis, these services can decrease the likelihood of emergency room visits and hospitalizations related to mental health issues. This not only benefits those in distress but also helps healthcare systems allocate resources more effectively.

Moreover, crisis hotlines and text lines play a significant role in raising awareness and educating the public about mental health. Many of these services engage in outreach initiatives to inform communities about mental health issues and promote available resources. By fostering awareness, these services encourage a culture of openness, enabling more individuals to seek help when they need it.

Technological advancements have also enhanced the reach and efficiency of crisis hotlines and text lines. Many services now offer mobile apps and online chat options, making it easier for individuals to access help discreetly. This is particularly important for younger generations who may prefer texting or online communication over traditional phone calls, allowing them to seek support in a manner that feels comfortable.

In conclusion, the significance of crisis hotlines and text lines in supporting mental health cannot be emphasized enough. They provide invaluable, accessible resources for individuals in crisis, offering immediate support, guidance, and education. As society continues to recognize the importance of mental well-being, advocating for the sustainability and expansion of these services is essential. By doing so, we contribute to a healthier, more connected community where individuals feel empowered to seek help and support one another.

Chapter Thirty Three:

Local Mental Health Services

Local mental health services play a crucial role in supporting individuals facing various mental health challenges. These services encompass a wide range of programs and resources designed to promote mental well-being, provide therapy and counseling, and offer crisis intervention. The goal of local mental health services is to create a supportive environment where individuals can access the care they need in a timely manner.

One of the primary components of local mental health services is community mental health centers. These centers provide a variety of services, including individual and group therapy, medication management, and psychoeducation. They often serve as a first point of contact for individuals seeking help, offering a welcoming space where people can discuss their concerns without stigma.

In addition to community mental health centers, many localities offer specialized programs targeting specific populations, such as children, adolescents, veterans, and the elderly. These programs are designed to address the unique needs of each group, ensuring that services are both relevant and effective. For instance, youth programs may incorporate school-based mental health services, while veteran programs might include trauma-focused therapies.

Crisis intervention services are another critical aspect of local mental health services. These services respond to individuals in immediate distress, providing support through hotlines, crisis centers, or mobile crisis teams. The goal is to stabilize the individual and connect them with ongoing care, reducing the likelihood of hospitalization or further escalation of the crisis.

Access to mental health services can be influenced by various factors, including socioeconomic status, cultural background, and geographic location. Local mental health services often work to address these disparities by providing sliding scale fees, bilingual services, and outreach programs to underserved communities. This commitment to accessibility ensures that everyone can receive the care they need, regardless of their circumstances.

Education and prevention are also key components of local mental health services. Many organizations prioritize mental health education initiatives to raise awareness about mental health issues and reduce stigma. Workshops, community events, and school programs aim to empower individuals with knowledge and coping strategies, promoting mental wellness across the community.

Local mental health services often collaborate with other community organizations, such as schools, hospitals, and social service agencies, to create a comprehensive support network. This collaboration enhances the continuity of care and ensures that individuals receive holistic support that addresses not only their mental health needs but also other factors that may impact their well-being, such as housing and employment.

Telehealth has become an increasingly important tool in local mental health services, especially in the wake of the COVID-19 pandemic. Many providers now offer virtual therapy sessions, allowing individuals to access care from the comfort of their homes. This flexibility can be particularly beneficial for those with mobility challenges or those living in remote areas where in-person services may be limited.

Despite the positive strides made in local mental health services, challenges remain. Funding constraints often limit the availability of services, forcing many organizations to operate with fewer resources. Additionally, there may still be stigma associated with seeking mental health support, which can deter individuals from accessing necessary services. Advocacy for increased funding and awareness is essential to overcome these barriers.

The integration of mental health services into broader health care systems is another area of focus. By recognizing the connection between physical and mental health, local services can better address the overall well-being of individuals. This integrative approach can lead to improved outcomes, as mental health care becomes a routine part of health care rather than a separate entity.

Family involvement is often encouraged in local mental health services, particularly when working with children and adolescents. Family therapy and support groups can help educate family members about mental health issues and equip them with strategies to support their loved ones. This involvement fosters a more supportive home environment, which is vital for recovery and resilience.

Local mental health services are invaluable resources that provide essential support to individuals facing mental health challenges. By offering a range of services, promoting accessibility, and fostering community awareness, these services contribute significantly to the overall well-being of individuals and communities. Continued investment in and advocacy for these services is crucial in ensuring that everyone has access to the mental health care they need.

Ultimately, the effectiveness of local mental health services hinges on community involvement and support. Encouraging open conversations about mental health, advocating for those in need, and participating in local initiatives can help create an environment where mental health is prioritized. As communities rally together to support mental health, the impact can be profound, leading to healthier, more resilient populations.

Local mental health services are essential in addressing the mental health needs of communities. They provide a variety of resources and programs aimed at helping individuals manage mental health disorders, cope with life challenges, and enhance overall emotional well-being. These services are designed to be accessible and tailored to meet the diverse needs of different populations, ensuring that everyone can find support appropriate to their circumstances.

Community mental health centers serve as the cornerstone of local mental health services. These centers provide comprehensive services, including psychotherapy, counseling, medication management, and crisis intervention. They often have a multidisciplinary team of professionals, such as psychologists, social workers, and psychiatric nurses, who work collaboratively to create individualized treatment plans. This holistic approach ensures that care is tailored to each person's unique needs and circumstances.

Specialized programs are also critical in addressing the needs of specific groups, such as children, adolescents, and marginalized populations. For example, youth mental health programs often incorporate school-based services, making it easier for students to access support. Similarly, programs for veterans may focus on trauma-informed care, addressing the specific mental health challenges faced by those who have served in the military. These targeted services help ensure that individuals receive the most relevant and effective interventions.

Crisis intervention services are vital for individuals experiencing acute mental health crises. These services include hotlines, crisis centers, and mobile crisis teams that provide immediate support and stabilization. Having access to these services can prevent escalation and reduce the need for hospitalization, allowing individuals to receive timely assistance and connect with ongoing care. This immediate support can be life-saving, particularly in moments of acute distress.

Education and outreach initiatives are integral to local mental health services, aiming to reduce stigma and promote awareness of mental health issues. By providing workshops, community events, and educational resources, these programs empower individuals to recognize the signs of mental health challenges and seek help. This proactive approach fosters a more informed community, encouraging conversations about mental health and ultimately creating a more supportive environment for those in need.

Collaboration between local mental health services and other community organizations is essential for providing holistic support. By partnering with schools, healthcare providers, and social service agencies, mental health services can create a comprehensive network that addresses the various factors affecting an individual's well-being. This integrated approach enhances the effectiveness of care, ensuring that individuals receive support that encompasses not only their mental health needs but also social, economic, and physical health factors.

Despite the critical role of local mental health services, challenges such as funding limitations and societal stigma persist. Many organizations struggle with inadequate funding, which can hinder their ability to offer a full range of services or expand their reach to underserved populations. Furthermore, stigma surrounding mental health can prevent individuals from seeking help, highlighting the need for ongoing advocacy and education to promote understanding and acceptance.

In conclusion, local mental health services are fundamental in fostering community well-being. By providing accessible care, specialized programs, crisis intervention, and educational initiatives, these services play a vital role in supporting individuals facing mental health challenges. Ongoing advocacy for funding, awareness, and collaboration is essential to ensure that these services can continue to thrive and meet the needs of the communities they serve. As communities work together to prioritize mental health, they contribute to the overall resilience and health of their populations.

Chapter Thirty Four:

Creating an Emergency Plan

Creating an emergency plan surrounding mental health is crucial for individuals who may experience mental health crises. Such a plan can provide guidance and support during times of distress. Here are twelve important aspects to consider when developing an emergency plan for mental health:

1. Identify Triggers: Begin by identifying triggers that may lead to a mental health crisis. Understanding what may exacerbate symptoms can help in creating a plan to mitigate these triggers or cope with them effectively.

2. Establish Support System: Build a support system of trusted individuals who can provide assistance during an emergency. This may include friends, family members, therapists, or support groups.

3. Contact Information: Ensure that all relevant contact information, including emergency hotlines, mental health professionals, and loved ones, is easily accessible in the plan.

1. Crisis Response Steps: Outline specific steps to take in case of a mental health crisis, such as who to contact first, where to go for help, and what immediate actions to take.

1. Medication Management: If the individual is on medication, include details about dosage, frequency, and emergency procedures in case medication is lost or

unavailable.

6. Self-Care Strategies: Incorporate self-care strategies that have been effective in managing mental health challenges. This can include mindfulness techniques, relaxation exercises, or grounding activities.

7. Triggers to Avoid: Identify triggers to avoid during a crisis and outline strategies to steer clear of situations or environments that may worsen mental health symptoms.

8. Emergency Accommodations: Plan for emergency accommodations if the individual needs a safe space to stay during a crisis, such as a friend's home or a mental health facility.

9. Legal and Medical Information: Include important legal and medical information, such as health insurance details, advance directives, and any legal documents related to mental health care.

10. Communication Plan: Develop a communication plan for informing key individuals about the mental health crisis, including how to communicate effectively during times of distress.

11. Follow-Up Care: Outline follow-up care procedures, including scheduling appointments with mental health professionals, checking in with support systems, and monitoring progress after the crisis.

12. Regular Review and Updates: Regularly review and update the emergency plan to ensure that it remains relevant and effective in addressing the individual's mental health needs.

By incorporating these elements into an emergency plan surrounding mental health, individuals can feel more prepared and supported in managing mental health crises effectively. It is essential to tailor the plan to the individual's specific needs and preferences to ensure its effectiveness in times of need.

1. Accessibility of the Plan: Ensure that the emergency plan is easily accessible at all times. Consider keeping copies of the

plan in multiple locations, such as on a smartphone, in a wallet or purse, and at home. This accessibility can ensure that the plan can be quickly referenced and followed during a crisis.

14. Training for Support System: Provide training to the individuals in the support system on how to recognize signs of a mental health crisis and how to effectively support and assist the individual in distress. This training can empower the support system to respond appropriately and compassionately during emergencies.

15. Confidentiality and Privacy: Emphasize the importance of confidentiality and privacy within the emergency plan. Clearly outline who has access to the plan and how sensitive information will be handled to ensure the individual's trust and comfort in utilizing the plan.

16. Involvement of Healthcare Providers: Involve healthcare providers, such as therapists, psychiatrists, or primary care physicians, in the creation of the emergency plan. Collaborating with healthcare professionals can ensure that the plan aligns with the individual's treatment goals and clinical recommendations.

17. Community Resources:Research and include information about community resources and mental health services that can offer support during a crisis. This may include crisis hotlines, local mental health clinics, support groups, and online resources for immediate assistance.

1. Emergency Contacts:Clearly list emergency contacts in the plan, including names, phone numbers, and relationships to the individual. This information should be easily accessible and prominently displayed to expedite communication and support during emergencies.

19. De-Escalation Techniques: Incorporate de-escalation techniques and strategies for managing crisis situations effectively. These techniques may involve calming exercises, breathing techniques, or communication approaches to help defuse heightened emotions and distress.

20. Practice Scenarios: Regularly practice scenarios outlined in the emergency plan with the support system to ensure everyone understands their roles and responsibilities. Practicing can enhance preparedness and coordination during a real mental health crisis.

By addressing these additional aspects in the emergency plan surrounding mental health, individuals can strengthen their resilience and readiness to navigate challenging situations with the necessary support and guidance. Each element plays a vital role in ensuring a comprehensive and effective response to mental health emergencies.

Chapter Thirty Five:

Real-Life Stories of Overcoming Despair

Overcoming mental health challenges can be an arduous journey, but the stories of individuals who have triumphed over despair serve as beacons of hope for many. One such story is that of Sarah, who battled severe depression for years. Through therapy and medication, Sarah slowly began to see light at the end of the tunnel. With a strong support system of friends and family, Sarah learned coping mechanisms that helped her manage her condition on a daily basis. Today, Sarah not only leads a fulfilling life but also volunteers at a mental health support group to help others facing similar struggles.

Another inspiring tale is that of Michael, who struggled with anxiety and panic attacks since his teenage years. Despite feeling overwhelmed at times, Michael sought professional help and underwent cognitive-behavioral therapy. Through therapy, he learned to challenge his negative thought patterns and gradually regained control over his anxiety. Michael's journey serves as a reminder that with determination and the right support, it is possible to overcome even the most debilitating mental health conditions.

One remarkable story is that of Maria, who faced post-traumatic stress disorder (PTSD) after a traumatic event. For years, Maria avoided seeking help, believing that she could handle her symptoms alone. However, with the encouragement of a close friend, Maria eventually reached out to a therapist specializing in trauma counseling. Through therapy, Maria confronted her past traumas and began to heal. Today, Maria advocates for destigmatizing mental health issues and encourages others to seek help when needed.

A story that resonates with many is that of David, who battled addiction and depression for years. Despite numerous setbacks, David found the strength to seek treatment at a rehabilitation center. Through a combination of therapy, support groups, and medication, David slowly rebuilt his life and found a renewed sense of purpose. Today, David shares his story at addiction recovery seminars to inspire others struggling with similar challenges.

The journey of Emily, who grappled with bipolar disorder, is equally inspiring. Despite facing periods of intense highs and lows, Emily refused to let her condition define her. With the guidance of a psychiatrist, Emily found the right medication regimen that stabilized her mood swings. Through therapy, she learned to recognize early warning signs of relapse and developed healthy coping strategies. Emily now leads a balanced life and uses her experiences to advocate for mental health awareness in her community.

One particularly moving story is that of James, who contemplated suicide during his darkest moments of depression. With the support of a crisis hotline, James was able to speak openly about his struggles and receive immediate help. Through a combination of therapy, medication, and support from loved ones, James gradually found reasons to keep living. Today, James volunteers at a suicide prevention hotline, offering hope and compassion to those in crisis.

The story of Rachel, who battled an eating disorder for years, sheds light on the complexities of mental health struggles. Through intensive therapy and nutritional counseling, Rachel confronted the underlying issues fueling her disorder. With unwavering determination, Rachel challenged distorted beliefs about body image and food. Today, Rachel is a vocal advocate for eating disorder awareness, using her journey to inspire others to seek help and embrace recovery.

The journey of Carlos, who faced debilitating social anxiety, highlights the transformative power of exposure therapy. Despite feeling paralyzed by fear in social situations, Carlos worked with a therapist to gradually confront his anxieties. Through repeated exposure to triggering scenarios, Carlos learned to manage his anxiety and build confidence in social settings. Today, Carlos leads a fulfilling social life and encourages others to confront their fears in a supportive environment.

The story of Lisa, who experienced severe trauma in her past, showcases the resilience of the human spirit. Despite grappling with complex PTSD, Lisa embarked on a healing journey through trauma-focused therapy. By processing past traumas and learning healthy coping strategies, Lisa was able to reclaim her sense of safety and empowerment. Today, Lisa volunteers at a trauma support group, offering empathy and understanding to survivors of abuse and violence.

The journey of Alex, who struggled with self-harm and suicidal thoughts, demonstrates the importance of seeking professional help during times of crisis. Through intensive therapy and medication management, Alex learned healthier ways to cope with emotional pain. With support from a psychiatrist and a dedicated therapist, Alex gradually overcame the urge to self-harm and found hope for the future. Today, Alex advocates for destigmatizing mental health discussions and encourages others to prioritize their well-being.

The story of Maya, who battled depression and addiction simultaneously, underscores the interconnected nature of mental health struggles. Through a dual diagnosis treatment program, Maya received specialized care that addressed both her mental health and substance use issues. With the guidance of therapists and addiction counselors, Maya learned to navigate triggers and develop a relapse prevention plan. Today, Maya is in recovery and serves as a beacon of hope for individuals facing co-occurring disorders.

The journey of Kevin, who faced severe anxiety and obsessive-compulsive disorder (OCD), exemplifies the transformative power of exposure and response prevention therapy. Despite feeling consumed by intrusive thoughts and rituals, Kevin worked with a therapist to gradually confront his fears and reduce compulsive behaviors. Through consistent practice and a supportive treatment team, Kevin learned to manage his symptoms and regain control over his life. Today, Kevin shares his story to raise awareness about OCD and inspire others to seek evidence-based treatments.

One poignant story is that of Sophia, who battled severe depression and self-esteem issues stemming from childhood trauma. Through individual therapy and group counseling, Sophia learned to explore her past experiences and challenge negative beliefs about herself. With the support of her therapist and peers, Sophia gradually rebuilt her self-worth and developed healthier coping mechanisms. Today, Sophia advocates for mental health resources in underserved communities, helping others access the support they need to heal.

The journey of Jack, who faced intense phobias and panic attacks, demonstrates the transformative impact of exposure therapy and mindfulness practices. Despite feeling overwhelmed by irrational fears, Jack worked with a therapist to gradually expose himself to triggering stimuli in a controlled environment. Through mindfulness techniques, Jack learned to ground himself in the present moment and manage his anxiety effectively. Today, Jack leads a more empowered life, sharing his journey to inspire others to confront their fears with courage and resilience.

The story of Lily, who struggled with complex grief and survivor's guilt, highlights the importance of grief counseling and peer support groups. After losing a loved one in a tragic accident, Lily found solace in connecting with others who understood her pain. Through grief counseling sessions and group therapy, Lily processed her emotions and learned to honor her loved one's memory while also focusing on her own healing. Today, Lily volunteers at a bereavement support center, offering comfort and empathy to those navigating loss.

The journey of Thomas, who grappled with schizophrenia and auditory hallucinations, underscores the significance of medication management and psychoeducation. Through a comprehensive treatment plan that included antipsychotic medication and cognitive-behavioral therapy, Thomas gained insight into his symptoms and learned to differentiate between reality and delusions. With the guidance of his psychiatrist and therapist, Thomas developed coping strategies to manage his condition effectively. Today, Thomas advocates for mental health awareness and challenges misconceptions about schizophrenia.

The story of Ava, who faced debilitating social isolation and feelings of worthlessness, showcases the impact of peer support networks and community resources. Despite struggling with loneliness and low self-esteem, Ava found connection and belonging in a local support group for individuals with similar experiences. Through shared stories and mutual encouragement, Ava discovered a sense of belonging and acceptance that helped her combat feelings of isolation. Today, Ava volunteers at a community center, creating safe spaces for individuals to connect and share their struggles without judgment.

The journey of Jacob, who experienced severe mood swings and emotional dysregulation, illustrates the benefits of dialectical behavior therapy (DBT) and emotion regulation skills training. Through a specialized DBT program, Jacob learned to identify and manage intense emotions, reduce impulsive behaviors, and improve interpersonal relationships. With the guidance of his therapist and the support of a skills training group, Jacob developed a toolbox of coping strategies that empowered him to navigate life's challenges more effectively. Today, Jacob leads a more balanced life and mentors others in developing emotional resilience.

The story of Olivia, who grappled with body dysmorphic disorder (BDD) and obsessive-compulsive behaviors, sheds light on the importance of exposure therapy and cognitive restructuring. Through targeted interventions that challenged distorted beliefs about her appearance and reduced compulsive rituals, Olivia gained a new perspective on beauty and self-acceptance. With the support of a specialized treatment team, Olivia learned to embrace her unique features and cultivate self-confidence. Today, Olivia advocates for body positivity and mental health awareness, encouraging others to seek help for BDD.

The journey of Nathan, who faced debilitating perfectionism and performance anxiety, highlights the transformative power of acceptance and commitment therapy (ACT). Despite struggling with unrealistic expectations and fear of failure, Nathan engaged in ACT sessions that focused on mindfulness, values clarification, and psychological flexibility. Through experiential exercises and cognitive defusion techniques, Nathan learned to embrace imperfection, let go of unattainable standards, and live in alignment with his core values. Today, Nathan leads a more authentic life and shares his journey to inspire others to prioritize self-compassion over self-criticism.

The story of Mia, who grappled with self-esteem issues and disordered eating behaviors, emphasizes the role of holistic treatment approaches in addressing complex mental health challenges. Through an integrative treatment plan that combined individual therapy, nutritional counseling, and body-positive interventions, Mia embarked on a journey of self-discovery and self-acceptance. With the support of a multidisciplinary team of professionals, Mia learned to cultivate a healthy relationship with food, exercise, and her body. Today, Mia advocates for holistic wellness and encourages others to prioritize self-care and self-love in their recovery journey.

The journey of Lucas, who faced trauma-induced phobias and nightmares, showcases the effectiveness of eye movement desensitization and reprocessing (EMDR) therapy in processing traumatic memories. Through EMDR sessions that targeted specific triggers and reprocessed distressing memories, Lucas experienced significant relief from his symptoms and gained a greater sense of control over his reactions. With the guidance of his therapist and the use of bilateral stimulation techniques, Lucas was able to integrate past traumas and reduce the intensity of his phobias. Today, Lucas leads a more peaceful life and advocates for trauma-informed care in mental health treatment.

The story of Isabella, who battled chronic pain and depression, underscores the importance of integrated care models that address both physical and mental health needs. Through a collaborative approach involving pain management specialists, mental health professionals, and holistic practitioners, Isabella received comprehensive treatment that targeted the underlying causes of her symptoms. By addressing the mind-body connection and implementing interventions such as cognitive-behavioral therapy, mindfulness practices, and physical therapy, Isabella experienced improvements in both her physical well-being and emotional resilience. Today, Isabella advocates for a holistic approach to health care that recognizes the interconnectedness of physical and mental health.

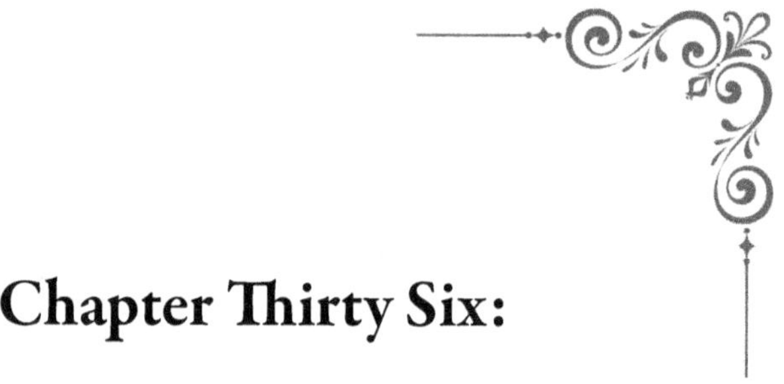

Chapter Thirty Six:

The Role of Resilience in Recovery

Resilience plays a crucial role in supporting mental health and aiding in the recovery process for individuals facing various challenges. The ability to bounce back from adversity and adapt to difficult situations is a key component of mental well-being. Individuals who possess resilience are better equipped to cope with stress, trauma, and setbacks, ultimately leading to improved mental health outcomes.

One way resilience supports mental health is by enhancing an individual's ability to regulate emotions. Resilient individuals are more adept at managing their feelings and responding to stressful situations in a healthy manner. This emotional regulation can prevent the escalation of negative emotions and reduce the risk of developing mental health disorders such as anxiety or depression.

Moreover, resilience fosters a sense of empowerment and self-efficacy in individuals. When facing challenges, resilient individuals believe in their ability to overcome obstacles and navigate difficult circumstances. This belief in one's own capacity to cope and succeed can boost self-esteem and contribute to a positive self-image, which are essential components of mental well-being.

In addition, resilience promotes adaptive coping strategies that help individuals effectively deal with stressors. Rather than resorting to harmful coping mechanisms like substance abuse or avoidance, resilient individuals are more likely to utilize healthy coping strategies such as seeking social support, practicing mindfulness, or engaging in physical activity. These positive coping mechanisms can protect mental health and facilitate recovery from challenging experiences.

Resilience also plays a role in fostering social connections and support networks, which are vital for maintaining mental health. Resilient individuals tend to have strong relationships with family, friends, or community members who provide emotional support, encouragement, and practical assistance during difficult times. These social connections serve as protective factors against mental health issues and contribute to overall well-being.

Furthermore, resilience helps individuals develop a sense of purpose and meaning in life, which are important aspects of mental health recovery. Resilient individuals are able to find meaning in their experiences, even in the face of adversity, and use these challenges as opportunities for growth and personal development. This sense of purpose can instill hope and motivation, driving individuals towards recovery and a sense of fulfillment.

Resilience also plays a role in fostering adaptability and flexibility in individuals. In today's rapidly changing world, the ability to adapt to new circumstances and bounce back from setbacks is essential for maintaining mental health. Resilient individuals are more open to change, willing to learn from their experiences, and able to adjust their goals and expectations as needed, which contributes to their overall well-being.

Moreover, resilience can act as a buffer against the negative effects of stress on mental health. Individuals with high levels of resilience are better able to withstand the impact of stressors and maintain their mental well-being in the face of adversity. This ability to resist the detrimental effects of stress can prevent the development of stress-related mental health disorders and promote recovery from existing conditions.

Resilience also promotes a positive outlook on life and a sense of optimism about the future. Resilient individuals are more likely to focus on the possibilities for growth and improvement, rather than dwelling on past failures or setbacks. This optimistic mindset can enhance mental health by fostering hope, resilience, and a belief in one's ability to overcome challenges and achieve personal goals.

Furthermore, resilience is associated with increased psychological flexibility, which is the ability to adapt to changing circumstances and think creatively about solutions to problems. Individuals with high levels of resilience are more likely to approach challenges with a flexible mindset, exploring different perspectives and adapting their strategies as needed. This psychological flexibility can enhance mental health by reducing rigidity and promoting problem-solving skills.

In addition, resilience is linked to greater emotional intelligence, which is the ability to recognize, understand, and manage one's own emotions as well as those of others. Resilient individuals are better equipped to navigate complex emotional situations, communicate effectively with others, and build strong relationships. This emotional intelligence contributes to mental health by promoting self-awareness, empathy, and healthy interpersonal interactions.

Overall, the role of resilience in supporting mental health and recovery cannot be overstated. By enhancing emotional regulation, fostering self-efficacy, promoting adaptive coping strategies, fostering social connections, instilling a sense of purpose, fostering adaptability, acting as a buffer against stress, promoting optimism, enhancing psychological flexibility, and increasing emotional intelligence, resilience plays a vital role in promoting mental well-being and aiding individuals in their recovery journey.

Resilience is a fundamental trait that significantly influences mental health outcomes and recovery processes. Individuals with resilience possess the capacity to adapt and thrive in the face of adversity, which is essential for maintaining mental well-being. By cultivating resilience, individuals can effectively navigate challenging circumstances and bounce back from setbacks, ultimately supporting their journey towards recovery and improved mental health.

One key aspect of resilience in mental health is its role in promoting emotional regulation. Resilient individuals demonstrate a heightened ability to manage their emotions and cope with stress in a healthy manner. This emotional regulation not only safeguards against the development of mental health disorders but also contributes to overall emotional well-being by preventing the escalation of negative emotions and promoting a sense of balance and stability.

Furthermore, resilience empowers individuals by fostering a belief in their own capabilities and self-efficacy. When faced with obstacles, resilient individuals maintain a positive outlook and confidence in their ability to overcome challenges. This sense of empowerment boosts self-esteem and cultivates a resilient mindset that is instrumental in supporting mental health recovery and personal growth.

Resilience also plays a crucial role in promoting the adoption of adaptive coping strategies. Rather than resorting to maladaptive behaviors, resilient individuals are more likely to engage in positive coping mechanisms such as seeking social support, practicing mindfulness, or engaging in activities that promote well-being. These healthy coping strategies not only enhance resilience but also contribute to the overall maintenance of mental health and recovery from adverse experiences.

Moreover, resilience fosters the development of strong social connections and support networks, which serve as protective factors for mental health. Resilient individuals tend to have robust relationships with others who provide emotional support, encouragement, and practical assistance during challenging times.

These social connections act as a source of strength and resilience, facilitating recovery and promoting psychological well-being.

Additionally, resilience encourages individuals to find purpose and meaning in their experiences, even amidst adversity. Resilient individuals are able to derive lessons and growth from difficult situations, transforming challenges into opportunities for personal development. This sense of purpose instills hope, motivation, and a sense of direction, which are essential components of mental health recovery and overall well-being.

Furthermore, resilience fosters adaptability and flexibility in individuals, enabling them to navigate change and uncertainty with resilience. In a rapidly evolving world, the ability to adapt to new circumstances and bounce back from setbacks is crucial for mental health. Resilient individuals demonstrate a willingness to learn, grow, and adjust their goals in response to challenges, contributing to their overall psychological well-being.

Resilience also acts as a buffer against the detrimental effects of stress on mental health. Individuals with high levels of resilience are better equipped to withstand stressors and maintain their mental well-being in the face of adversity. This resilience to stress helps prevent the development of stress-related mental health issues and supports individuals in their recovery journey by promoting emotional resilience and psychological strength.

In conclusion, resilience plays a multifaceted role in supporting mental health and recovery by enhancing emotional regulation, fostering self-empowerment, promoting adaptive coping strategies, cultivating social connections, fostering purpose and meaning, encouraging adaptability, acting as a buffer against stress, and promoting overall psychological well-being. By cultivating resilience, individuals can navigate challenges with strength and resilience, ultimately supporting their journey towards mental health recovery and well-being.

Chapter Thirty Seven:

Learning from Others' Experiences

Learning from the experiences of others can be a valuable source of support and guidance for individuals striving to maintain or improve their mental health. By listening to and understanding the stories of others, individuals can gain insights, perspectives, and coping strategies that may be beneficial in their own mental health journey. The importance of learning from others' experiences lies in the potential for shared wisdom, empathy, and inspiration to foster personal growth and resilience in the face of mental health challenges.

One significant benefit of learning from others' experiences is the opportunity to gain new perspectives and insights into mental health issues. By hearing about the struggles, triumphs, and coping mechanisms of others, individuals can broaden their understanding of mental health and develop a more nuanced view of their own challenges. This expanded perspective can help individuals reframe their own experiences, normalize their emotions, and feel a sense of connection and solidarity with others facing similar issues.

Moreover, learning from others' experiences can provide valuable coping strategies and tools for managing mental health challenges. Individuals can draw inspiration from the resilience, creativity, and problem-solving abilities of others in navigating difficult emotions and situations. By learning about effective coping mechanisms and self-care practices from others, individuals can enhance their own mental health toolkit and develop personalized strategies for maintaining well-being.

Additionally, hearing about others' experiences can instill a sense of hope and optimism in individuals struggling with mental health issues. Stories of recovery, growth, and resilience from others can serve as beacons of light in times of darkness, offering reassurance that healing and transformation are possible. This sense of hope can motivate individuals to persevere through challenges, seek support, and take proactive steps towards improving their mental health.

Learning from others' experiences also promotes empathy and understanding towards oneself and others. By listening to the stories of individuals with diverse backgrounds and experiences, individuals can cultivate compassion, reduce stigma, and foster a sense of connection with others. This empathy not only enhances interpersonal relationships but also promotes self-acceptance, self-compassion, and a non-judgmental attitude towards one's own mental health struggles.

Furthermore, sharing and learning from others' experiences can help individuals feel less alone in their mental health journey. The realization that others have faced similar challenges, emotions, and setbacks can reduce feelings of isolation and foster a sense of belonging and community. Connecting with others who have walked similar paths can provide comfort, validation, and reassurance that one is not alone in their struggles.

Moreover, learning from others' experiences can serve as a source of motivation and inspiration for individuals seeking to improve their mental health. Hearing about the growth, achievements, and resilience of others can ignite a sense of possibility, purpose, and determination in individuals, encouraging them to set goals, seek help, and take proactive steps towards recovery and well-being. These stories of inspiration can fuel individuals' motivation to overcome obstacles and strive for positive change in their lives.

Learning from others' experiences also facilitates personal growth and self-discovery by encouraging individuals to reflect on their own beliefs, values, and coping strategies. By comparing and contrasting their experiences with those of others, individuals can gain new insights into themselves, identify areas for growth, and explore different approaches to managing their mental health. This process of self-reflection can promote self-awareness, self-acceptance, and personal development.

Furthermore, learning from others' experiences can help individuals build resilience and adaptability in the face of adversity. Hearing about how others have navigated challenges, coped with setbacks, and bounced back from difficult situations can provide valuable lessons in resilience-building and problem-solving. By learning from the experiences of resilient individuals, individuals can cultivate a mindset of perseverance, flexibility, and resourcefulness in managing their mental health.

In addition, learning from others' experiences can enhance individuals' social support networks and sense of belonging. By connecting with peers, mentors, or support groups who share similar experiences, individuals can build relationships based on trust, understanding, and mutual support. These connections can provide emotional validation, practical advice, and a sense of camaraderie that can strengthen individuals' resilience and well-being.

Moreover, learning from others' experiences can promote a sense of empowerment and agency in individuals by highlighting the possibilities for personal growth and change. By witnessing the transformative journeys of others, individuals can gain confidence in their own ability to overcome challenges, make positive changes, and take control of their mental health. This sense of empowerment can inspire individuals to set boundaries, advocate for their needs, and make choices that support their well-being.

In conclusion, the importance of learning from others' experiences in supporting mental health lies in its potential to provide insights, coping strategies, inspiration, empathy, connection, motivation, personal growth, resilience, social support, and empowerment. By listening to and sharing stories of triumph, struggle, and recovery, individuals can gain valuable perspectives, tools, and sources of strength that can aid them in their own mental health journey. Embracing the wisdom and experiences of others can be a transformative and affirming process that fosters growth, resilience, and well-being in individuals striving to navigate the complexities of mental health.

Learning from the experiences of others is a powerful tool in promoting mental health and well-being. By actively engaging with the stories and insights shared by individuals who have faced similar challenges, individuals can gain valuable perspectives and strategies to navigate their own mental health journey. The wisdom and lessons learned from others' experiences can offer comfort, guidance, and inspiration to those seeking support and understanding in managing their mental health.

One of the key benefits of learning from others' experiences is the opportunity to gain a deeper understanding of mental health issues. By listening to personal narratives and accounts of struggles and triumphs, individuals can expand their knowledge and awareness of different aspects of mental health. This increased understanding can help individuals normalize their experiences, reduce feelings of isolation, and foster a sense of connection with others who may be going through similar challenges.

Moreover, learning from others' experiences can provide practical coping strategies and tools for managing mental health concerns. Hearing about the resilience and adaptive strategies employed by others can offer new approaches for individuals to cope with stress, regulate emotions, and maintain well-being. By incorporating these learned techniques into their own lives, individuals can enhance their ability to navigate difficult situations and promote their mental health.

Additionally, stories of hope and recovery shared by others can serve as sources of inspiration and motivation for individuals struggling with mental health issues. Witnessing the transformation and growth of individuals who have overcome adversity can instill a sense of optimism and belief in the possibility of healing and recovery. This inspiration can empower individuals to seek help, set goals, and take positive steps towards improving their mental well-being.

Learning from others' experiences also cultivates empathy and understanding towards oneself and others. By engaging with diverse narratives and perspectives, individuals can develop compassion, reduce self-judgment, and foster a sense of connectedness with others. This empathy not only enhances interpersonal relationships but also promotes self-acceptance, self-compassion, and a non-judgmental attitude towards one's own mental health struggles.

Furthermore, sharing and learning from others' experiences can create a sense of belonging and community for individuals navigating mental health challenges. Connecting with others who have walked similar paths can provide a sense of validation, support, and camaraderie. This shared experience fosters a supportive environment where individuals can feel understood, accepted, and less alone in their struggles, ultimately promoting their mental well-being.

Moreover, learning from others' experiences encourages individuals to engage in self-reflection and personal growth. By comparing their own experiences with those of others, individuals can gain insights into their beliefs, values, and coping mechanisms. This process of reflection enables individuals to identify areas for growth, challenge limiting beliefs, and explore new ways of approaching their mental health, leading to greater self-awareness and personal development.

Learning from others' experiences can also facilitate the development of resilience and adaptability in individuals facing mental health challenges. By learning how others have coped with setbacks, managed stress, and overcome obstacles, individuals can gain valuable lessons in resilience-building and problem-solving. These insights can help individuals cultivate a mindset of perseverance, flexibility, and resourcefulness, equipping them to navigate future challenges with strength and resilience.

In addition, connecting with peers and mentors who share similar experiences can enhance individuals' social support networks and sense of empowerment. By building relationships based on trust, understanding, and mutual support, individuals can access emotional validation, practical advice, and encouragement in their mental health journey. These supportive connections provide a sense of security, belonging, and empowerment that can bolster individuals' resilience and well-being.

In conclusion, learning from the experiences of others is a transformative process that offers individuals valuable insights, coping strategies, inspiration, empathy, connection, motivation, personal growth, resilience, social support, and empowerment in managing their mental health. By embracing the stories and wisdom shared by others, individuals can draw strength, guidance, and hope to navigate the complexities of mental health with courage and resilience. The collective wisdom and experiences of individuals form a tapestry of support and understanding that can empower individuals on their journey towards mental well-being.

Chapter Thirty Eight:

Nutrition and Mental Health
Nutrition plays a crucial role in supporting mental health and well-being. The food we consume not only fuels our bodies but also directly impacts our brain function, mood, and overall mental health. A balanced and nutrient-rich diet is essential for maintaining optimal brain health and supporting emotional well-being. By understanding the importance of nutrition in mental health, individuals can make informed choices about their diet to promote cognitive function, mood regulation, and overall psychological well-being.

First and foremost, nutrition provides the building blocks for brain health and neurotransmitter production. Certain nutrients, such as omega-3 fatty acids, vitamins, minerals, and antioxidants, play key roles in supporting brain function and neurotransmitter synthesis. Consuming a diet rich in these nutrients can enhance cognitive performance, improve concentration, and support mental clarity, ultimately contributing to better mental health outcomes.

Moreover, nutrition influences mood regulation and emotional well-being through its impact on neurotransmitters like serotonin and dopamine. Serotonin, often referred to as the "feel-good" neurotransmitter, is synthesized from the amino acid tryptophan found in protein-rich foods. Consuming foods that support serotonin production can help regulate mood, reduce feelings of anxiety and depression, and promote emotional stability. Similarly, dopamine, known for its role in motivation and pleasure, can be influenced by the intake of certain nutrients, such as tyrosine found in protein sources.

Additionally, a balanced and diverse diet can help regulate blood sugar levels and prevent fluctuations that can impact mood and energy levels. Consuming complex carbohydrates, fiber-rich foods, and sources of protein can help stabilize blood sugar levels, preventing rapid spikes and crashes that can lead to mood swings, irritability, and fatigue. By maintaining stable blood sugar levels through proper nutrition, individuals can promote sustained energy levels and emotional balance.

Furthermore, nutrition plays a key role in reducing inflammation in the body, which has been linked to the development of mental health disorders such as depression and anxiety. Consuming anti-inflammatory foods rich in antioxidants, omega-3 fatty acids, and phytonutrients can help combat oxidative stress, reduce inflammation, and support a healthy immune system. By incorporating these foods into their diet, individuals can protect their brain health and reduce the risk of mental health conditions associated with inflammation.

In addition, gut health and the gut-brain axis play a significant role in mental health, with emerging research highlighting the link between the gut microbiome and brain function. The microbiota in the gut produce neurotransmitters, regulate inflammation, and communicate with the brain through the gut-brain axis, influencing mood, cognition, and behavior. Consuming a diet rich in fiber, prebiotics, and probiotics can support a healthy gut microbiome, improve digestion, and positively impact mental health outcomes.

Moreover, nutrition impacts stress levels and the body's response to stress, with certain nutrients playing a role in the production of stress hormones like cortisol. Consuming foods rich in magnesium, vitamin C, and B vitamins can support the body's stress response system, reduce the impact of chronic stress on mental health, and promote resilience. By nourishing the body with stress-reducing nutrients, individuals can better manage stress, anxiety, and the negative effects of prolonged stress on mental well-being.

Furthermore, proper nutrition is essential for supporting cognitive function, memory, and focus, all of which are vital components of mental well-being. Nutrients such as antioxidants, omega-3 fatty acids, and B vitamins have been shown to enhance cognitive performance, protect brain cells from damage, and support neuroplasticity. Consuming a diet rich in these nutrients can improve cognitive function, enhance memory retention, and promote mental clarity, contributing to overall mental health and well-being.

Additionally, nutrition plays a role in the prevention and management of mental health disorders such as depression, anxiety, and cognitive decline. Research has shown that certain dietary patterns, such as the Mediterranean diet rich in fruits, vegetables, whole grains, and healthy fats, are associated with a lower risk of depression and cognitive impairment. By adopting a diet that prioritizes nutrient-dense foods and promotes brain health, individuals can reduce their risk of developing mental health conditions and support their mental well-being.

In conclusion, the importance of nutrition in mental health cannot be overstated, as the food we consume directly impacts our brain function, mood, and overall well-being. By prioritizing a balanced and nutrient-rich diet that supports brain health, neurotransmitter production, mood regulation, and cognitive function, individuals can enhance their mental health outcomes and promote emotional well-being. Understanding the link between nutrition and mental health empowers individuals to make informed dietary choices that support their brain health, reduce inflammation, regulate stress, and enhance cognitive function, ultimately contributing to a holistic approach to mental health and well-being.

Nutrition is a fundamental pillar of mental health, influencing brain function, mood regulation, and emotional well-being. A diet rich in essential nutrients such as omega-3 fatty acids, vitamins, minerals, and antioxidants is crucial for supporting optimal brain health and neurotransmitter synthesis. These nutrients serve as the building blocks for neurotransmitters like serotonin and dopamine, which play key roles in regulating mood, emotions, and cognitive function. By consuming a varied and nutrient-dense diet, individuals can provide their brains with the necessary resources to function optimally and promote mental well-being.

The impact of nutrition on mood regulation cannot be understated, as certain foods contain components that directly influence neurotransmitter production and balance. For instance, foods rich in tryptophan can support serotonin synthesis, promoting feelings of well-being and happiness. Similarly, nutrients like tyrosine found in protein sources can contribute to dopamine production, enhancing motivation and pleasure. By incorporating these mood-supporting nutrients into their diet, individuals can help stabilize their emotions and promote mental stability.

In addition to mood regulation, nutrition also plays a crucial role in maintaining stable blood sugar levels, which are essential for sustained energy and emotional balance. Consuming complex carbohydrates, fiber-rich foods, and adequate protein sources can help prevent blood sugar fluctuations that can lead to mood swings, irritability, and fatigue. By prioritizing a balanced diet that supports blood sugar regulation, individuals can promote consistent energy levels and emotional well-being throughout the day.

Furthermore, the anti-inflammatory properties of certain foods can have a profound impact on mental health, as chronic inflammation has been linked to conditions like depression and anxiety. Consuming foods high in antioxidants, omega-3 fatty acids, and phytonutrients can help reduce inflammation, combat oxidative stress, and support the body's immune response. By incorporating anti-inflammatory foods into their diet, individuals can protect their brain health, reduce the risk of mental health disorders, and promote overall well-being.

The connection between gut health and mental health is another important aspect of nutrition, as the gut microbiome plays a significant role in neurotransmitter production, inflammation regulation, and communication with the brain. A diet rich in fiber, prebiotics, and probiotics can support a healthy gut microbiome, improve digestion, and positively impact mental health outcomes. By nurturing their gut health through proper nutrition, individuals can enhance their mood, cognition, and overall mental well-being.

Moreover, nutrition influences the body's response to stress, with certain nutrients playing a role in the production of stress hormones like cortisol. Consuming foods rich in magnesium, vitamin C, and B vitamins can support the body's stress response system, reduce the impact of chronic stress on mental health, and promote resilience. By incorporating stress-reducing nutrients into their diet, individuals can better manage stress, anxiety, and the physiological effects of prolonged stress on mental well-being.

Cognitive function, memory retention, and focus are also influenced by nutrition, with specific nutrients supporting brain health and neuroplasticity. Antioxidants, omega-3 fatty acids, and B vitamins have been shown to enhance cognitive performance, protect brain cells, and promote neural connectivity. By consuming a diet that prioritizes these brain-boosting nutrients, individuals can improve their cognitive function, memory recall, and mental clarity, contributing to overall mental health and well-being.

Nutrition also plays a pivotal role in the prevention and management of mental health disorders, with research indicating that dietary patterns can influence the risk of conditions like depression, anxiety, and cognitive decline. Diets rich in fruits, vegetables, whole grains, and healthy fats, such as the Mediterranean diet, have been associated with lower rates of depression and cognitive impairment. By adopting a nutrient-dense diet that supports brain health and overall well-being, individuals can reduce their susceptibility to mental health conditions and promote long-term mental wellness.

In conclusion, the profound impact of nutrition on mental health underscores the importance of making informed dietary choices to support brain function, mood regulation, cognitive performance, and emotional well-being. By recognizing the link between nutrition and mental health, individuals can prioritize a balanced and nutrient-rich diet that provides the essential nutrients needed for optimal brain health and neurotransmitter balance. Embracing a holistic approach to mental health that includes a focus on nutrition empowers individuals to take proactive steps towards enhancing their mental well-being and achieving a healthier relationship with food and their minds.

Chapter Thirty Nine:

The Importance of Sleep

Sleep plays a vital role in promoting mental health and overall well-being. Adequate and restful sleep is essential for cognitive function, emotional regulation, stress management, and mood stability. The quality and quantity of sleep directly impact various aspects of mental health, including memory consolidation, decision-making, problem-solving, and resilience to stress. Understanding the importance of sleep for mental health is crucial for individuals to prioritize healthy sleep habits and optimize their psychological well-being.

One of the primary functions of sleep is to support cognitive performance and memory consolidation. During sleep, the brain processes information acquired during the day, consolidates memories, and strengthens neural connections essential for learning and memory retention. Insufficient or poor-quality sleep can impair cognitive function, memory recall, and information processing, leading to difficulties in concentration, decision-making, and overall cognitive performance.

Furthermore, sleep plays a critical role in emotional regulation and mood stability. Adequate sleep is essential for managing emotions, processing stress, and maintaining psychological resilience. Sleep deprivation can disrupt emotional regulation processes, leading to increased irritability, mood swings, heightened stress responses, and a greater susceptibility to mood disorders such as anxiety and depression. Prioritizing quality sleep can help individuals regulate their emotions effectively and promote mental well-being.

In addition to emotional regulation, sleep has a profound impact on stress management and resilience. Restorative sleep is crucial for the body to recover from daily stressors, regulate stress hormones like cortisol, and support the immune system. Chronic sleep deprivation can elevate stress levels, weaken the body's ability to cope with stress, and increase the risk of developing stress-related mental health conditions. By prioritizing adequate sleep, individuals can enhance their resilience to stress and better manage life's challenges.

Moreover, sleep is essential for brain health and neural restoration. During sleep, the brain undergoes crucial processes that promote cellular repair, remove toxins, and support overall brain function. Chronic sleep deprivation has been linked to cognitive decline, impaired brain function, and an increased risk of neurodegenerative disorders. By getting sufficient sleep, individuals can support their brain health, enhance cognitive function, and reduce the risk of cognitive impairment over time.

Furthermore, sleep influences decision-making, problem-solving, and creativity. Adequate sleep fosters cognitive flexibility, enhances problem-solving abilities, and promotes creative thinking. Sleep deprivation can impair cognitive processes, reduce cognitive flexibility, and hinder decision-making skills, leading to decreased productivity and performance. Prioritizing restful sleep can help individuals think more clearly, make better decisions, and approach challenges with greater creativity and innovation.

Additionally, sleep plays a crucial role in maintaining a healthy circadian rhythm, which regulates the body's internal clock and various physiological processes. Disruptions to the circadian rhythm, such as irregular sleep patterns or sleep disturbances, can impact hormone regulation, metabolism, immune function, and mental health. Establishing a consistent sleep schedule and creating a sleep-conducive environment can help individuals align their circadian rhythm, promote hormonal balance, and support overall health and well-being.

Moreover, sleep is essential for physical health and immune function, which are closely linked to mental health. Restorative sleep allows the body to repair tissues, strengthen the immune system, and reduce inflammation. Sleep deprivation, on the other hand, compromises immune function, increases inflammation, and raises the risk of developing physical health problems that can impact mental well-being. Prioritizing quality sleep can boost immune function, reduce inflammation, and support overall physical and mental health.

In addition to its direct effects on mental health, sleep also influences interpersonal relationships and social interactions. Adequate sleep enhances communication skills, empathy, and social behavior, while sleep deprivation can lead to irritability, mood disturbances, and impaired social interactions. By getting enough restful sleep, individuals can improve their social interactions, strengthen relationships, and foster positive connections with others, ultimately contributing to their overall mental well-being.

Furthermore, sleep is essential for regulating appetite, metabolism, and weight management, all of which can impact mental health. Sleep plays a role in appetite regulation by influencing hunger hormones like leptin and ghrelin. Inadequate sleep disrupts these hormones, leading to increased appetite, cravings for unhealthy foods, and weight gain. Poor sleep habits can contribute to metabolic imbalances, obesity, and related health conditions that can negatively affect mental health. Prioritizing sufficient sleep can support healthy eating habits, weight management, and metabolic health, promoting overall well-being.

Additionally, sleep hygiene practices, such as creating a comfortable sleep environment, establishing a relaxing bedtime routine, and avoiding stimulants before bed, are essential for promoting restful sleep and optimal mental health. Creating a sleep-conducive environment can help individuals unwind, relax, and prepare for restorative sleep. By incorporating healthy sleep habits into their daily routine, individuals can improve the quality and duration of their sleep, leading to better mental health outcomes and enhanced overall well-being.

In conclusion, the importance of sleep for mental health cannot be overstated, as adequate and restful sleep is essential for cognitive function, emotional regulation, stress management, and overall well-being. Prioritizing healthy sleep habits, such as maintaining a consistent sleep schedule, creating a comfortable sleep environment, and practicing relaxation techniques, can significantly impact mental health outcomes. By recognizing the critical role of sleep in promoting mental well-being, individuals can take proactive steps to prioritize quality sleep, support their brain health, enhance emotional resilience, and improve overall mental health and quality of life.

Sleep is a fundamental pillar of mental health, playing a crucial role in cognitive function, emotional regulation, stress management, and overall well-being. Adequate and restful sleep is essential for memory consolidation, learning, decision-making, and problem-solving. The brain processes information acquired during the day and consolidates memories during sleep, strengthening neural connections vital for cognitive performance. Insufficient or poor-quality sleep can impair cognitive function, memory recall, and concentration, affecting overall mental clarity and performance.

Emotional regulation and mood stability are significantly influenced by sleep quality. Adequate sleep is essential for processing emotions, managing stress, and maintaining psychological resilience.

Sleep deprivation can disrupt emotional regulation processes, leading to increased irritability, mood swings, and a higher susceptibility to mood disorders like anxiety and depression. Prioritizing quality sleep enables individuals to regulate their emotions effectively, cope with stress, and promote mental well-being.

Furthermore, sleep plays a critical role in stress management and resilience. Restorative sleep allows the body to recover from daily stressors, regulate stress hormones like cortisol, and support the immune system. Chronic sleep deprivation can elevate stress levels, weaken the body's ability to cope with stress, and increase the risk of developing stress-related mental health conditions. By prioritizing adequate sleep, individuals can enhance their resilience to stress, improve coping mechanisms, and maintain psychological well-being.

In addition to emotional and cognitive functions, sleep is essential for brain health and neural restoration. While sleeping, the brain undergoes vital processes that promote cellular repair, remove toxins, and support overall brain function. Chronic sleep deprivation has been associated with cognitive decline, impaired brain function, and an increased risk of neurodegenerative disorders. Getting sufficient sleep is crucial for supporting brain health, enhancing cognitive function, and reducing the risk of cognitive impairment.

Sleep also influences decision-making, problem-solving, and creativity. Adequate sleep promotes cognitive flexibility, enhances problem-solving abilities, and fosters creative thinking. Sleep deprivation can impair cognitive processes, reduce cognitive flexibility, and hinder decision-making skills, leading to decreased productivity and performance. Prioritizing restful sleep helps individuals think clearly, make sound decisions, and approach challenges with creativity and innovation.

Moreover, sleep is essential for maintaining a healthy circadian rhythm, which regulates various physiological processes, including hormone regulation, metabolism, and immune function. Disruptions to the circadian rhythm, such as irregular sleep patterns or sleep disturbances, can impact hormonal balance, metabolism, and overall mental health. Establishing a consistent sleep schedule and creating a sleep-conducive environment can help individuals align their circadian rhythm, promote hormonal balance, and support overall health and well-being.

In addition to its direct effects on mental health, sleep also influences physical health, immune function, interpersonal relationships, and weight management. Adequate sleep supports immune function, reduces inflammation, enhances social interactions, and regulates appetite and metabolism. Poor sleep habits can lead to compromised immune function, increased inflammation, impaired social interactions, and disruptions in appetite regulation, potentially affecting both physical and mental well-being. Prioritizing quality sleep is essential for supporting overall health, enhancing interpersonal relationships, and promoting optimal mental well-being.

By incorporating healthy sleep practices into daily routines and recognizing the critical role of sleep in mental health, individuals can take proactive steps to prioritize restful sleep, support brain health, enhance emotional resilience, and improve overall well-being. Embracing the importance of sleep as a key component of mental health can lead to positive outcomes in cognitive function, emotional well-being, stress management, and overall quality of life.

Chapter Forty:

E ngaging in Relaxation Techniques
Engaging in relaxation techniques is a beneficial practice that can have a profound impact on mental health and overall well-being. Relaxation techniques encompass a variety of strategies and activities designed to promote relaxation, reduce stress, and enhance feelings of calmness and inner peace. These techniques can help individuals manage anxiety, improve mood, increase self-awareness, and cultivate a sense of balance in their lives. By incorporating relaxation techniques into daily routines, individuals can effectively cope with stress, promote mental clarity, and support their emotional and psychological health.

One commonly practiced relaxation technique is deep breathing exercises, which involve taking slow, deep breaths to activate the body's relaxation response. Deep breathing can help reduce anxiety, lower blood pressure, and promote a sense of calm. By focusing on their breath and engaging in rhythmic breathing patterns, individuals can center themselves, alleviate tension, and enhance their overall well-being. Deep breathing exercises are easily accessible and can be practiced anywhere, making them a convenient tool for relaxation.

Another popular relaxation technique is progressive muscle relaxation, which involves systematically tensing and relaxing different muscle groups to release physical tension and promote relaxation. By consciously tensing and then relaxing muscle groups throughout the body, individuals can increase body awareness, reduce muscle stiffness, and experience a deep sense of relaxation. Progressive muscle relaxation can be particularly beneficial for individuals who carry physical stress and tension in their bodies, helping them unwind and release built-up stress.

Mindfulness meditation is a powerful relaxation technique that involves focusing on the present moment without judgment. Through mindfulness practices, individuals can cultivate awareness, reduce rumination, and develop a greater sense of clarity and perspective. Mindfulness meditation can help individuals manage stress, improve concentration, and enhance emotional well-being by fostering a non-reactive and accepting attitude towards their thoughts and feelings. Regular practice of mindfulness meditation can lead to increased resilience, improved emotional regulation, and a greater sense of inner peace.

Guided imagery is another effective relaxation technique that involves visualizing calming and peaceful scenes or experiences to evoke a sense of relaxation and mental clarity. By creating vivid mental images of serene landscapes, soothing environments, or positive outcomes, individuals can reduce anxiety, enhance relaxation, and promote a sense of well-being. Guided imagery can be practiced independently or with the guidance of a trained professional or audio recording, making it a versatile and accessible relaxation tool for managing stress and promoting mental health.

Progressive relaxation techniques, such as autogenic training, involve focusing on physical sensations and promoting a sense of relaxation through self-suggestion and visualization. Autogenic training aims to create a state of deep relaxation by focusing on sensations like warmth, heaviness, and calmness in different parts of the body. By repeating affirmations and visualizing sensations of relaxation, individuals can induce a state of calm and reduce stress levels. Autogenic training can be an effective technique for promoting relaxation, enhancing self-awareness, and fostering a mind-body connection.

Yoga and tai chi are ancient practices that combine physical movement, breath control, and mindfulness to promote relaxation, flexibility, and overall well-being. Both yoga and tai chi have been shown to reduce stress, increase body awareness, and improve mental health by integrating movement with breath awareness and meditation. These practices can help individuals release tension, improve posture, and cultivate a sense of inner peace through gentle, flowing movements and mindful breathing techniques. Regular practice of yoga or tai chi can enhance physical and mental well-being, reduce stress levels, and promote relaxation.

Aromatherapy is a relaxation technique that involves using essential oils derived from plants to promote relaxation, reduce stress, and enhance mood. Inhalation or topical application of essential oils can have calming effects on the mind and body, triggering positive emotional responses and promoting relaxation. Scents like lavender, chamomile, and bergamot are commonly used in aromatherapy to induce feelings of relaxation, reduce anxiety, and create a calming atmosphere. Aromatherapy can be incorporated into daily routines through diffusers, massage oils, or bath products, making it a convenient and enjoyable relaxation practice.

Music therapy is a relaxation technique that utilizes music and sound to promote relaxation, reduce stress, and improve emotional well-being. Listening to calming music, playing musical instruments, or engaging in rhythmic activities can have a soothing effect on the mind and body, helping individuals unwind and release tension. Music therapy has been shown to reduce anxiety, enhance mood, and promote relaxation by stimulating the brain's emotional centers and promoting a sense of harmony and tranquility. Incorporating music therapy into daily routines can be a creative and enjoyable way to manage stress and support mental health.

Journaling is a relaxation technique that involves writing down thoughts, feelings, and experiences to promote self-reflection, emotional processing, and stress relief. Journaling can help individuals express emotions, gain insight into their thoughts and behaviors, and reduce psychological distress. By documenting their thoughts and emotions in a journal, individuals can identify patterns, set goals, and work through challenging emotions, leading to increased self-awareness and emotional well-being. Regular journaling can be a therapeutic practice for managing stress, enhancing self-care, and fostering personal growth.

Nature therapy, or ecotherapy, is a relaxation technique that involves spending time in natural environments to promote relaxation, reduce stress, and improve mental health. Connecting with nature through activities like hiking, gardening, or simply spending time outdoors can have a calming effect on the mind and body, reducing anxiety and enhancing well-being. Nature therapy has been associated with improved mood, reduced stress levels, and increased feelings of relaxation and rejuvenation. Immersing oneself in nature can be a powerful relaxation practice that fosters a sense of connection with the natural world and promotes overall mental well-being.

Laughter therapy is a relaxation technique that involves engaging in activities that promote laughter and humor to reduce stress, enhance mood, and improve emotional well-being. Laughter has been shown to have numerous mental health benefits, including reducing anxiety, boosting mood, and promoting relaxation by releasing endorphins and reducing stress hormones. Engaging in laughter therapy through activities like watching comedies, socializing with friends, or practicing laughter yoga can be a fun and effective way to manage stress, improve emotional health, and foster a positive outlook on life.

In conclusion, engaging in relaxation techniques is a valuable practice for promoting mental health, managing stress, and enhancing overall well-being. By incorporating a variety of relaxation techniques into daily routines, individuals can cultivate a sense of calm, reduce anxiety, improve emotional regulation, and support their psychological health. Whether through deep breathing exercises, mindfulness meditation, guided imagery, or other relaxation practices, individuals can find effective ways to unwind, release tension, and nurture their mental well-being. Embracing relaxation techniques as part of a holistic self-care routine empowers individuals to prioritize their mental health, cope with life's challenges, and cultivate a sense of balance and peace in their lives.

Engaging in relaxation techniques is a powerful way to promote mental health, manage stress, and enhance overall well-being. By incorporating these practices into daily routines, individuals can experience a profound impact on their emotional state, cognitive function, and physical health. Relaxation techniques encompass a wide range of strategies, such as deep breathing exercises, progressive muscle relaxation, mindfulness meditation, guided imagery, and more, each offering unique benefits for relaxation and stress reduction. These techniques provide individuals with effective tools to cope with anxiety, improve mood, increase self-awareness, and cultivate a sense of inner peace.

Deep breathing exercises are a simple yet effective relaxation technique that helps activate the body's relaxation response. By focusing on slow, deep breaths, individuals can reduce anxiety, lower blood pressure, and promote a sense of calmness and relaxation. Deep breathing can be practiced anywhere and at any time, making it a convenient tool for managing stress and promoting emotional well-being. This technique is particularly beneficial for individuals looking to center themselves, alleviate tension, and enhance their overall sense of well-being.

Progressive muscle relaxation involves systematically tensing and relaxing different muscle groups in the body to release physical tension and promote relaxation. By engaging in this practice, individuals can increase body awareness, reduce muscle stiffness, and experience a deep sense of relaxation. Progressive muscle relaxation is an effective technique for unwinding and releasing built-up stress, making it a valuable tool for those seeking to alleviate physical tension and promote overall relaxation.

Mindfulness meditation is a powerful relaxation technique that involves focusing on the present moment without judgment. Through mindfulness practices, individuals can cultivate awareness, reduce rumination, and develop greater mental clarity and emotional balance. Mindfulness meditation can help individuals manage stress, improve concentration, and enhance emotional well-being by fostering a non-reactive and accepting attitude towards thoughts and feelings. Regular practice of mindfulness meditation can lead to increased resilience, improved emotional regulation, and a greater sense of inner peace.

Guided imagery is another effective relaxation technique that involves visualizing calming and peaceful scenes or experiences to evoke relaxation and mental clarity. By creating vivid mental images of serene landscapes or positive outcomes, individuals can reduce anxiety, enhance relaxation, and promote a sense of well-being. Guided imagery can be practiced independently or with the guidance of a professional or audio recording, making it a versatile tool for managing stress and supporting mental health.

Yoga and tai chi are ancient practices that combine physical movement, breath control, and mindfulness to promote relaxation, flexibility, and overall well-being. Both practices have been shown to reduce stress, increase body awareness, and improve mental health by integrating movement with breath awareness and meditation. Through gentle, flowing movements and mindful breathing techniques, yoga and tai chi help individuals release tension, improve posture, and cultivate a sense of inner peace. Regular practice of these disciplines can enhance physical and mental well-being, reduce stress levels, and promote relaxation.

Chapter Forty One:

Understanding Your Emotions

Understanding your emotions is a crucial aspect of mental health that often goes overlooked. Emotions are complex reactions that involve physical, cognitive, and behavioral components. They can significantly influence how we perceive ourselves and the world around us. Recognizing and understanding your emotions is the first step toward managing them effectively, leading to improved mental well-being.

Emotions can be categorized into primary and secondary emotions. Primary emotions are the immediate responses to stimuli, such as happiness, sadness, anger, fear, and surprise. These emotions are universal and instinctual, often serving as signals to guide our behavior. Secondary emotions, on the other hand, are more complex and can arise from how we interpret or react to our primary emotions. For instance, feeling ashamed of being angry can lead to guilt, which complicates our emotional landscape.

The importance of emotional awareness cannot be overstated. Being aware of your emotions allows you to identify triggers and patterns in your behavior. This understanding can help you develop coping strategies to manage stress and anxiety. Keeping a journal can be a helpful tool in this process, allowing you to express your feelings and recognize trends over time. Reflecting on your emotions can also enhance self-awareness and lead to greater emotional intelligence.

Coping with negative emotions is an essential part of maintaining mental health. Negative emotions, such as anger, sadness, or fear, are natural and can serve important purposes. For example, fear can protect you from danger, while sadness can signal the need for support. However, when these emotions become overwhelming, they can lead to mental health issues such as depression or anxiety. Therefore, finding healthy outlets for these emotions, such as talking to a friend or engaging in physical activity, is vital.

Emotional regulation is another critical component of mental health. This refers to the ability to manage and respond to your emotions in a healthy way. Techniques such as mindfulness, deep breathing, and cognitive restructuring can help you gain control over your emotional responses. By practicing these techniques, you can learn to pause and reflect before reacting, allowing for more thoughtful and constructive responses to challenging situations.

Understanding the impact of emotions on physical health is also essential. There is a significant connection between mental and physical health, and prolonged negative emotions can manifest in physical symptoms. Stress, for instance, can lead to headaches, fatigue, and a weakened immune system. Therefore, managing your emotions effectively can have a positive impact on your overall health and well-being.

Seeking professional help is often a beneficial step for those struggling with their emotions. Therapists and counselors can provide valuable insights and coping strategies tailored to your specific needs. They can help you explore the root causes of your emotions and offer tools to manage them effectively. Therapy is not just for those with severe mental health issues; it can be a useful resource for anyone seeking to improve their emotional well-being.

Building a support network is another vital aspect of understanding your emotions. Surrounding yourself with friends, family, or support groups can provide a safe space to share your feelings. Social connections can offer perspective and validation, making it easier to cope with difficult emotions. Engaging with others who understand your experiences can also foster a sense of belonging and reduce feelings of isolation.

Additionally, practicing self-compassion is crucial in understanding your emotions. Being kind to yourself during difficult times can help mitigate the impact of negative emotions. Self-compassion involves recognizing that everyone struggles with their feelings and that it's okay to experience a range of emotions. Treating yourself with the same kindness you would offer a friend can promote resilience and emotional healing.

The role of creativity in emotional expression should not be overlooked. Engaging in creative activities, such as painting, writing, or music, can provide a powerful outlet for emotions. Creativity allows for self-expression and can be a therapeutic process, helping to clarify feelings and reduce anxiety. This form of expression can also lead to a sense of accomplishment and joy, further contributing to mental health.

Finally, understanding your emotions is an ongoing journey. Emotions are fluid and can change from moment to moment, influenced by various factors such as environment, relationships, and personal experiences. Embracing this fluidity and allowing yourself to feel a range of emotions without judgment can lead to greater emotional resilience. Continuous self-reflection and a commitment to personal growth are key to navigating the complexities of your emotional landscape.

In conclusion, understanding your emotions is fundamental to maintaining mental health. It involves recognizing the different types of emotions, developing coping strategies, and seeking support when needed. By fostering emotional awareness and practicing self-compassion, you can cultivate a healthier relationship with your emotions, ultimately leading to improved mental well-being.

Understanding your emotions is vital for maintaining mental health, as it allows you to navigate the complexities of your feelings and reactions. Emotions are multifaceted, encompassing physical sensations, thoughts, and behavioral responses. By developing a deeper awareness of your emotions, you can better manage them, leading to enhanced mental well-being and a more fulfilling life.

Emotions can be broadly categorized into primary and secondary types. Primary emotions are instinctual responses that arise immediately in reaction to stimuli, such as joy, sadness, anger, fear, and surprise. These emotions serve as essential signals that guide our behavior and decision-making processes. In contrast, secondary emotions are more nuanced and typically emerge from our interpretations of primary emotions. For instance, feeling angry may lead to guilt if you believe that expressing anger is inappropriate. Understanding these distinctions can help you unravel the complexity of your emotional experiences.

Emotional awareness is crucial for self-understanding and personal growth. By identifying your emotions and their triggers, you can uncover patterns in your behavior and responses. Keeping a journal can be an effective way to document your feelings and reflect on them over time. This practice not only promotes emotional clarity but also enhances self-awareness, allowing you to recognize how your emotions influence your thoughts and actions.

Coping with negative emotions is an integral part of maintaining mental health. Emotions like anger, sadness, and fear are natural and can serve important functions in our lives. For example, fear can alert us to potential dangers, while sadness can signal the need for support from others. However, when negative emotions become overwhelming, they can lead to mental health challenges such as anxiety or depression. Finding healthy ways to express and cope with these emotions, such as through physical activity or talking with a friend, is essential for emotional resilience.

Emotional regulation is another critical aspect of mental well-being. This involves managing your emotional responses in a constructive manner. Techniques such as mindfulness, deep breathing, and cognitive restructuring can help you gain greater control over your emotions. By learning to pause and reflect before reacting, you can respond to challenging situations with thoughtfulness rather than impulsivity. This practice can lead to healthier relationships and improved mental health.

The connection between emotions and physical health is significant. Prolonged negative emotions can manifest in physical symptoms, such as headaches, fatigue, and a weakened immune system. This mind-body connection underscores the importance of emotional management for overall health. By addressing your emotions, you can positively influence your physical well-being and reduce the risk of stress-related health issues.

Seeking professional help can also be a beneficial step for those struggling with their emotions. Therapists and counselors offer valuable insights and coping strategies tailored to individual needs. They can help you explore the root causes of your emotions and provide tools to manage them effectively. Therapy is not solely for those facing severe mental health issues; it can be a valuable resource for anyone looking to enhance their emotional well-being.

Building a support network is another vital component of understanding your emotions. Surrounding yourself with friends, family, or support groups creates a safe space for sharing feelings. Social connections can offer perspective, validation, and encouragement, making it easier to cope with difficult emotions. Engaging with others who share similar experiences fosters a sense of belonging and can help diminish feelings of isolation.

Practicing self-compassion is essential for emotional understanding and resilience. Being kind to yourself during challenging times allows you to acknowledge your emotions without judgment. Everyone experiences struggles, and it's important to remember that it's okay to feel a range of emotions. Treating yourself with the same kindness you would offer a friend can promote healing and resilience as you navigate your emotional landscape.

Finally, understanding your emotions is an ongoing journey that requires continuous self-reflection and growth. Emotions are dynamic and can change based on various factors, such as your environment and personal experiences. Embracing this fluidity and allowing yourself to experience a wide range of emotions can lead to greater emotional resilience. By committing to this journey, you can cultivate a healthier relationship with your emotions, ultimately enhancing your mental well-being and quality of life.

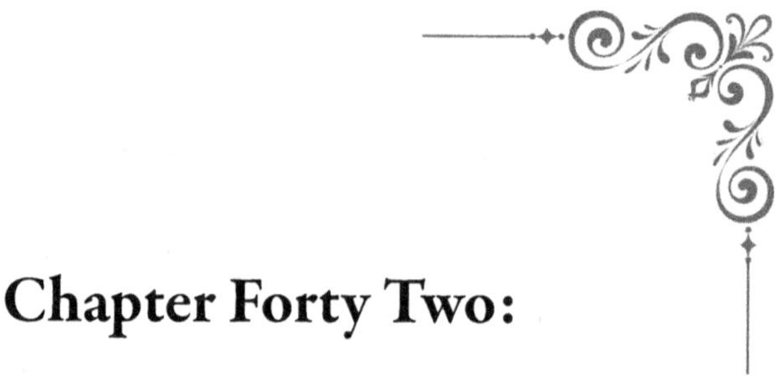

Chapter Forty Two:

Developing Empathy and Compassion
Mental health is an integral aspect of overall well-being, yet it often remains shrouded in stigma and misunderstanding. Developing empathy and compassion towards individuals dealing with mental health issues is crucial for fostering a supportive society. Empathy allows us to understand and share the feelings of others, while compassion drives us to take action to alleviate their suffering. Together, these qualities can create a more inclusive and understanding environment for those facing mental health challenges.

Empathy plays a vital role in breaking down the barriers of stigma associated with mental health. When we take the time to listen and understand the experiences of those struggling with mental illness, we begin to challenge preconceived notions and stereotypes. This understanding can help shift societal attitudes, making it easier for individuals to seek help without fear of judgment. As people become more empathetic, they contribute to a culture that values mental wellness and supports those who are affected.

Compassion, on the other hand, motivates us to take concrete actions that can improve the lives of others. It prompts us to offer support, whether that be through active listening, providing resources, or simply being present for someone in need. Such actions can make a significant difference in the lives of individuals coping with mental health challenges, helping them feel less isolated and more valued. When compassion is cultivated within communities, it creates a ripple effect that encourages others to engage in acts of kindness.

One of the key benefits of developing empathy and compassion is that it enhances our relationships. When we approach others with an open heart and a willingness to understand their struggles, we foster deeper connections. This is particularly important in a world where mental health issues can create feelings of isolation. Building compassionate relationships can provide individuals with a sense of belonging and support, which is essential for recovery and healing.

Furthermore, empathy and compassion can improve our own mental health. Engaging in acts of kindness and understanding not only benefits others but also elevates our own well-being. Studies have shown that helping others can lead to increased feelings of happiness and fulfillment. By developing these qualities, we create a positive feedback loop that nurtures our mental health while simultaneously supporting those around us.

In educational settings, teaching empathy and compassion can have a profound impact on students' understanding of mental health. Incorporating these values into the curriculum can help young people become more aware of mental health issues and how to address them compassionately. This foundational understanding can equip future generations with the tools they need to foster a more empathetic society, ultimately leading to better mental health outcomes for all.

The workplace also stands to benefit from an emphasis on empathy and compassion. Employers who cultivate a culture of understanding are more likely to retain employees and create a more productive work environment. When individuals feel supported and understood in their mental health journeys, they are better equipped to contribute to their teams. This can lead to reduced absenteeism and increased job satisfaction, creating a win-win situation for both employees and employers.

In the realm of healthcare, empathy and compassion are essential components of effective patient care. Mental health professionals who approach their patients with understanding and kindness are more likely to build trust and rapport. This can lead to better treatment outcomes, as patients feel safe to share their experiences and engage in their recovery process. By prioritizing empathy in mental health treatment, we can create a more compassionate healthcare system.

Advocacy for mental health awareness is also strengthened by empathy and compassion. Individuals who have a personal understanding of mental health struggles are often the most effective advocates. Their ability to share their experiences with empathy can resonate with others, fostering a sense of community and encouraging further dialogue about mental health. This grassroots approach to advocacy can lead to systemic changes that benefit those affected by mental illness.

Moreover, developing empathy and compassion is a lifelong journey. It requires ongoing reflection and a commitment to understanding the experiences of others. Engaging in conversations about mental health, participating in community support initiatives, and educating ourselves about mental health issues are all ways to nurture these qualities. As we grow in our empathy and compassion, we become better equipped to support those around us.

In conclusion, the importance of developing empathy and compassion around mental health cannot be overstated. These qualities are essential for breaking down stigma, enhancing relationships, and improving overall mental health outcomes. By fostering a culture of understanding and kindness, we can create a more inclusive society where individuals feel safe and supported in their mental health journeys. It is a collective responsibility to cultivate empathy and compassion, paving the way for a brighter future for all.

Expanding on the significance of developing empathy and compassion in the context of mental health, it is essential to recognize the role of personal stories in fostering understanding. When individuals share their experiences with mental health challenges, they humanize the issue and allow others to see beyond clinical definitions. Personal narratives can evoke empathy in listeners, making them more receptive to the realities surrounding mental illness. This connection can lead to increased awareness and a collective push towards a more compassionate society.

Another critical aspect is the role of social media in shaping perceptions of mental health. In recent years, platforms like Instagram, Twitter, and Facebook have become avenues for individuals to express their struggles openly. These platforms can serve as powerful tools for empathy and compassion by creating communities where individuals feel safe to share their stories. When followers engage with these narratives positively, it can foster a sense of understanding and solidarity, breaking down the walls of isolation that often accompany mental health issues.

In the context of familial relationships, empathy and compassion can be transformative. Family members who cultivate these qualities can create a safe space for loved ones dealing with mental health challenges. This support can encourage open communication and strengthen family bonds, making it easier for individuals to seek help when needed. Empathetic family dynamics can also significantly reduce feelings of shame and guilt often associated with mental illness, paving the way for healing and recovery.

Moreover, developing empathy and compassion can play a vital role in reducing suicide rates. When individuals feel understood and supported, they are less likely to experience feelings of hopelessness and despair. Community initiatives that promote mental health awareness and encourage open discussions can help identify individuals in crisis and connect them with necessary resources. By fostering a culture of compassion, we can create an environment where individuals feel comfortable reaching out for help, potentially saving lives.

Additionally, workplaces that prioritize empathy and compassion can enhance overall productivity and morale. Organizations that provide mental health training for employees can cultivate a culture of understanding, equipping staff with the tools to support one another. Such initiatives not only benefit employees' mental health but also contribute to a more cohesive and motivated team. A compassionate workplace environment encourages open dialogue about mental health, helping to normalize conversations that were once considered taboo.

Educational institutions must also recognize the importance of empathy and compassion in shaping young minds. By integrating social-emotional learning into the curriculum, schools can teach students to recognize their emotions and those of others. This approach not only fosters empathy but also equips students with conflict resolution skills and emotional intelligence. As students learn to navigate their own feelings and understand their peers, they become more empathetic individuals, prepared to contribute positively to society.

Furthermore, the role of community organizations in promoting empathy and compassion cannot be overlooked. Local initiatives that offer mental health support, awareness campaigns, and workshops can help create a more informed public. These organizations often serve as a bridge between individuals in need and the resources available to them. By actively participating in community efforts, individuals can contribute to a culture that values empathy and compassion while also enhancing their understanding of mental health.

Lastly, the journey toward developing empathy and compassion is ongoing and requires commitment from all members of society. It involves continuous learning, unlearning biases, and actively engaging in conversations about mental health. Building these qualities takes time, but the rewards are profound. As we work towards fostering empathy and compassion, we contribute to the creation of a society where mental health is prioritized, and individuals feel supported in their journeys toward wellness.

In summary, developing empathy and compassion around mental health is a multifaceted endeavor that requires participation from individuals, families, workplaces, educational institutions, and communities. By prioritizing understanding and kindness, we can cultivate a society that values mental well-being, reduces stigma, and supports those facing mental health challenges. It is a collective effort that promises to yield significant benefits for everyone involved.

Chapter Forty Three:

Managing Stress Effectively

Stress is an inevitable part of life, but how we manage it can significantly impact our mental health. Understanding the importance of effective stress management is crucial for maintaining emotional well-being and fostering resilience in the face of challenges. Stress can arise from various sources, including work, relationships, and personal challenges, and if left unmanaged, it can lead to serious mental health issues such as anxiety and depression.

One of the primary reasons effective stress management is essential is that chronic stress can have detrimental effects on both physical and mental health. Prolonged exposure to stress can lead to a range of physical health issues, including cardiovascular disease, digestive problems, and weakened immune function. When the body is in a constant state of stress, it can also contribute to mental health problems, making it crucial to develop strategies for managing stress effectively to preserve overall health.

Managing stress helps individuals maintain a sense of control over their lives. When stress becomes overwhelming, it can create feelings of helplessness and hopelessness. By implementing effective stress management techniques, individuals can regain a sense of agency and empowerment. This can involve setting realistic goals, prioritizing tasks, and learning to say no, ultimately leading to improved mental clarity and reduced anxiety.

Moreover, effective stress management enhances emotional regulation. Learning to identify and cope with stressors allows individuals to process their emotions more effectively. By employing techniques such as mindfulness, meditation, or journaling, individuals can cultivate greater self-awareness and emotional intelligence. This heightened awareness can help in identifying triggers and developing healthier responses to stress, ultimately supporting mental health.

Social support plays a vital role in managing stress effectively. Engaging with friends, family, or support groups can provide a valuable outlet for expressing feelings and sharing experiences. Such connections can reduce feelings of isolation and foster a sense of belonging, making it easier to cope with stress. Building a robust support network can be a protective factor against the negative effects of stress, enhancing overall mental well-being.

In addition to social support, incorporating regular physical activity into one's routine is another effective stress management strategy. Exercise has been shown to release endorphins, which are natural mood boosters. Physical activity can also serve as a distraction from stressors, allowing individuals to clear their minds and focus on their well-being. Whether through walking, yoga, or team sports, finding an enjoyable form of exercise can significantly improve mental health.

Time management is another critical aspect of stress management. Many individuals experience stress due to feeling overwhelmed by competing demands on their time. By developing effective time management skills, individuals can prioritize tasks, set boundaries, and allocate time for self-care. This can lead to a more balanced lifestyle, reducing stress levels and promoting a healthier outlook on life.

Another important consideration is the impact of nutrition on stress levels. A well-balanced diet rich in essential nutrients can support mental health and resilience. Foods high in omega-3 fatty acids, antioxidants, and vitamins can help regulate mood and reduce stress. Conversely, excessive consumption of caffeine, sugar, or processed foods can exacerbate stress levels. Making mindful dietary choices can be an effective strategy for managing stress and supporting overall mental health.

Sleep plays a crucial role in stress management as well. Poor sleep quality can amplify stress and negatively impact mental health. Establishing a consistent sleep routine, creating a calming bedtime environment, and practicing relaxation techniques can improve sleep quality and help individuals manage stress more effectively. Prioritizing restorative sleep is essential for maintaining emotional balance and resilience.

In the workplace, fostering a culture that prioritizes mental health and stress management is essential. Employers can implement policies that promote work-life balance, such as flexible working hours or mental health days. Additionally, providing resources for stress management, such as workshops or access to counseling, can empower employees to take charge of their mental well-being. A supportive work environment not only enhances employee morale but also boosts productivity and reduces burnout.

Furthermore, seeking professional help can be a vital step in managing stress effectively. Mental health professionals, such as therapists or counselors, can provide valuable guidance and support tailored to individual needs. They can help individuals develop coping strategies, explore underlying issues, and navigate life's challenges more effectively. Professional support can be a game-changer for those struggling with chronic stress or mental health concerns.

Ultimately, managing stress effectively is an ongoing process that requires self-awareness and commitment. It is essential to recognize that different strategies work for different individuals, and finding the right approach may take time. By exploring various techniques, individuals can discover what resonates with them and build a personalized stress management toolkit that supports their mental health.

In conclusion, the importance of managing stress effectively cannot be overstated. It is a critical component of maintaining mental health and overall well-being. By implementing effective stress management techniques, individuals can reduce the negative impact of stress, enhance emotional resilience, and foster a healthier, more balanced life. Prioritizing stress management is an investment in oneself that pays dividends in mental health and quality of life.

Stress is an unavoidable aspect of life that everyone experiences at some point. However, how we manage this stress can significantly influence our mental health and overall well-being. Effective stress management is essential for maintaining emotional stability and fostering resilience in the face of life's challenges. When stress is left unchecked, it can lead to serious mental health issues, including anxiety, depression, and burnout. Understanding the importance of managing stress effectively is crucial for supporting mental health.

Chronic stress can have detrimental effects not only on mental health but also on physical health. Prolonged exposure to stress can result in various health problems, such as cardiovascular issues, digestive disorders, and a weakened immune system. When the body remains in a constant state of stress, it can create a cycle of mental health problems, which emphasizes the need for effective stress management techniques. By learning to identify and manage stressors, individuals can protect their mental and physical health.

One of the primary benefits of managing stress effectively is the restoration of a sense of control over one's life. When stress becomes overwhelming, feelings of helplessness can arise. However, by implementing stress management strategies, such as setting realistic goals, prioritizing tasks, and learning to say no, individuals can regain a sense of agency. This empowerment can lead to improved mental clarity and reduced anxiety, ultimately enhancing overall emotional well-being.

Social support is another crucial element in managing stress effectively. Engaging with friends, family, or support groups can provide individuals with an outlet for expressing their feelings and sharing experiences. Connecting with others helps reduce feelings of isolation and fosters a sense of belonging, making it easier to cope with stress. Building a solid support network can serve as a protective factor against the negative effects of stress, enhancing mental health and resilience.

Incorporating regular physical activity into one's routine is an effective strategy for managing stress. Exercise has been shown to release endorphins, which are natural mood boosters, and serve as a distraction from stressors. Engaging in enjoyable forms of exercise whether it be walking, yoga, or team sports can significantly improve mental health. Physical activity not only helps alleviate stress but also promotes overall well-being and resilience.

Time management is a critical aspect of stress management as well. Many individuals experience stress due to feeling overwhelmed by competing demands on their time. Developing effective time management skills allows individuals to prioritize tasks, set boundaries, and allocate time for self-care. This can lead to a more balanced lifestyle, ultimately reducing stress levels and promoting a healthier outlook on life. By managing time effectively, individuals can create space for relaxation and rejuvenation.

In addition to these strategies, seeking professional help can be vital for those struggling with chronic stress. Mental health professionals, such as therapists or counselors, can provide valuable guidance tailored to individual needs. They can assist individuals in developing coping strategies, exploring underlying issues, and navigating life's challenges more effectively. Professional support can be transformative in managing stress and improving mental health.

In conclusion, managing stress effectively is essential for maintaining mental health and overall well-being. By implementing various stress management techniques, individuals can reduce the negative impact of stress and enhance emotional resilience. Prioritizing stress management is an investment in oneself that leads to improved mental health, healthier relationships, and a better quality of life. A proactive approach to stress management empowers individuals to navigate life's challenges with confidence and strength.

Chapter Forty Four:

Nurturing Healthy Relationships

Nurturing healthy relationships is essential for maintaining good mental health. Our connections with others can significantly influence our emotional well-being. Positive relationships provide a support system that can help us navigate life's challenges, reduce stress, and enhance our overall happiness. When we cultivate these connections, we foster an environment where we can share our thoughts and feelings freely, promoting understanding and empathy.

One of the foundational elements of nurturing healthy relationships is effective communication. Open and honest dialogue allows individuals to express their needs, concerns, and emotions without fear of judgment. When both parties feel heard and valued, it creates a safe space for vulnerability. This transparency not only strengthens bonds but also mitigates misunderstandings that can lead to conflict and emotional distress.

Empathy plays a crucial role in nurturing relationships. By putting ourselves in others' shoes, we can better understand their perspectives and emotions. This practice fosters compassion and connection, enabling us to support our loved ones in meaningful ways. When we demonstrate empathy, we validate others' feelings, which can be incredibly healing for both parties involved.

Setting healthy boundaries is another key aspect of nurturing relationships. Boundaries help establish what is acceptable and what is not, allowing individuals to feel safe and respected. When boundaries are clearly defined, it reduces the likelihood of resentment and conflict. Moreover, respecting each other's boundaries reinforces trust, which is vital for any healthy relationship.

The quality of our relationships can greatly impact our mental health. Positive relationships are associated with lower levels of anxiety and depression, while toxic relationships can contribute to emotional turmoil. It is essential to recognize when a relationship is harmful and to take steps to address or distance ourselves from negative influences. Surrounding ourselves with supportive and uplifting individuals can significantly enhance our emotional resilience.

In nurturing healthy relationships, it is also important to practice gratitude. Expressing appreciation for the people in our lives fosters a sense of connection and positivity. Simple gestures, such as saying "thank you" or acknowledging someone's efforts, can strengthen bonds and promote a supportive atmosphere. Gratitude can also shift our focus from negativity to the positive aspects of our relationships.

Engaging in shared activities can further enhance relationships. Whether it's participating in a hobby, exercising together, or simply spending quality time, these shared experiences create lasting memories and deepen connections. Engaging in enjoyable activities together can also serve as a natural stress reliever, allowing individuals to unwind and enjoy each other's company without the pressures of daily life.

Conflict resolution is an inevitable aspect of any relationship. However, how we approach conflicts can determine the health of our relationships. Instead of resorting to blame or avoidance, addressing issues with a problem-solving mindset can lead to growth and understanding. Learning to navigate disagreements respectfully can strengthen the bond between individuals and foster a greater sense of teamwork.

Mental health awareness within relationships is crucial. Understanding each other's mental health needs and being supportive during difficult times can create a nurturing environment. When partners, friends, or family members are aware of each other's emotional states, they can offer appropriate support and encouragement. This awareness can also help in recognizing signs of distress early on, allowing for timely intervention.

Self-care plays a significant role in nurturing relationships as well. When individuals prioritize their own mental health, they are better equipped to be present and supportive in their relationships. Engaging in self-care practices, such as mindfulness, exercise, or pursuing personal interests, can enhance one's emotional well-being. A healthy individual contributes positively to their relationships, creating a cycle of support and care.

Nurturing healthy relationships also involves being adaptable. Life is full of changes, and relationships must evolve to thrive. Being open to change and willing to adjust expectations can help individuals navigate transitions together. Whether it's a new job, relocation, or personal growth, adapting to these changes can strengthen the bond and foster resilience.

In conclusion, nurturing healthy relationships is a vital component of mental health. By fostering open communication, empathy, and mutual respect, individuals can create supportive environments that enhance emotional well-being. Recognizing the impact of relationships on mental health encourages us to invest time and energy into cultivating connections that promote happiness and resilience. As we prioritize our relationships, we not only improve our own mental health but also contribute positively to the well-being of those around us.

Nurturing healthy relationships is fundamental to maintaining good mental health. Our connections with others can significantly impact our emotional well-being, acting as a buffer against stress and promoting happiness. Strong, supportive relationships provide a foundation that helps us cope with life's challenges, allowing us to share our thoughts and feelings openly. This sharing creates an environment where empathy and understanding can thrive, essential components for fostering mental wellness.

Effective communication is one of the cornerstones of nurturing healthy relationships. When individuals engage in open and honest dialogue, they foster a sense of safety and trust. This communication allows both parties to express their feelings, needs, and concerns without fear of judgment. When people feel heard and validated, it strengthens the bond between them and reduces the potential for misunderstandings, which can lead to emotional distress and conflict.

Empathy is another critical element in nurturing relationships. By trying to understand another person's perspective, we can forge deeper connections and demonstrate compassion. This practice not only helps in validating the feelings of others but also promotes a sense of belonging and emotional safety. Empathy encourages individuals to support one another through difficult times, reinforcing the idea that they are not alone in their struggles.

Setting healthy boundaries is essential for maintaining respect and trust in relationships. Clearly defined boundaries outline what is acceptable behavior and what is not, helping individuals feel secure. When boundaries are respected, it minimizes the risk of resentment and emotional turmoil. Moreover, healthy boundaries enable individuals to prioritize their own needs while still being available for others, creating a balanced dynamic.

The impact of relationships on mental health cannot be overstated. Positive relationships are linked to lower levels of anxiety and depression, while toxic relationships can exacerbate emotional suffering. Recognizing when a relationship is harmful is crucial, as distancing oneself from negative influences can lead to improved mental well-being. Surrounding ourselves with supportive and positive individuals enhances our emotional resilience and overall happiness.

Practicing gratitude within relationships can further strengthen bonds. Expressing appreciation for loved ones fosters a sense of connection and positivity. Simple acts of gratitude, such as acknowledging someone's efforts or saying "thank you," can make a significant difference in how individuals feel within their relationships. This focus on positivity can help shift attention away from negativity, reinforcing the good in our connections.

Shared activities can also play a vital role in nurturing relationships. Engaging in hobbies, exercising, or simply spending quality time together strengthens the emotional bond between individuals. These shared experiences create lasting memories and provide a natural way to relieve stress. Enjoying activities together allows individuals to connect on a deeper level and enjoy each other's company without the distractions of daily life.

Conflict resolution is an inevitable aspect of any relationship. However, how conflicts are approached can significantly influence the health of the relationship. A constructive approach to disagreements, focusing on problem-solving rather than blame can lead to growth and understanding. Learning to navigate conflicts with respect and empathy can strengthen the bond between individuals and foster a sense of teamwork.

Awareness of mental health within relationships is crucial for providing support. Understanding each other's mental health needs allows individuals to be there for one another during tough times. When partners, friends, or family members are attuned to each other's emotional states, they can offer timely support and encouragement. This awareness creates a nurturing environment where individuals feel comfortable seeking help when needed.

In conclusion, nurturing healthy relationships is a vital aspect of mental health. By prioritizing open communication, empathy, and mutual respect, individuals can create supportive environments that enhance emotional well-being. Recognizing the profound impact of relationships on mental health encourages a commitment to cultivating connections that promote happiness and resilience. Ultimately, investing in our relationships not only improves our own mental health but also contributes positively to the well-being of those we care about.

Chapter Forty Five:

Letting Go of Toxic Connections

Letting go of toxic connections is crucial for maintaining good mental health and well-being. Toxic relationships can take many forms, including friendships, romantic partnerships, or even family dynamics. These connections often drain our emotional energy, contribute to feelings of anxiety and depression, and create an overall sense of imbalance in our lives. Recognizing and addressing these unhealthy relationships is a vital step toward fostering a healthier mindset and emotional resilience.

A toxic relationship typically involves patterns of manipulation, control, and negativity. Such dynamics can leave individuals feeling unsupported or belittled, which can lead to a decline in self-esteem and self-worth. When someone consistently undermines our confidence or disregards our feelings, it can create an internal struggle, making it challenging to maintain a positive self-image. By letting go of these toxic connections, we allow ourselves the opportunity to rebuild our self-esteem and focus on healthier interactions.

The emotional and mental toll of toxic relationships can be profound. They can lead to chronic stress, anxiety, and even depression. When we are consistently exposed to negativity, our mental health can deteriorate, making it difficult to cope with everyday challenges. Breaking free from such relationships can serve as a form of self-care, allowing individuals to prioritize their mental well-being and seek environments that foster positivity and growth.

Letting go of toxic connections can also pave the way for healthier relationships. When we remove individuals who drain our energy or create emotional turmoil, we create space for connections that uplift and support us. Healthy relationships are characterized by mutual respect, understanding, and encouragement, leading to a more fulfilling social life. By focusing on building positive connections, individuals can develop a strong support system that enhances their mental health.

Additionally, the process of letting go can lead to personal growth. When individuals distance themselves from toxic relationships, they often gain clarity about their own values and needs. This self-discovery can empower them to set healthier boundaries and make more informed choices about the relationships they cultivate. Understanding what constitutes a healthy relationship can enhance individuals' ability to attract supportive and positive connections in the future.

It is important to acknowledge that letting go of toxic connections may not always be easy. Emotional attachments can make it challenging to sever ties, even when we recognize that a relationship is harmful. Feelings of guilt, fear of loneliness, or worry about the reactions of others can create significant barriers. However, prioritizing mental health requires courage and a commitment to self-care, which may involve difficult decisions.

Support from friends, family, or mental health professionals can be invaluable during this process. Talking about the challenges of letting go can provide individuals with the encouragement and validation they need to make necessary changes. Seeking guidance from a therapist or counselor can also offer tools and strategies for navigating the complexities of toxic relationships, promoting healing and growth.

Moreover, letting go of toxic connections can have a ripple effect on overall well-being. When individuals prioritize their mental health by distancing themselves from negativity, they often experience improvements in various aspects of their lives. This may include increased productivity, better physical health, and enhanced emotional stability. The positive changes that come from fostering healthy relationships can lead to an overall sense of fulfillment and joy.

It is essential to remember that letting go does not mean abandoning compassion or empathy for the other person. It is entirely possible to care for someone while recognizing that the relationship is unhealthy. Setting boundaries and choosing to distance oneself can be an act of self-love and self-respect. Sometimes, stepping away from a toxic connection is the kindest choice one can make for both parties involved.

As individuals let go of toxic relationships, they often find that they can engage more deeply in their own interests and passions. Freed from the weight of negativity, they can explore new hobbies, reconnect with old friends, or invest time in self-improvement. This renewed focus on oneself can lead to greater self-awareness and fulfillment, ultimately enhancing mental health and well-being.

In conclusion, letting go of toxic connections is a vital step in nurturing mental health. While it can be a challenging process, the benefits of distancing oneself from negativity far outweigh the difficulties. By prioritizing self-care and making room for healthier relationships, individuals can foster emotional resilience and create a more positive, fulfilling life. Ultimately, letting go allows us to reclaim our power, fostering connections that uplift and inspire us on our journey toward mental well-being.

Letting go of toxic connections is not just beneficial; it is often essential for personal and psychological growth. Toxic relationships can create a cycle of negativity that perpetuates feelings of inadequacy, anxiety, and depression. When individuals remain in these unhealthy dynamics, they may find themselves caught in a pattern of emotional distress that seems inescapable. The first step in breaking this cycle is recognizing the signs of toxicity and understanding that prioritizing one's mental health is not only acceptable but necessary.

One common characteristic of toxic relationships is the presence of constant criticism or judgment. When someone continually points out our flaws or belittles us, it can erode our self-confidence over time. This behavior can lead to a diminished sense of self-worth, causing individuals to doubt their abilities and decisions. Letting go of such connections allows for the reclamation of one's self-esteem and the opportunity to surround oneself with people who foster positivity and support.

Another significant impact of toxic relationships is the drain on emotional energy. Engaging with individuals who are consistently negative or demanding can leave us feeling exhausted and depleted. This emotional fatigue can affect various aspects of life, including work performance, personal interests, and our ability to engage in healthy relationships. By distancing ourselves from these draining connections, we can reclaim our energy and direct it toward pursuits that bring joy and fulfillment.

The fear of loneliness often serves as a barrier to letting go of toxic relationships. Many individuals worry that breaking free from such connections will leave them isolated or unsupported. However, it is essential to recognize that loneliness is often a temporary state. As individuals prioritize their mental health and seek out healthier relationships, they are likely to attract positive connections that provide true companionship and support.

Letting go can also lead to the development of healthier coping mechanisms. In toxic relationships, individuals may resort to unhealthy behaviors as a means of coping with stress or emotional pain. These may include substance abuse, avoidance behaviors, or self-isolation. By removing toxic influences, individuals often find that they can engage in healthier coping strategies, such as seeking social support, practicing mindfulness, or pursuing hobbies that bring them joy.

The importance of setting boundaries cannot be overstated when it comes to letting go of toxic connections. Establishing boundaries is a crucial skill that allows individuals to protect their emotional well-being. This might involve clearly communicating one's needs or deciding to limit contact with certain individuals. Learning to assertively set boundaries can empower individuals to take control of their relationships and prioritize their mental health.

Additionally, the process of letting go can serve as a catalyst for personal reflection and growth. It encourages individuals to evaluate their values, needs, and desires within relationships. This self-reflection can lead to greater self-awareness and a clearer understanding of what constitutes a healthy relationship. Armed with this knowledge, individuals can make more informed choices in future connections, ensuring they prioritize their mental well-being.

Letting go of toxic connections can also positively influence our relationships with others. When we free ourselves from negativity, we often become more available and open to building healthy relationships. This newfound emotional space can foster connections that are characterized by mutual respect, understanding, and support. Healthy relationships not only enhance our emotional well-being but also provide a network of support during challenging times.

Moreover, the journey of letting go can empower individuals to take responsibility for their own happiness. In toxic relationships, it is easy to feel trapped and dependent on the other person for validation and support. However, by recognizing that one has the power to choose their connections, individuals can reclaim their autonomy and work toward building a life filled with joy and fulfillment. This empowerment is a crucial step toward achieving lasting mental well-being.

It is also vital to acknowledge the role of forgiveness in the process of letting go. While it may be challenging to forgive those who have caused emotional pain, holding onto resentment can further perpetuate feelings of negativity and stress. Forgiveness does not mean condoning harmful behavior; rather, it is about freeing oneself from the emotional burden of anger and hurt. This process can be liberating, allowing individuals to move forward and focus on their own healing.

In conclusion, the importance of letting go of toxic connections cannot be overstated when it comes to nurturing mental health. While the process may be challenging, the benefits of distancing oneself from negativity far outweigh the difficulties. By prioritizing self-care, setting boundaries, and seeking supportive relationships, individuals can foster emotional resilience and create a more positive, fulfilling life. Ultimately, letting go is not just about severing ties; it is a powerful act of self-love that leads to a healthier, more balanced existence.

Chapter Forty Six:

The Importance of Forgiveness

Forgiveness is often viewed as a noble virtue, but its significance extends far beyond moral or ethical considerations. In the realm of mental health, forgiveness plays a crucial role in emotional well-being, providing individuals with a pathway to healing and personal growth. It allows individuals to release feelings of resentment, anger, and hurt, which can otherwise hinder mental health. By understanding the importance of forgiveness, individuals can cultivate a mindset that promotes inner peace and emotional resilience.

One of the most profound benefits of forgiveness is its ability to reduce stress and anxiety. Holding onto grudges and negative feelings can create a cycle of emotional turmoil that weighs heavily on the mind. Research has shown that unresolved anger and resentment can lead to increased levels of cortisol, the stress hormone, which can negatively impact both mental and physical health. By choosing to forgive, individuals can alleviate this emotional burden and promote a sense of calm and tranquility.

Forgiveness also plays a vital role in improving interpersonal relationships. When individuals hold onto past grievances, it can create barriers that prevent healthy communication and connection with others. By forgiving, individuals can open the door to reconciliation and understanding, fostering healthier relationships. This not only enhances the quality of social interactions but also contributes to a sense of belonging, which is essential for mental well-being.

The act of forgiveness can also empower individuals to take control of their emotional states. When people cling to negative feelings, they often feel victimized by their experiences. However, forgiveness shifts the focus from the actions of others to personal healing and growth. This shift in perspective can be incredibly liberating, as it allows individuals to reclaim their emotional power and move forward without the weight of past hurts.

Moreover, forgiveness is closely linked to improved mental health outcomes. Studies have consistently shown that individuals who practice forgiveness experience lower levels of depression, anxiety, and stress. These positive mental health outcomes can be attributed to the release of negative emotions, which creates space for more positive feelings such as joy, empathy, and compassion. This emotional shift can significantly enhance overall well-being.

Additionally, forgiveness fosters resilience. Life is filled with challenges and disappointments, and the ability to forgive helps individuals bounce back from adversity. When individuals practice forgiveness, they develop the emotional tools necessary to navigate difficult situations without becoming overwhelmed by negative emotions. This resilience is essential for maintaining mental health, as it enables individuals to cope effectively with stress and setbacks.

Forgiveness can also enhance self-esteem and self-worth. When individuals choose to forgive, they engage in a process of self-reflection that can lead to a deeper understanding of their values and priorities. This introspection often results in greater self-acceptance and a positive self-image. As individuals learn to forgive themselves and others, they cultivate a sense of compassion that can improve their relationship with themselves, further supporting mental health.

The journey toward forgiveness is often a personal and transformative one. It requires individuals to confront their emotions, acknowledge their pain, and make a conscious choice to let go of resentment. This process can lead to significant personal growth, as individuals learn valuable lessons about empathy, compassion, and the complexity of human relationships. This growth fosters a greater understanding of oneself and others, contributing to improved mental health.

Forgiveness does not mean condoning harmful behavior or forgetting past hurts. Instead, it is about acknowledging the pain while making a deliberate choice to release its hold on one's life. This distinction is essential, as it empowers individuals to prioritize their mental health without minimizing their experiences. Embracing this understanding allows for a healthier approach to forgiveness that respects personal boundaries.

Furthermore, forgiveness can lead to a greater sense of inner peace and emotional stability. By letting go of negative feelings, individuals often find that they can experience life more fully and authentically. This newfound freedom from resentment allows for greater emotional clarity, enabling individuals to focus on what truly matters in their lives. This sense of peace is vital for maintaining mental health, as it fosters a more positive outlook on life.

Practicing forgiveness can also have a ripple effect on those around us. When individuals embrace forgiveness, they often inspire others to do the same. This creates an environment where compassion and empathy flourish, fostering a sense of community and support. Such positive social dynamics can enhance mental health, as strong social connections are essential for emotional well-being.

In addition, forgiveness can be a powerful tool for personal empowerment and agency. By choosing to forgive, individuals reclaim control over their emotional responses and life narratives.

This sense of agency is crucial for mental health, as it reinforces the idea that individuals have the power to shape their experiences and responses. This empowerment can lead to greater resilience and a more positive outlook on life.

Lastly, forgiveness is a lifelong journey that requires ongoing commitment and practice. It is important to recognize that forgiveness is not a one-time event but rather an ongoing process that may require time and effort. As individuals encounter new challenges and experiences, they may find themselves needing to revisit the concept of forgiveness. Engaging in this process regularly can help individuals maintain emotional balance and foster a deeper understanding of both themselves and their relationships with others. Embracing forgiveness as a continuous practice can create lasting changes in one's emotional landscape, leading to sustained improvements in mental health.

Incorporating forgiveness into daily life can take various forms, such as journaling, meditation, or engaging in discussions with trusted friends or therapists. These practices allow individuals to explore their feelings, process their experiences, and ultimately work towards letting go of resentment. By actively engaging in these activities, individuals can create a safe space for reflection and healing, reinforcing the importance of forgiveness within their mental health journey.

One effective strategy for cultivating forgiveness is to develop a compassionate mindset. When individuals can view their experiences and the actions of others through a lens of empathy, it becomes easier to understand the motivations and circumstances that led to hurtful behavior. This shift in perspective can significantly reduce feelings of anger and resentment, making it easier to move toward forgiveness. By fostering compassion for both oneself and others, individuals can create a more supportive emotional environment that nurtures mental health.

Another approach to embracing forgiveness involves setting realistic expectations. It is essential to recognize that forgiveness is not a linear process, and individuals may experience setbacks along the way. Emotions can be complex and multifaceted, and it is normal to feel a mix of anger, sadness, and relief as one navigates the journey of forgiveness. By allowing oneself the grace to feel and process these emotions, individuals can cultivate a more forgiving attitude toward themselves, enhancing their overall mental well-being.

Forgiveness can also be facilitated through the practice of gratitude. Focusing on the positive aspects of life, even amidst challenging circumstances, can help shift one's mindset from negativity to appreciation. By recognizing the lessons learned from difficult experiences and the growth that has emerged, individuals can cultivate a greater sense of acceptance and understanding. This practice not only fosters forgiveness but also promotes a more optimistic outlook on life, which is essential for mental health.

Moreover, engaging in acts of kindness and compassion can reinforce the practice of forgiveness. When individuals focus on extending kindness to others, they often find that their own feelings of resentment and negativity begin to dissipate. This reciprocal relationship between kindness and forgiveness can create a more positive emotional environment, further supporting mental well-being. By actively participating in acts of compassion, individuals can foster a sense of connection and purpose that enhances their overall mental health.

It is also important to recognize that some relationships may be beyond repair, and in such cases, forgiveness may involve letting go rather than reconciliation. Understanding that it is possible to forgive someone while choosing not to maintain a relationship can be a powerful realization. This process allows individuals to release the emotional weight without feeling obligated to continue engaging with a toxic or harmful connection. This form of forgiveness serves as an act of self-care, prioritizing one's mental health and emotional well-being.

In conclusion, the importance of forgiveness in supporting mental health cannot be overstated. By letting go of resentment, embracing compassion, and engaging in practices that foster emotional healing, individuals can create a more positive and resilient mindset. Forgiveness is a powerful tool that allows individuals to reclaim their emotional well-being and navigate life's challenges with greater ease. Ultimately, the journey toward forgiveness is a deeply personal one that can lead to profound growth, healing, and enhanced mental health for individuals willing to embrace the process.

Chapter Forty Seven:

Accepting That Recovery Takes Time
Recovery from mental health issues is a nuanced journey that varies greatly from person to person. One of the most critical lessons individuals must learn is that recovery is not a race; it is a gradual process that requires patience, self-compassion, and understanding. The societal pressures to "get better" quickly can be overwhelming, but accepting that recovery takes time is essential for fostering a healthier mindset and life.

The first step in accepting the timeline of recovery is recognizing that mental health struggles are complex and multifaceted. Unlike physical injuries, where the healing process can often be straightforward and predictable, mental health recovery involves emotional, psychological, and social dimensions. Each individual's experience is unique, influenced by factors such as personal history, support systems, and the nature of their challenges. Understanding this complexity helps to cultivate a more realistic perspective on what recovery entails.

Many people seeking recovery may feel discouraged when progress appears slow. It is vital to celebrate small victories along the way, as these milestones can significantly contribute to overall well-being. For instance, acknowledging days when one feels slightly better, engages in self-care, or reaches out for support can foster a sense of accomplishment. This practice helps to reinforce a positive outlook and encourages continued effort in the recovery journey.

Another aspect of accepting that recovery takes time is recognizing the role of setbacks. Setbacks can be disheartening, but they are often a natural part of the process. Rather than viewing them as failures, it is beneficial to see them as opportunities for growth and learning. Understanding that setbacks do not negate progress can provide a healthier framework for navigating the complexities of recovery.

Support systems play a crucial role in mental health recovery. Engaging with friends, family, or support groups can offer individuals a sense of belonging and understanding during challenging times. When individuals accept that recovery is a process, they may be more open to seeking help and sharing their experiences with others. This connection can be incredibly healing and can reinforce the notion that they are not alone in their journey.

Self-compassion is another critical component of accepting that recovery takes time. Many individuals are quick to judge themselves harshly for perceived shortcomings in their progress. Embracing self-compassion involves treating oneself with the same kindness and understanding that one would offer a friend. This shift in mindset can create a more supportive internal dialogue, essential for fostering resilience and patience.

Mindfulness practices can also aid in accepting the timeline of recovery. Mindfulness encourages individuals to remain present and acknowledge their thoughts and feelings without judgment. This practice can help individuals develop a greater awareness of their emotional state and reduce anxiety about the future. By focusing on the present moment, individuals may find it easier to accept where they are in their recovery journey.

Another important aspect of acceptance is the acknowledgment that recovery is not linear. There will be good days and bad days, and this fluctuation is entirely normal. By reframing expectations and allowing for variability in emotions and experiences, individuals can reduce feelings of frustration and disappointment. This perspective fosters resilience and encourages individuals to keep moving forward, even when progress feels slow.

Education about mental health can also play a vital role in acceptance. Understanding the nature of mental health disorders, treatment options, and recovery processes can empower individuals to navigate their journey more effectively. Knowledge helps demystify the experience and allows individuals to approach their recovery with a more informed mindset, reducing feelings of fear or uncertainty.

Therapeutic interventions can facilitate acceptance of the time it takes to recover. Therapy provides a safe space for individuals to explore their thoughts and feelings about their mental health challenges. Skilled therapists can help individuals set realistic goals, process emotions, and develop coping strategies. This professional support can be invaluable in reinforcing the understanding that recovery is a journey, not a destination.

It's also essential to create a routine that includes self-care practices. Integrating regular physical activity, healthy eating, and adequate sleep can significantly impact mental health and recovery. By committing to these practices, individuals can foster a sense of stability and control over their lives, which can be empowering during the recovery process. It is crucial to recognize that self-care is not a quick fix but rather a sustained effort that contributes to overall well-being.

Building resilience is another vital aspect of accepting that recovery takes time. Resilience is the ability to bounce back from adversity, and it can be cultivated through various practices, including developing problem-solving skills, fostering connections, and maintaining a hopeful outlook. By focusing on resilience, individuals can approach their recovery with a more optimistic perspective, understanding that setbacks do not define them.

Engaging in creative outlets can also support mental health recovery. Activities such as art, writing, music, or dance can serve as powerful forms of expression and emotional release. These creative practices can provide individuals with a sense of purpose and fulfillment, helping them to process their emotions while accepting that recovery takes time.

Finally, it is essential to remind oneself that everyone's journey is unique. Comparing one's progress to others can lead to feelings of inadequacy and frustration. Each person's path is shaped by their individual experiences, coping mechanisms, and circumstances. By focusing on personal progress rather than external comparisons, individuals can cultivate a more fulfilling and authentic recovery journey. Embracing uniqueness allows for a deeper appreciation of one's growth and the challenges overcome along the way.

In the context of accepting that recovery takes time, setting realistic expectations is crucial. Individuals often have an inherent desire for quick fixes or instantaneous results, especially in a world that promotes rapid solutions. However, recognizing that meaningful change often unfolds gradually can help to alleviate pressure. By establishing achievable short-term goals, individuals can create a sense of direction and accomplishment while still remaining committed to their long-term recovery.

Moreover, cultivating patience is a vital skill in the recovery process. Patience allows individuals to navigate the ups and downs without becoming overwhelmed by frustration or despair. Practicing mindfulness can enhance this patience, as it encourages individuals to stay grounded in the present moment. By learning to appreciate the journey itself, individuals can find value and meaning even in the slower phases of their recovery.

It is also beneficial to engage in community resources and activities that promote mental well-being. Many communities offer programs, workshops, and support groups that foster connection and understanding among individuals facing similar challenges. Participating in these activities can not only provide valuable insights but also reinforce the message that recovery is a shared experience. Connecting with others can alleviate feelings of isolation and instill hope.

As individuals progress in their recovery, it can be empowering to share their stories and experiences with others. This act of sharing can be cathartic and may encourage others who are struggling. By openly discussing the challenges and triumphs of their recovery journey, individuals can contribute to a broader conversation about mental health, helping to reduce stigma and promoting understanding that recovery is a process that deserves time and compassion.

Reflecting on one's journey can also be a powerful tool for acceptance. Keeping a journal or creating a visual representation of progress can help individuals see how far they have come, even when it feels like they are still far from their goals. This reflective practice allows for recognition of growth, resilience, and perseverance, reinforcing the understanding that recovery is a continuous journey rather than a destination.

Lastly, it is essential to cultivate a mindset of gratitude. Recognizing the positive aspects of life, even amidst struggles, can shift focus away from negativity. Gratitude can enhance emotional well-being and foster a more optimistic outlook on recovery. By appreciating the small things, support from loved ones, moments of joy, or personal insights, individuals can nurture a sense of hope and motivation as they navigate their unique recovery paths.

In conclusion, accepting that recovery takes time is a vital lesson in supporting mental health. Embracing the complexity of this journey, celebrating small victories, and fostering self-compassion can significantly impact individuals' experiences. By prioritizing patience, resilience, and community connection, individuals can create a holistic approach to recovery that honors their unique journeys. Ultimately, accepting the timeline of recovery allows for a more compassionate and fulfilling path toward mental well-being.

Chapter Forty Eight:

Celebrating Small Victories
Celebrating small victories is an essential practice in supporting mental health and well-being. The journey of mental health recovery can often feel overwhelming, with its peaks and valleys sometimes leading to discouragement. Acknowledging and celebrating small achievements can provide individuals with the motivation and encouragement needed to continue on their path to recovery. This practice fosters a positive mindset and can significantly enhance emotional resilience.

Firstly, small victories serve as reminders of progress. In the context of mental health, success is not solely defined by significant milestones, such as completing a treatment program or being free from symptoms. Instead, it encompasses everyday achievements, like getting out of bed, engaging in a conversation, or practicing self-care. Recognizing these moments helps individuals to appreciate their journey and reinforces the idea that every step forward, no matter how small, is valuable.

Celebrating small victories also plays a crucial role in building self-esteem. Many individuals struggling with mental health issues experience feelings of inadequacy and self-doubt. By taking the time to acknowledge achievements, individuals can combat negative self-perceptions and cultivate a more positive self-image. This process helps to create a sense of agency, empowering individuals to take charge of their recovery journey.

Moreover, celebrating small victories can foster motivation. When individuals recognize their progress, it can ignite a sense of hope and encourage them to set and pursue new goals. This motivation is particularly important during challenging times when individuals may feel stuck or disheartened. By focusing on incremental achievements, individuals can maintain a forward momentum, which is crucial for sustaining long-term recovery efforts.

Another important aspect of celebrating small victories is that it promotes a positive mindset. Focusing on achievements rather than setbacks allows individuals to cultivate gratitude and appreciation for their journey. This shift in perspective can significantly influence overall mental health and well-being, as a positive mindset is associated with reduced stress, anxiety, and depressive symptoms. It encourages individuals to view their challenges through a lens of possibility and growth.

Creating a ritual or habit around celebrating small victories can also enhance the experience. Whether through journaling, sharing with friends, or engaging in a favorite activity, establishing a consistent practice of recognition can reinforce the importance of these moments. For instance, writing down daily achievements in a gratitude journal not only helps to document progress but also serves as a source of inspiration during difficult times.

In addition to personal benefits, celebrating small victories can strengthen social connections. Sharing achievements with friends, family, or support groups fosters a sense of community and belonging. When individuals celebrate their progress with others, it can create opportunities for connection and encouragement. This social support is crucial for mental health, as it reminds individuals that they are not alone in their journey.

Furthermore, celebrating small victories can help to build resilience. Resilience is the ability to bounce back from adversity and adapt to challenges. By recognizing and celebrating achievements, individuals can cultivate a sense of hope and determination. This resilience can be invaluable when faced with setbacks, as it encourages individuals to persevere and continue working toward their goals.

In the workplace, celebrating small victories can also contribute to a positive organizational culture. Employers who recognize employees' incremental achievements foster an environment of support and encouragement. This practice not only enhances employee morale but can also lead to increased productivity and job satisfaction. In turn, a positive workplace culture has a ripple effect on employees' mental health and overall well-being.

Education about the importance of celebrating small victories can also empower individuals in their recovery journeys. Mental health professionals can incorporate this practice into therapy sessions, emphasizing the value of recognizing progress. By equipping individuals with the tools and language to celebrate their achievements, therapists can help clients cultivate a proactive and positive approach to mental health.

Additionally, celebrating small victories can serve as a form of self-reward. When individuals acknowledge their achievements, they can treat themselves to something enjoyable, whether it's a favorite snack, a relaxing bath, or a fun outing. These self-rewards reinforce positive behaviors and encourage continued effort in the recovery process.

In conclusion, celebrating small victories is a vital practice in supporting mental health. By recognizing and appreciating incremental achievements, individuals can foster a sense of progress, build self-esteem, and cultivate a positive mindset. This practice not only enhances personal well-being but also strengthens social connections and resilience. Ultimately, celebrating small victories is a powerful tool in the journey toward mental health recovery, reminding individuals that every step forward is worthy of recognition and celebration.

Celebrating small victories is a vital aspect of mental health support and recovery. The journey to improved mental health can often feel daunting, filled with challenges and setbacks. Recognizing and celebrating small achievements along the way can provide individuals with the motivation, encouragement, and hope necessary to persevere. This practice helps to cultivate a positive mindset, fostering emotional resilience and overall well-being.

One of the primary reasons for celebrating small victories is that they serve as tangible reminders of progress. In the realm of mental health, success is not always marked by significant milestones. Instead, it often consists of daily accomplishments, such as getting out of bed, engaging in social interactions, or practicing self-care. Acknowledging these small wins allows individuals to appreciate their journey and reinforces the notion that every step forward, regardless of size, is meaningful and contributes to overall recovery.

In addition to recognizing progress, celebrating small victories can significantly boost self-esteem. Many individuals experiencing mental health challenges struggle with feelings of inadequacy and self-doubt. By taking the time to acknowledge and celebrate their achievements, individuals can combat negative self-perceptions and foster a more positive self-image. This process empowers them to take control of their recovery journey, reinforcing their belief in their ability to grow and change.

Moreover, celebrating small victories can serve as a powerful motivator. Recognizing progress can ignite hope and inspire individuals to set new goals for themselves. This motivation becomes especially crucial during difficult times when feelings of stagnation may arise. Focusing on incremental achievements helps maintain forward momentum, encouraging individuals to keep striving toward their objectives and reinforcing the importance of persistence in recovery.

The act of celebrating small victories also promotes a positive mindset. By focusing on achievements rather than setbacks, individuals can cultivate gratitude and appreciation for their journey. This shift in perspective has a profound impact on overall mental health, as a positive outlook is linked to reduced levels of stress, anxiety, and depression. Emphasizing small victories allows individuals to view their challenges through a lens of growth and potential, fostering resilience in the face of adversity.

Creating a ritual around the celebration of small victories can enhance the experience even further. Establishing a consistent practice such as journaling accomplishments, sharing successes with friends, or engaging in enjoyable activities, reinforces the significance of these moments. For instance, maintaining a gratitude journal where individuals document daily achievements can serve as a source of inspiration during tougher times, reminding them of their progress and resilience.

Furthermore, social connections can be strengthened through the celebration of small victories. Sharing achievements with friends, family, or support groups fosters a sense of community and belonging. When individuals celebrate their progress with others, it creates opportunities for connection and encouragement. This social support is crucial for mental health, as it helps individuals feel less isolated and more motivated in their recovery journeys.

In conclusion, celebrating small victories is essential for supporting mental health and well-being. By recognizing and valuing incremental achievements, individuals can foster a sense of progress, build self-esteem, and cultivate a positive mindset. This practice not only enhances personal well-being but also strengthens social connections and resilience. Ultimately, celebrating small victories serves as a powerful tool in the journey toward mental health recovery, reminding individuals that every step forward is worthy of recognition and celebration.

Chapter Forty Nine:

Moving Forward: Life After Crisis
Experiencing a crisis can be a profoundly challenging and transformative event in a person's life. Whether it is a mental health crisis, a traumatic experience, or a significant life change, the aftermath can leave individuals feeling disoriented, vulnerable, and uncertain about their future. Moving forward after such crises is essential for mental health recovery, requiring a thoughtful approach that emphasizes resilience, self-compassion, and growth.

The first step in moving forward is acknowledging the impact of the crisis. It is crucial for individuals to process what they have experienced, allowing space for feelings of grief, anger, or confusion. Denying or suppressing these emotions can hinder recovery and lead to further mental health challenges. By taking the time to reflect on their experiences, individuals can begin to understand the lessons learned and how they can use these insights to foster personal growth.

Building a support network is another critical component of moving forward after a crisis. This network can include friends, family, mental health professionals, or support groups. Connecting with others who have experienced similar challenges can provide a sense of belonging and understanding. Support from loved ones can also provide encouragement and reassurance during difficult times, reminding individuals that they are not alone in their journey.

Self-care is an important practice in the aftermath of a crisis. Individuals should prioritize their physical, emotional, and mental well-being by engaging in activities that promote relaxation and rejuvenation. This can include exercise, mindfulness practices, hobbies, or simply spending time in nature. By caring for themselves, individuals can rebuild their strength and resilience, setting the foundation for a healthier future.

Establishing new routines can also play a significant role in moving forward. Crises can disrupt daily life, making it essential to create structure and stability. Routines can provide a sense of normalcy and control, helping individuals navigate their day-to-day responsibilities with greater ease. Incorporating small, manageable goals into these routines can foster a sense of accomplishment and motivation as individuals work toward recovery.

Embracing change and adaptability is crucial when moving forward after a crisis. Life may never return to the way it was before, and individuals must learn to accept this new reality. By cultivating an open mindset and a willingness to adapt, individuals can discover new opportunities for growth and fulfillment. This adaptability can lead to personal development and a deeper understanding of oneself and one's values.

Moreover, practicing self-compassion is essential during this transitional phase. Individuals often hold themselves to high standards, which can lead to feelings of guilt or shame when they struggle to cope. By practicing self-kindness and understanding, individuals can create a nurturing inner dialogue that encourages healing. This compassion allows for a more compassionate approach to setbacks, recognizing that recovery is not linear and that it is okay to ask for help when needed.

Setting realistic goals can help individuals maintain focus and direction in their recovery journey. These goals should be specific, measurable, achievable, relevant, and time-bound (SMART).

Breaking larger goals into smaller, manageable steps can prevent feelings of overwhelm and create a sense of progress. Celebrating these small victories along the way reinforces motivation and encourages individuals to continue moving forward.

Engaging in new interests and activities can also foster personal growth after a crisis. Exploring new hobbies, volunteering, or pursuing educational opportunities can provide individuals with a renewed sense of purpose and fulfillment. These activities not only serve as distractions but also help individuals reconnect with their passions and develop new skills, enhancing their overall well-being.

Mindfulness and grounding techniques can be beneficial tools for individuals navigating life after a crisis. Practicing mindfulness encourages individuals to stay present and observe their thoughts and feelings without judgment. Grounding techniques can help individuals connect with their surroundings and reduce feelings of anxiety or distress. By incorporating these practices into their daily routines, individuals can cultivate a greater sense of calm and clarity.

Revisiting and redefining personal values can also be a transformative process in moving forward. Crises often prompt individuals to reflect on what truly matters to them. By identifying and prioritizing their core values, individuals can align their actions and decisions with what is most important in their lives. This alignment can lead to a greater sense of fulfillment and purpose, guiding individuals on their path to recovery.

Additionally, seeking professional help can be an invaluable resource in the recovery process. Mental health professionals can provide guidance, support, and tools to help individuals navigate their feelings and experiences. Therapy can offer a safe space for individuals to explore their emotions, process their experiences, and develop coping strategies. Engaging in therapy can empower individuals to take charge of their mental health and work toward healing.

Lastly, it's important to remember that moving forward is a journey, not a destination. Each individual's path to recovery is unique, and there is no set timeline for healing. Embracing the ups and downs of this journey can help individuals cultivate resilience and adaptability. By focusing on progress rather than perfection, individuals can create a more compassionate relationship with themselves and their recovery process.

In conclusion, moving forward after a crisis is a multifaceted journey that requires patience, self-compassion, and a proactive approach to mental health. Acknowledging the impact of the crisis and allowing oneself to feel and process the associated emotions is crucial for healing. This initial step paves the way for personal growth and understanding, setting the stage for a more resilient future.

Building a robust support network is equally important in this journey. Surrounding oneself with friends, family, and supportive communities provides essential encouragement and understanding. The shared experiences and perspectives from others can help individuals feel less isolated and more empowered to face the challenges ahead. This sense of connection fosters resilience and can be a source of strength during difficult moments.

Self-care practices play a foundational role in recovery after a crisis. Prioritizing physical, emotional, and mental well-being through activities that promote relaxation and rejuvenation is vital. By engaging in self-care routines, individuals can rebuild their strength and resilience, allowing them to navigate the complexities of life after a crisis with greater ease. This commitment to self-care reinforces the understanding that mental health is a priority, not an afterthought.

Establishing new routines can create stability in a post-crisis life. Routine provides a sense of normalcy and control, which can be especially comforting during uncertain times. By setting small, achievable goals within these routines, individuals can foster a sense of accomplishment and motivation. This structured approach helps individuals feel more grounded as they work toward recovery and healing.

Additionally, embracing change and practicing self-compassion are vital components of moving forward. Life after a crisis may not resemble what it once was, and accepting this new reality can be challenging. By cultivating an open mindset and practicing kindness toward oneself, individuals can navigate the ups and downs of recovery with greater ease. This compassion allows for a more nurturing approach to setbacks, recognizing that healing is a process that takes time and effort.

Engaging in new interests and exploring personal values can also enhance the recovery experience. These activities provide opportunities for growth and self-discovery, helping individuals reconnect with their passions. As they explore new avenues, they can gain a deeper understanding of themselves, which can guide their decisions and actions in the future. This journey of self-exploration is essential for cultivating a fulfilling life after a crisis.

In summary, moving forward after a crisis involves a combination of self-awareness, support, and proactive engagement in life. By acknowledging emotions, building supportive networks, prioritizing self-care, and embracing change, individuals can foster resilience and growth. Each step taken in this journey contributes to a stronger foundation for mental health and well-being, allowing individuals to navigate life's challenges with confidence and hope. The path to recovery may be complex, but it is also an opportunity for profound transformation and renewal.

Chapter Fifty:

Embracing Life: Finding Joy and Purpose Again

Embracing life after facing challenges, whether they stem from mental health struggles, personal crises, or significant life changes, is an essential aspect of healing and growth. The journey back to joy and purpose can often feel overwhelming, but it is also an opportunity for profound transformation. By actively seeking ways to reconnect with life, individuals can foster resilience and create a fulfilling existence.

The first step in this journey is acknowledging the feelings of loss or disconnection that may have arisen during difficult times. It is imperative to allow oneself to experience these emotions fully. Suppressing feelings of sadness, frustration, or confusion can impede the healing process. By giving voice to these feelings, whether through journaling, talking to a friend, or engaging in therapy, individuals can begin to understand their experiences and pave the way for recovery.

Finding joy again often involves rediscovering passions and interests that may have been sidelined during challenging periods. Individuals should take time to explore activities that once brought them happiness, whether it's painting, hiking, reading, or cooking. Engaging in these activities can reignite a sense of joy and remind individuals of the simple pleasures life has to offer. If old interests no longer resonate, trying new hobbies can open up exciting avenues for exploration and creativity.

Additionally, cultivating gratitude can significantly enhance one's ability to embrace life. Practicing gratitude involves consciously focusing on the positive aspects of life and acknowledging the small wins and joys that occur daily. Keeping a gratitude journal or simply taking a moment each day to reflect on what one is thankful for can shift perspectives, helping individuals to see the beauty and hope in their surroundings, even amidst struggles.

Building meaningful relationships is another vital component of finding joy and purpose again. Social connections play a crucial role in mental health, as they provide support, understanding, and a sense of belonging. Individuals should prioritize nurturing existing relationships and seeking out new connections. Engaging in community activities, support groups, or social clubs can help individuals connect with like-minded people, fostering friendships that can enrich their lives.

Setting intentions and goals can also guide individuals toward a more purposeful existence. Intentions can be small, daily affirmations or larger life goals that give direction and meaning to one's actions. By identifying what truly matters and aligning daily activities with those values, individuals can cultivate a sense of purpose. This practice encourages mindfulness and helps individuals stay focused on what brings them joy.

Incorporating mindfulness practices into daily routines can deepen the experience of embracing life. Mindfulness involves being present in the moment and observing thoughts and feelings without judgment. Techniques such as meditation, deep breathing, or yoga can help individuals cultivate a greater awareness of their inner experiences, enabling them to appreciate life's moments more fully. This heightened awareness can lead to a more profound sense of connection with oneself and the world.

Moreover, embracing life often requires letting go of perfectionism and embracing imperfection. Many individuals struggle with self-criticism and unrealistic expectations, which can hinder the ability to find joy. By accepting that imperfections are a natural part of life and that mistakes are opportunities for growth, individuals can foster a more compassionate relationship with themselves. This mindset shift allows for greater exploration and enjoyment of life's experiences.

Volunteering and giving back to the community can also enhance one's sense of purpose. Helping others not only contributes to positive societal change but also fosters a sense of fulfillment and joy within oneself. Engaging in acts of kindness, whether through formal volunteering or simple gestures of support, can create meaningful connections and enhance overall well-being.

Creating a positive environment can also significantly impact one's ability to embrace life. Surrounding oneself with uplifting people, engaging in inspiring activities, and curating a physical space that reflects personal values and aesthetics can contribute to mental well-being. A nurturing environment encourages positivity and creativity, making it easier to find joy and purpose in daily life.

Incorporating physical activity into one's routine is another powerful way to support mental health and foster joy. Exercise releases endorphins, which are natural mood lifters. Whether it's going for a walk, practicing yoga, or participating in sports, finding enjoyable forms of movement can enhance physical health and contribute to emotional well-being. The connection between the body and mind is vital, and physical activity can be a gateway to feeling more alive and engaged.

As individuals embrace life, it is essential to practice self-compassion throughout the journey. There will be ups and downs, and it's important to recognize that healing and growth take time. Being gentle with oneself during difficult moments allows individuals to maintain a sense of hope and resilience. Self-compassion encourages individuals to treat themselves with the same kindness and understanding they would offer a friend facing similar challenges.

In conclusion, embracing life and finding joy and purpose again is a dynamic process involving self-exploration, connection, and growth. By acknowledging emotions, rediscovering passions, cultivating gratitude, and building relationships, individuals can foster a renewed sense of engagement with life. This journey is deeply personal and unique for each individual, but certain universal themes can guide the way toward a more fulfilling existence. As individuals navigate this path, it is essential to remain open to the experiences that life presents, understanding that each moment carries the potential for joy and discovery.

A significant aspect of embracing life is the willingness to face fears and uncertainties head-on. Often, the fear of failure or rejection can hold individuals back from pursuing new opportunities or experiences. By confronting these fears and taking small, courageous steps outside of their comfort zones, individuals can build confidence and resilience. Each step taken, no matter how small, reinforces the belief that they are capable of overcoming challenges and embracing life's possibilities.

Additionally, nurturing creativity is a powerful way to find joy and purpose. Creative expression can take many forms, including art, music, writing, or dance. Engaging in creative activities allows individuals to explore their emotions, share their stories, and connect with their inner selves. This form of expression can be liberating and therapeutic, providing an outlet for feelings that may otherwise remain unexpressed. Creativity fosters a sense of playfulness and experimentation, encouraging individuals to embrace life with curiosity and enthusiasm.

Furthermore, the practice of acceptance plays a crucial role in the journey of embracing life. Accepting one's circumstances, past experiences, and emotions can be a transformative process. It allows individuals to release the burden of regret and disappointment, making room for healing and new possibilities. Acceptance does not mean resignation; rather, it is an acknowledgment of reality that empowers individuals to move forward with clarity and purpose.

Engaging with nature is another significant way to reconnect with life. Spending time outdoors can have a profound impact on mental health, providing a sense of peace and grounding. Nature has a unique ability to inspire awe and wonder, reminding individuals of the beauty and interconnectedness of all living things. Whether it's a stroll in the park, a hike in the mountains, or simply sitting by a lake, immersing oneself in nature can rejuvenate the spirit and foster a deeper appreciation for life.

Moreover, the importance of humor and playfulness cannot be overstated in the pursuit of joy. Laughter is a natural antidote to stress and can create a sense of connection with others. Finding joy in the small, everyday moments, whether through a funny movie, playful interaction with friends, or a lighthearted conversation, can uplift spirits and enhance overall well-being. Embracing a playful attitude can encourage individuals to take life less seriously and enjoy the journey.

Establishing healthy boundaries is also essential in the quest for joy and purpose. Individuals should evaluate the relationships and commitments in their lives to ensure they are aligned with their values and well-being. Setting boundaries allows individuals to protect their time and energy, creating space for activities and relationships that bring them fulfillment. By prioritizing what truly matters, individuals can cultivate an environment conducive to joy.

As individuals continue to embrace life, it is beneficial to engage in lifelong learning. This can encompass formal education, personal development, or acquiring new skills. The pursuit of knowledge fosters a sense of curiosity and growth, empowering individuals to adapt and thrive in an ever-changing world. Lifelong learning can open doors to new opportunities, perspectives, and experiences, enhancing overall life satisfaction.

In addition, practicing mindfulness can deepen the experience of embracing life. Mindfulness encourages individuals to be fully present in each moment, cultivating an awareness of thoughts, emotions, and sensations without judgment. This practice helps individuals appreciate the richness of life, fostering a deeper connection with themselves and their surroundings. By incorporating mindfulness into daily routines, individuals can enhance their overall sense of well-being.

The journey of embracing life is also about serving others and contributing to something greater than oneself. Engaging in acts of kindness, whether through volunteering, mentoring, or simply being there for someone in need, can create a profound sense of purpose. Helping others fosters a sense of connection and community, reinforcing the understanding that we are all part of a larger tapestry of human experience. This sense of interconnectedness can deepen one's appreciation for life.

Finally, it is important to celebrate progress and honor the journey. Recognizing and celebrating achievements no matter how small reinforces a sense of accomplishment and motivation. Reflecting on the challenges faced and the growth experienced can provide valuable insights into one's strength and resilience. By honoring the journey, individuals can maintain a positive outlook and continue to embrace life with hope and enthusiasm.

In summary, embracing life and finding joy and purpose again is a multifaceted journey that encompasses self-discovery, connection, and growth. By acknowledging emotions, rediscovering passions, nurturing relationships, and engaging in meaningful activities, individuals can create a fulfilling existence. This journey is not always linear, but with patience, resilience, and an open heart, individuals can cultivate a life rich with joy and purpose.

Conclusion

In conclusion, it's vital to recognize the significance of perseverance, especially when navigating the turbulent waters of mental health challenges. The feelings you experience in the moment can often feel overwhelming, leading to a sense of hopelessness; however, it's crucial to remember that these emotions are not permanent. By allowing yourself the grace of time, another day, another week, another month, or another year, you can begin to see the light at the end of the tunnel.

You are far from alone in your struggles; many people face mental health issues at various points in their lives, and it is entirely normal to feel this way. It's essential to reach out for support, whether it's confiding in a friend, family member, or a mental health professional. There is a myriad of resources available to help you through this journey.

Endurance is key, keep pushing forward, even when the road seems daunting. Acknowledging your feelings and seeking help can pave the way to healing. Remember, hope is a powerful ally hold on to it, and never, ever give up. Your story is still being written, and brighter days are ahead.

You are not alone, and your feelings are valid. Embrace the journey, and keep enduring.

Amanda Ventura

Don't miss out!

Visit the website below and you can sign up to receive emails whenever Amanda Ventura publishes a new book. There's no charge and no obligation.

https://books2read.com/r/B-A-AQBIC-IBODF

BOOKS 2 READ

Connecting independent readers to independent writers.

Also by Amanda Ventura

Echoes Of Divinity
Determined Heart
Rising From The Ashes
Unyielding Faith
Vanessa's Miracle, A Journey Through Kidney Cancer
Prioritizing Mental Health: A Guide to Overcoming Despair and
Rediscovering Hope

About the Author

Amanda Ventura, a linguist originally from Texas, has a strong enthusiasm for languages, writing, and culture. Her unique personal experiences have the potential to resonate deeply with many, and she aims to share her story to inspire and connect with a global audience. Amanda Ventura aims to make a positive societal impact by sharing her experiences.

Read more at https://www.amazon.com/author/venturaamanda.